GOLDENEYE GUIDEBOOK

Exploring
THE COTSWOLDS

William Fricker

BATH
BROADWAY
BURFORD
CHELTENHAM
CHIPPING CAMPDEN
CIRENCESTER
STRATFORD-UPON-AVON

To Carolina, My Cotswold Love

Author: William Fricker

Photography: William Fricker (unless credited with image)

The 6th edition published by Goldeneye, Broad Street, Penryn, TR10 8JL

Text copyright

Photographs

Maps copyright

Art direction: William Fricker

Book design and layout: camouka.co.uk

Editor: Izy Fricker

Printed in the Czech Republic

Abbreviations in Text	
C14	14th Century
Mar-Oct	1 March to 31 October (inc.)
NT	National Trust property
EH	English Heritage property
BHs	Bank Holidays
W/Es	Weekends
East	Easter
E/C	Early Closing
TIC	Tourist Information Centre
M	Monday
Tu	Tuesday
W	Wednesday
Th	Thursday
F	Friday
Sa	Saturday
Su	Sunday
ss	Supplied by Subject (reference images)

All Rights Reserved

No part of this publication may be reproduced or transmitted in any form or by any means, electronic or mechanical including photocopy, recording or any other information storage or retrieval system, without prior permission in writing from the publisher. A CIP catalogue record for this book is available from the British Library.

Correct Information:
The contents of this publication were believed to be correct and accurate at the time of printing. However, Goldeneye accepts no responsibility for any errors, omissions or changes in the details given, or for the consequences arising thereto, from the use of this book. However, the publishers would greatly appreciate your time in notifying us of any changes or new attractions (or places to eat, drink and stay) that you consider merit inclusion in the next edition. Your comments are most welcome, for we value the views and suggestions of our readers. Please write to: The Editor, Goldeneye, Broad Street, Penryn TR10 8JL, UK.

Keble's Bridge, Eastleach

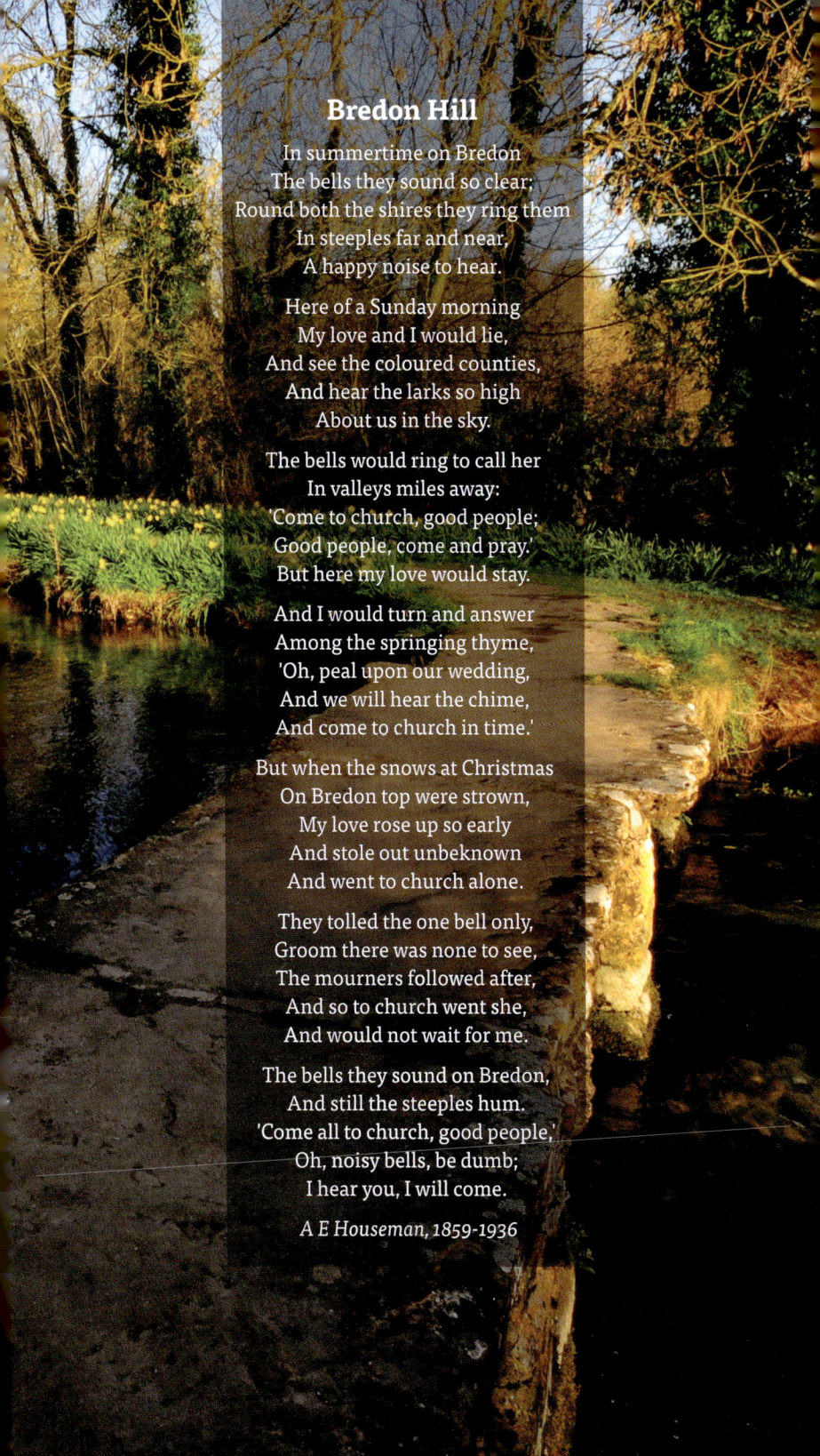

Bredon Hill

In summertime on Bredon
The bells they sound so clear;
Round both the shires they ring them
In steeples far and near,
A happy noise to hear.

Here of a Sunday morning
My love and I would lie,
And see the coloured counties,
And hear the larks so high
About us in the sky.

The bells would ring to call her
In valleys miles away:
'Come to church, good people;
Good people, come and pray.'
But here my love would stay.

And I would turn and answer
Among the springing thyme,
'Oh, peal upon our wedding,
And we will hear the chime,
And come to church in time.'

But when the snows at Christmas
On Bredon top were strown,
My love rose up so early
And stole out unbeknown
And went to church alone.

They tolled the one bell only,
Groom there was none to see,
The mourners followed after,
And so to church went she,
And would not wait for me.

The bells they sound on Bredon,
And still the steeples hum.
'Come all to church, good people,'
Oh, noisy bells, be dumb;
I hear you, I will come.

A E Houseman, 1859-1936

PREFACE

I have a close relationship with all the areas I have produced guidebooks for. As with siblings these relationships differ in style and intensity and develop over time. None of the other regions is quite as close to me as the Cotswolds...my regional twin, if you like.

The Cotswolds were once my base for 30 years. For 20 of those years I lived and managed Goldeneye from Cheltenham. I walked, drove and cycled around the area researching, writing and taking photographs for Goldeneye's Map-Guides and Photographic Books. I played cricket in many of the towns and villages (eventually, ending up at Sheepscombe, on Laurie Lee Field - strange and ironic for his prose set me on this journey of adventure many years ago), and sampled many a brew in the local hostelries. I eventually married a Cotswold girl and our wedding took place in Gloucester Cathedral. A privilege rarely granted to those outside the Church. It so happened that her Grandfather had been Vicar of Guiting Power for 25-years, and had collapsed and died on the High Altar of the Cathedral whilst taking a service. A unique event that gave us entry to the inner sanctum. My original cartographer David Cox has lived all his life in West Oxfordshire, and I have the use of many researchers who ply me with new and up-to-date information. My visits to the area are frequent and intense. Our Cotswold credentials are significant and deeply ingrained and this Guidebook represents the sum of our collective years and all the knowledge and opinions that engenders.

Having produced the Cotswold Map-Guide for many years it had been a long-standing ambition to extend that publication and to produce a book on this scale. My intention that it be practical and easy-to-use. A book that is clear to navigate, fun to read and a pleasure to turn the page. One that will encourage you to delve beyond the surface of the region. There aren't enough pages in this fifth edition to fit in everything and so future editions of the book will be refined on a constant, annual basis – in parallel, I hope with your relationship with the region. For this is more than a simple guidebook - it is meant to be a souvenir and an object to treasure.

As well as photography, I have included contemporary and traditional paintings to provide a different perspective. The touring maps offer an immense amount of detail not necessarily common to guidebooks. This has saved me a lot of unnecessary descriptive prose. But, the major difference of this Guidebook compared to many others on the market (who first commission a writer, then gather the images from various picture libraries) is that I have researched, written it and taken 80% of the photographs. Repeated visits to chosen sites at different times of the day or year in differing lights and weather has given me a greater insight into my subject and has helped create an intense labour of love. Goldeneye's small enthusiastic team work closely together on each guidebook. And they

PREFACE

Guiting Power

build up an undiluted passion for each region as well as for the guidebooks in the series. So, thank you Phil (book designer), Dave (cartographer) and Izy (editor), for sharing this incredible journey.

In the last couple of years my movements have been restricted due to COVID, and also having a young daughter bed bound for seven-years with Severe M.E. It occurred to me that walking, visiting country pubs, gardens, beaches and mountains was a privilege I had always taken for granted. Indeed, these sentiments have deepened by the day as I note the endless misery of families seeking to survive in Ukraine, Afghanistan and Syria. The horrors of war pale in comparison with the restrictions of Lock Down and a reminder that these restrictions are insignificant compared to the suffering of the Ukrainians, Afghanis and Syrians.

Peace is the only battle worth waging - **Albert Camus**

Peace is its own reward - **M Ghandi**

There are many religions, but there is only one morality - **John Ruskin**

So, be with good cheer and a hearty breakfast inside you. Go forth and take advantage of these English hills and villages while you can.

NEW FOR THIS EDITION:

More variance in the Eating Out options – I have included a whole variety of options such as Light Bites (cafés, coffee shops, tea rooms and delis). Inns With Rooms and Traditional Inns with pub-grub as well as sophisticated Dining Pubs and more Farm Shops.

Navigation & Clarity – For ease of use the area is split into five regions. At the start of each is an area map followed by the respective guide text and illustrations. Each section is colour-coded and the area maps either overlap or juxtapose to allow easy navigation. We have also re-designed the pages with new typography and many new images to provide a cleaner, clearer presentation.

I believe the Cotswolds to be a truly magical destination, whether you have a short break, a week, are alone or with friends and family. Whether you have a particular interest in the English landscape and village life, literary and music festivals, gardens and historic 'wool' churches or simple hedonism. There are no shortages of options available to you. Take a deep breath of country air, shrug off your working persona and live the life fantastic.

William Fricker, June 2023

The Glebe, Bourton-on-the-Water

CONTENTS

1	Title Page	• 112	**THE EAST COTSWOLDS**
2	Locator Map	114	Burford, Witney Map
4	Credits	116	Burford, Witney Guide
5	A E Houseman's Poem - Bredon Hill	124	Chipping Norton, Great Tew, Woodstock Map
6	Preface	126	Chipping Norton, Great Tew, Woodstock Guide
9	Contents		
10	Introduction	• 134	**THE CENTRAL WOLDS**
12	Recommendations	136	Bourton-On-The-Water, Stow, The Slaughters Map
14	Which Village to Visit	138	Bourton-On-The-Water, Stow, The Slaughters Guide
16	Where to Stay	140	In Memoriam To The Fallen - Poppies In A Cotswold Garden
22	The Value & Survival of Hospitality	148	Stow Horse Fair
24	Where to Eat & Drink	153	Winchcombe Gargoyles
28	The Golden Fleece of the Cotswold Sheep	154	Cotswold Churches
		156	Cheltenham, Gloucester, Tewkesbury Map
• 30	**THE SOUTH WEST COTSWOLDS**	158	Cheltenham, Gloucester, Tewkesbury Guide
32	Bath, Bradford-On-Avon, Castle Combe Map	166	Gloucester Cathedral
34	Bath, Bradford-On-Avon, Castle Combe Guide	170	Medieval Tewkesbury
48	Chipping Sodbury Guide	172	Cotswold Stone
49	Chipping Sodbury Map	174	Estate & Tithe Barns
50	Cotswold Cottages	176	Saxton's Map 1576
52	Tetbury, Malmesbury, Wotton-Under-Edge Map	• 178	**THE NORTHERN COTSWOLDS**
54	Tetbury, Malmesbury, Wotton-Under-Edge Guide	180	Great Malvern, Pershore Map
62	Cotswold Hostelries	182	Great Malvern, Pershore Guide
64	Pub Signs	186	Broadway, Chipping Campden Map
		188	Broadway, Chipping Campden Guide
• 66	**THE SOUTH COTSWOLDS**	199	Stratford-Upon-Avon
68	Arlingham, Berkeley, Frampton-On-Severn Map	202	William Shakespeare
69	Arlingham, Berkeley, Frampton-On-Severn Guide	204	Banbury, Shipston Map
74	Stroud, Nailsworth, Painswick Map	206	Banbury, Shipston Guide
76	Stroud, Nailsworth, Painswick Guide	210	Doors
81	Laurie Lee Country	212	Contemporary Art
86	The Cotswold Horse	214	Calendar Of Events
88	Bibury, Cirencester, Fairford, Northleach Map	215	Tourist Information Centres
90	Bibury	216	Acknowledgments
92	Bibury, Cirencester, Fairford, Northleach Guide	217	Index to towns, villages, and places of interest described in the book
94	Cirencester	223	Map Symbols Explained
102	The Church of St Mary the Virgin, Fairford	224	About The Author & Photographer
108	The South Cotswolds		
110	Pastoral Scenes		

9

AN INTRODUCTION

What and where is the region known as the Cotswolds? To those who know it, this may seem like a silly question. However, it is a place that manifests itself in many different ways to different people. Even down to the area they would define as the Cotswolds on a map. To some fashionistas, and magazine editors, the Cotswolds runs comparison to the New York Hamptons and Tuscany. Whilst to others the name is synonymous with wool and hunting, stone walls and majestic churches.

The Cotswolds region is perched on the central section of a ridge of oolitic limestone. The geological structure has thus had a profound and lasting affect on the landscape, and 'look' of the area. The oolitic limestone that forms these hills has the appearance of 1000s of tiny balls, like fish roe and is between 200 and 175 million years old.

This ridge has been tilted on its side, and is run off with streams, and river valleys, that lead off in a south-easterly direction, to feed the Thames basin. On the western edge, the scarp is steep in places with outcrops of rounded hills, notably Cam Long Down, and Bredon Hill, and makes for fine walking country, and pleasing views across to the Malvern Hills and Wales

Linguistically, the Cotswolds derives its name from two Saxon words: 'Cote' - sheep fold, and 'Wold' - bare hill. This references the importance of sheep in the development of the area. And, it is to the Cotswold Lion sheep that one must look to for the origin of wealth and endeavour that brought prosperity to this region

Neolithic Man found refuge on these hills from the swamps of the Severn, and Thames flood plains. The Celtic Dobunni tribe established hill forts where they farmed, bartered their crafts and founded coinage before the Romans arrived. They were not a warlike tribe like their neighbours the Silurians (Welsh), and eased into a compatible relationship with the conquering Romans to build Corinium

Dobunnorum (Cirencester) into the second largest Roman settlement in Britain with a populace of 12,000 inhabitants.

The Saxon farmer laid the foundations of prosperity for the medieval wool merchants, and it was these merchants who built the great 'Wool' churches and the great manor houses.

Henry VIII's Dissolution of the Monasteries in the C16 saw the destruction of the Abbeys at Cirencester, Winchcombe, Hailes and Malmesbury. The first, and last battles of the English Civil War, 1641-1651, saw skirmishes at Edgehill, Lansdowne (Bath) and Stow-On-The Wold.

In the more peaceful C18, Bath and Cheltenham epitomised the elegance, hedonism and splendour of the Georgian era.

The landscape is rich in imagery: dry-stone walls divide the vast, sweeping sheep pastures and lazy, winding, trout streams meander through the rich pastureland. And, scattered across this landscape you will come across quaint hamlets undisturbed by coach, sightseer or time itself. All this makes for an idyllic scene rarely bettered in England.

In recent times this region's closeness to London has attracted wealthy residents, and an increase in second homes being bought by out-of-towners. This development brings with it all the associated benefits and disadvantages. Now the region attracts glitzy minor celebrities with their hangers-on in tow, and the seemingly necessary trumpet and fanfare. This has, of course, meant an increase of high-class restaurants and dining pubs which is of benefit to all (if you can afford their prices). And, of course, any money spent in the area ensures that the great historic buildings are being brought back to their original glory, and maintained for future generations – for which I for one, am very grateful.

Uley Bury, Downham Hill & Cam Long Down from Coaley Peak

⭐ RECOMMENDATIONS

Broadway Tower

A Day at Cheltenham Races or Andoversford Point-to-Point.

Slowly meander along the Windrush Valley in May or early June.

Christmas Carol Concert (or Evensong), or a simple visit to Gloucester Cathedral.

Climb Broadway Tower, to View the 13 Counties.

Enjoy a Theatrical Experience at the Royal Shakespeare Theatre, Stratford.

Follow the "Wool Trail" from the Cotswold Woollen Weavers, to the Cotswold Farm Park, to a "Wool" church.

Windy Red Acers, Westonbirt Arboretum

RECOMMENDATIONS

Follow the "Arts & Crafts Movement Trail" from Kelmscott Manor, to Sapperton Church, to The Wilson - Cheltenham's Art Gallery, to the Arts & Crafts Guild, Chipping Campden.

Visit an Event at The Classic Motor Hub, Bibury Airfield

The Rococo Gardens or Cerney House Gardens for the first snowdrops in February.

Mosaic of Spring, Chedworth Roman Villa

The Chedworth Roman Villa, followed by a walk and picnic in Chedworth Woods.

Walk a section of the Cotswold Way.

Climb Bredon Hill and listen to the skylark.

Lunch in a Country Pub.

Westonbirt Arboretum, in the Autumn, and Spring.

Andoversford Point-to-Point

The Classic Motor Hub, Bibury Airfield: 1953 Cooper-Alta – The Stirling Moss F2 Car ss

WHICH VILLAGE TO VISIT

The Cotswolds are noted for their wealth of beautiful villages. If you have a short time and wish to visit just one or two, this spread will point you in a direction that will not disappoint.

Cotswold villages are often grouped under the same name, for example: Upper and Lower Slaughter, Little and Great Tew, Duntisbourne Leer, Middle Duntisbourne and Dunstisbourne Abbots. And, if so named, it is well worth visiting the collective for they are never too far apart, and are often connected by footpaths. The reason for your visit may be to explore the church, or perhaps to visit the village pub and as luck would have it, it is often the case that the two are found opposite or next door to each other.

1 BIBURY

William Morris described Bibury as one of the prettiest villages in England. It attracts the crowds and is the stop-off point for many coach tours. It is a honey-pot village made up of rose-covered cottages set behind idyllic kitchen gardens.

2 BOURTON-ON-THE-WATER

One of the most popular destinations in the Cotswolds, and one that invites mixed opinions. It can be charming on a quiet, frostbitten morning when only the postman is out and about, but is best avoided on a busy bank holiday. Often described as 'The Venice of the Cotswolds' because the River Windrush is spanned with low, graceful bridges.

3 BROADWAY

'The Painted Lady of the Cotswolds' is a term often used to describe this beautiful village. The honey-coloured stone captivates the visitor today, as it did in the C19, when William Morris, and his pre-Raphaelite friends settled here.

4 BURFORD

A fine introduction to the area for there are splendid inns and pretty cottages hidden down the side streets. The churchyard is a quiet spot with some beautifully decorated table tombs.

5 CHIPPING CAMPDEN

If you chose to visit just one Cotswold village, make sure it's this one. There is no better introduction. The harmony of Cotswold stone mirrors the town's prosperity in the Middle Ages as the home of the wealthiest wool merchants.

WHICH VILLAGE TO VISIT

6 GREAT TEW

A sensationally beautiful village lined with ironstone cottages covered in thatch and stone tiles. Many fell into disrepair, but have now been restored to their former glory. Soho Farmhouse have recently opened a centre of hedonism and eco sensibilities.

7 PAINSWICK
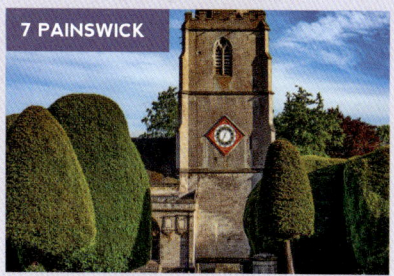

Its local description as 'The Queen of the Cotswolds' is fully justified. The houses have a Palladian quality about them. The Churchyard is famous for the legendary 99 yew trees. A centre for circular walks that features the Cotswold Way.

8 STANTON

A Charming village with houses of honey-coloured stone and the refurbished Mount Inn is a welcome refuge for those tackling the Cotswold Way or in need of sustenance. Horse riding centre.

9 UPPER & LOWER SLAUGHTER

One of the most popular of the twin villages in the Cotswolds connected by the Eye Stream and an easy-going footpath. Famous for the Old Mill and the three prestigious hotels: Lords Of The Manor, Lower Slaughter Manor House and The Slaughters Country Inn.

10 STANWAY

This village is dominated by the outstanding Manor House often featured in period TV dramas for in its grounds stands one of the country's finest tithe barns and across the road a thatched cricket pavilion is set on staddle stones. The Gatehouse is a marvel of architectural splendour.

WHERE TO STAY

Thyme, Southrop ss

This is a representative selection of what follows in this book and to make choosing your B&B, hotel or Inn an easy and quick process. We suggest you view their websites to find one that suits your tastes, expectations and budget. It is often the unexpected that will surprise you. Perhaps a luxurious bathroom, an exquisite view, attentive and discreet staff or a quirky and fun temperament that will draw you back again and again. In recent years the Cotswolds has seen a rebirth in the old-fashioned hostelry - Inns With Rooms. That these establishments are enthusiasts for fine dining is no accident. They would rather draw you to their tables and be able to offer a comfortable bed to sleep in and refresh you for another day, so as to spend more time at table.

Nowhere in England is the English Country Hotel more in evidence than within the Cotswold triangle. That these establishments are enthusiasts for fine dining is by no means an accident, and is a reflection on what the markets demands. But, whatever these businesses offer, when all is said and done you can not exchange charm, good manners and hospitality for material things. All are described in the following pages.

COUNTRY COTTAGE B&B

Bullocks Horn Cottage, Charlton.
01666 577600 bullockshorn.co.uk

Grey Cottage, Bath Road, Leonard Stanley.
01453 822515 grey-cottage.co.uk

Pinetum Lodge, Churcham. thepinetum.co.uk

COUNTRY HOUSE B&B

Clapton Manor, Clapton-on-the-Hill.
01451 810202 claptonmanor.co.uk

Eckington Manor Cookery School, Bredon.
01386 751600 eckingtonmanor.co.uk

Holmby House, Sibford Ferris. 01295 780140

Lower End House, Manor Road, Eckington.
01386 751600 eckingtonmanor.co.uk

Old Manor House, Halford. 01789 740264
oldmanor-halford.co.uk

Old Rectory, Cantax Hill, Lacock.
01249 730335 oldrectorylacock.co.uk

St Anne's B&B, Gloucester Street. Painswick.
01452 812879 st-annes-painswick.co.uk

Uplands House, Upton. 01295 678663
cotswolds-uplands.co.uk

Wren House, Donnington. 01451 831787
wrenhouse.net

COUNTRY HOUSE HOTELS

Bath Priory Hotel, Weston Road.
01225 331922 thebathpriory.co.uk

Buckland Manor Hotel, Nr Broadway.
01386 852626 bucklandmanor.co.uk

Cotswold House Hotel & Spa, The Square, Chipping Campden. 01386 840330
cotswoldhouse.com

Foxhill Manor. 01386 854200 foxhillmanor.com

WHERE TO STAY

Greenway, Shurdington. 01242 862352
thegreenwayhotelandspa.com

Lords of the Manor, Upper Slaughter.
01451 820243 lordsofthemanor.com

Lower Slaughter Manor House.
slaughtersmanor.co.uk

Manor House Hotel, Castle Combe.
01249 782206 exclusive.co.uk

Old Bell Hotel, Abbey Row. 01666 822344
oldbellhotel.co.uk

Rectory, Crudwell. 01666 577194
therectoryhotel.com

The Painswick. 01452 813289 thepainswick.co.uk

FARMHOUSE/BARN B&B

Barn B&B, Pensham. 01386 555270
pensham-barn.co.uk

Fosse Farm B&B, Castle Combe.
01249 782286. fossefarmhouse.com

Manor Farm, Weston Subedge.
01386 840390 manorfarmcotswolds.co.uk

Mount Pleasant Farm, Childswickham.
01386 853424 mountpleasantfarmbroadway.co.uk

North Farmcote, Winchcombe.
01242 602304 northfarmcote.co.uk

Salford Farm House, Salford Priors.
01386 870000 salfordfarmhouse.co.uk

Sudeley Hill Farm, Winchcombe.
01242 602344 cotswoldfarmstay.co.uk

Well Farm, Frampton Mansell.
07713 399613 well-farm.co.uk

West Farm, West Littleton. 07713 399613
westfarmandb.co.uk

Westley Farm, Chalford.
01285 760262 westleyfarm.co.uk

Weston Farm, Buscot Wick. 01367 252222

Whittington Lodge Farm, Whittington.
01242 820603 whittingtonlodgefarm.com

GUEST ACCOMMODATION (B&B)

Lacock Pottery, Lacock. 01249 730266

Moda House, Chipping Sodbury.
01454 312135 modahouse.co.uk

INNS WITH ROOMS

Amberley Inn. 01453 872565
theamberleyinn.co.uk

Angel Inn Hotel, Pershore.
01386 552046 angelpershore.co.uk

Bell Inn, Langford.

01367 860249 thebelllangford.com

Black Horse, Naunton. 01451 850565

Bull Inn, Charlbury. 01608 810689

Churchill Arms, Paxford. 01386 593159
churchillarms.co

Double Red Duke, Clanfield.
01367 810222 countrycreatures.com

38, The Park, Cheltenham ss

17

WHERE TO STAY

Wild Rabbit ss

Ebrington Arms, Ebrington.
01386 593123 theebringtonarms.co.uk

Eight Bells Inn. Church Street.
01386 840371 eightbellsinn.co.uk

Falkland Arms, Great Tew.
01608 683653 falklandarms.co.uk

Five Alls (The), Filkins.
01367 860875 thefiveallsfilkins.co.uk

Fleece, 11 Church Green, Witney.
01993 892270 fleecewitney.co.uk

Fleece Inn, Bretforton. 01386 831173
thefleeceinn.co.uk

Fox, Oddington. 01451 767000
foxoddington.com

George Hotel, Shipston-on-Stour.
01608 661453 georgeshipston.co.uk

Golden Heart, Birdlip. 01242 870261
thegoldenheart.co.uk

Highway Inn, 117 High Street, Burford.
01993 823661 thehighwayinn.co.uk

Horse & Groom, Bourton-on-the-Hill.
01386 700413 butcombe.com

Horse & Groom, Upper Oddington.
01451 830584 horseandgroomcotswolds.co.uk

Horse and Groom Inn, The Street, Charlton. 01666 823904 butcombe.com

Howard Arms, Ilmington. 01608 682226
howardarms.com

Inn For All Seasons, Little Barrington.
01451 844324 innforallseasons.com

Kings Arm's, Didmarton. 01454 238245
butcombe.com

Kings Arms, Stow-On-The-Wold.
01451 830364 thekingsarmsstow.co.uk

Kings Arms Hotel, Woodstock. 01993 813636
kingshotelwoodstock.co.uk

Kings Head Inn, Bledington. 01608 658365
thekingsheadinn.net

Lamb Inn, Burford. 01993 823155
cotswold-inns-hotels.co.uk/the-lamb-inn

Lamb Inn, Shipton-Under-Wychwood.
01993 832116 thelambshipton.com

Lion Inn, Winchcombe. 01242 603300
butcombe.com

Maytime, Asthall. 01993 822068
themaytime.com

Old Swan, Minster Lovell. 01993 862512
oldswan.co.uk

Plough (The), Kelmscott. 01367 253543
theploughinnkelmscott.com

Red Lion, Long Compton. 01608 684221
redlion-longcompton.co.uk

Cowley Manor ss

WHERE TO STAY

Redesdale Arms, Moreton-In-Marsh.
01608 650308 redesdalearms.com

Swan Inn, Swinbrook. 01993 823339
theswanswinbrook.co.uk

The Chequers at Churchill. 01608 659393
lionearth.co.uk

The Halfway at Kineton 07425 970507
thehalfwayatkineton.com

The Plough at Kingham. 01608 658327
thekinghamplough.co.uk

The Swan, Southrop. 01367 850205 thyme.co.uk

The Wild Rabbit, Kingham. 01608 658389
thewildrabbit.co.uk

Timbrell's Yard, Bradford-On-Avon.
01225 869492 timbrellsyard.com

The Trout, Tadpole Bridge. 01367 870382
butcombe.com

Wheatsheaf, Northleach. 01451 539889
cotswoldwheatsheaf.com

Wheelright Arms, Monkton Combe.
01225 722287
wheelwrightsarmsbath.co.uk

White Hart, Winchcombe. 01242 602359
whitehartwinchcombe.co.uk

LUXURIOUS B&B

Abbots Grange, Church Street, Broadway.
02081 338698 abbotsgrange.com

Eckington Manor, Hammock Road, Eckington. 01386 751600
eckingtonmanor.co.uk

Frampton Court, Frampton-On-Severn.
01452 740698 framptoncourtestate.co.uk

Slaughters Manor Hotel ss

The Boot, Barnsley ss

Greyhounds B&B, 19 Sheep Street, Burford.
01993 822780/07711 342608
greyhoundsburford.com

Manfred Schotten, Burford.
01993 822302 sportantiques.co.uk

Manor Farm House, Ab Lench.
01386 462226

Marlborough Arms, Woodstock. 01993 811227
themarlborougharms.co.uk

Mill Hay House, Broadway. 01386 852498
millhay.co.uk

No. 15 Great Pulteney Street, Bath.
01225 807105 guesthousehotels.co.uk

Oak House No.1 Hotel, The Chipping, Tetbury. 01666 505611 oakhouseno1.com

RUSTIC CAMPING

Cotswold Farm Park, Nr Bourton-on-the-Water. 01451 850307 cotswoldfarmpark.co.uk

Cotswold View Campsite, Charlbury.
01608 810314 cotswoldview.co.uk

Denfurlong Farm, Chedworth.
07707 181125 cotswoldcampsite.co.uk

Far Peak Camping, Northleach.
01285 700370 farpeakcamping.co.uk

Hayles Fruit Farm, Winchcombe.
01242 602123 haylesfruitfarm.co.uk

Abbey Home Farm, Burford Road, Cirencester. 01285 640441
theorganicfarmshop.co.uk

The Wildings, Bourton-on-the-Water. 01451 518869 thewildingscampsite.co.uk

WHERE TO STAY

Frampton Court (The Orangery)

SELF-CATERING

Arlington Mill, Bibury. manorcottages.co.uk

Frampton Court (The Orangery), Frampton-on-Severn. 01452 740698 framptoncourtestate.co.uk

Montreal House, Nr Barnsley. 01285 707785 montrealhouse.co.uk

Upper Court, Kemerton. 0333 335 5246 uppercourt.co.uk

SMALL HOTELS

Bay Tree Hotel, Sheep Street, Burford. 01993 822791 cotswold-inns-hotels.co.uk/the-bay-tree-hotel

Burford House, 99 High Street. Burford. 01993 823151 burford-house.co.uk

Castle Inn Hotel, Castle Combe. 01249 783030 exclusive.co.uk

Close Hotel, Tetbury. 01666 502272 cotswold-inns-hotels.co.uk

Cottage in The Wood, Holywell Road, Malvern. 01684 588860 cottageinthewood.co.uk

Ettington Park Hotel. 01789 450123 handpickedhotels.co.uk

Feathers Hotel, Woodstock. 01993 812291 feathers.co.uk

Hotel du Vin & Bistro, Cheltenham. 01242 370584 hotelduvin.com

New Inn, Coln St Aldwyn. 01285 750651 thenewinncoln.co.uk

No. 38 Evesham Road, Cheltenham. 01242 394014 no38thepark.com

No. 131 The Promenade, Cheltenham. 01242 822939 no131.com

Spa-Indoor Pool, Calcot Manor ss

WHERE TO STAY

Soho Farmhouse

Noel Arms Hotel, Chipping Campden.
01386 840317 bespokehotels.com

Ormond, Tetbury. 01666 505690
theormondtetbury.co.uk

Swan Hotel, Bibury. 01285 740695
cotswold-inns-hotels.co.uk

The Porch House, Stow-On-The-Wold.
01451 870048 porch-house.co.uk

The Slaughters Country Inn, Lower Slaughter. 01451 822145 theslaughtersinn.co.uk

Three Ways House Hotel, Mickleton. 01386 438429 threewayshousehotel.com

SPA & COUNTRY HOUSE HOTELS

Barnsley House, Nr Cirencester.
01285 740000 barnsleyhouse.com

Calcot Manor, Tetbury. 01666 890391
calcot.co

Combe Grove, Nr Bath. 01225 834644
combegrove.com

Cotswold House Hotel, Chipping Campden.
01386 840330 cotswoldhouse.com

Cowley Manor, Nr Cheltenham.
01242 870900 cowleymanorexperimental.com

Dormy House Hotel & Spa, Willersey Hill.
01386 852711 dormyhouse.co.uk

Ellenborough Park Hotel, Southam, Cheltenham. 01242 545454
ellenboroughpark.com

Ettington Park Hotel, Nr Stratford-Upon-Avon. 01789 450123 handpickedhotels.co.uk

15 Great Pulteney Street, Bath. 01225 807015
guesthousehotels.co.uk/no-15-bath

Lucknam Park, Colerne. 01225 742777
lucknampark.co.uk

Lygon Arms, Broadway. 01386 852255
lygonarmshotel.co.uk

Minster Mill, Minster Lovell. 01993 774441
minstermill.co.uk

Soho Farmhouse, Great Tew. 01608 691000
sohohouse.com

The Royal Crescent Hotel & Spa, 16 Royal Crescent, Bath. 01225 823333
royalcrescent.co.uk

Thyme Estate, Southrop. 01367 850174
thyme.co.uk

Whatley Manor, Easton Grey.
01666 822588 whatleymanor.com

Woolley Grange, Bradford-on-Avon.
01225 864705 woolleygrangehotel.co.uk

Wyck Hill House Hotel & Spa, Nr Stow-On-The-Wold. 01451 831936
wyckhillhousehotel.co.uk

THE VALUE & SURVIVAL OF HOSPITALITY

The Covid-19 Pandemic has been likened to a tsunami; b&bs, cafés, camp sites, hotels, inns/pubs, restaurants and self-catering businesses have been closed, some swept away for ever. Those with a will and an opportunity sold take-away meals to ease their cash flow, and the Government kept many businesses alive through the Furlough Scheme. But, this was all been for the short-term. The self-employed entrepreneur who placed all their savings into the business will not have wished to take on more debt and risk. A number of restaurateurs with a number of establishments have reduced them to one, or closed them for good. It is a hard game.

Indeed, the doyen, the original that created the genre of the English Country House Hotel, the Sharrow Bay in Cumbria went into administration. Covid-19 may not have been wholly responsible for its demise. Had it not addressed the new markets so steadfastly pursued by Barnsley House, The Painswick, Lords of the Manor? Today, these hotels need something extra, whether it be a brilliant chef or various hedonistic pleasures. They also need strong leadership, a passion and a vocation to serve. Others hung on by their fingertips in the hope that the months of Staycation restored their livelihoods. Then to top it all, Brexit and the lack of affordable housing exacerbated the staffing problems. Inns, hotels and restaurants have closed for two or three days each week. Whatever the outcome of all of this we wish them every success and good luck.

When we set out to up-date the Listings, what would we find? Who had closed down, What was new? Our policy has always been subjective. We like good manners, comfort, discretion, style and professional expertise. We like quirky personalities and value-for-money. We rarely include multiples. It is the Independent, free-spirited host/hostesses we are drawn to. So, we include the full gamut; the country house hotel, the lively Inn With Rooms, the wacky rustic camp site, the delicious deli and coffee shop. It is a wide range. Those that are in business will require your patience and good faith. Many will have lost staff and will have had to train the new. Their financial frailties will have been tested, but one hopes they will find new vigour to welcome you! In the article below an idyllic hostelry (Inn With Rooms/Small Hotel) is described. Many generations of the same family have run this business. They provide comfort, good manners, wholesome food, a refuge from this crazy world. They have no debt, no bank manager giving them grief. They have independence from a brewery. They are chilled. How many like them do you know in the UK?

AN EXTRACT FROM A WALKING MAN'S JOURNAL

Winter. For five months I had been tramping across Europe following paths, ancient tracks, canal and riverside paths. Where I could, I bought the local maps but very often I would just set my compass on a south-easterly bearing. Now I had reached a mountain range, and to cross a tricky col had decided to follow the old Pilgrim's path. I had heard it was way-marked and I needed an easy route down the mountain. Thing is, I missed it. A storm had come in. I had become disorientated and followed a parallel path that led me down into a valley where I had found refuge in a deserted barn.

For two or three days the storm raged. A helter-skelter of snow, hail and wind. I dined on packets of minestrone soup, chunks of brown bread, raisins, chorizo sausage and dark chocolate (always, chocolate in reserve).

On Saturday morning the day shone brightly. But, somehow I lost the path again, and found myself sliding down a rough track beside a torrent. Hopskipping over boulder to boulder, wet, cold, bedraggled, I slowly got off the mountain. By mid-afternoon I was pretty well beaten up and worried about where I could find refuge. A church bell woke me from my reverie. Through the mist I spied a mountain village. Entering the village a group were standing idly at the church's gate. Did they know of a local inn I could stay at? Oh yes. The inn was in that direction. I couldn't miss it.

I smelt the wood smoke before I saw it. A solid stone built building with large chimney stacks at either end. Lights ablaze inside. The Inn stood on its own. A couple of vehicles were parked to the side, behind wood neatly stacked.

I entered through a heavy wooden door. A large, hairy bearded man stood inside slicing thin pieces of meat. Above him hanging from the ceiling were hams and sausages. On seeing me he stopped, quickly came around the bar and took my pack off me.

"Yes, we have been waiting for you. We spied you on the mountain this morning and

THE VALUE & SURVIVAL OF HOSPITALITY

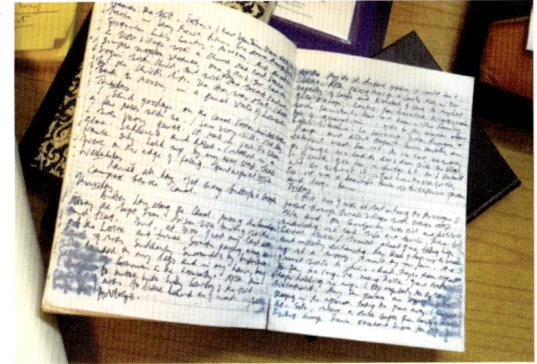
Journal

wondered when you would arrive…come in, come in, settle yourself down over there by the fire and I'll bring you some water - you must be dehydrated - No worries, a room has been prepared for you." I slumped into a threadbare armchair beside the blazing fire and looked about me; low beams, wooden panels and oil paintings of hunting scenes, mountains and torrential rivers. Animals heads; foxes, badgers, deer stood out on plinths….a long, bruegellesque table was set ready for a busy repast.

I fell asleep.

I dreamt I was standing beneath a waterfall, my face burnished by cool running water…. "Wake up, wake up." I looked into the brown eyes of a massive hairy beast who was licking my face. A wolf hound. The hound was pulled away and two little girls stood in front of me. Behind them stood one of the most beautiful women I had ever seen. "Hello, don't mind Wolfie. It's her way of saying welcome. I am Francesca and this is Flora and Isabella. I have drawn you a bath and there are clean clothes, I hope not too large for you, Andrea's, and if you don't mind taking these off upstairs we can get them into the wash." I noticed my boots had been pulled off me and my bare feet were being nibbled by Wolfie. My boots had been cleaned and polished and were sitting beside the fire. Laughter and the noise of people having a good time were somewhere in the distance.

While I was taking all this in Francesca continued: "We have been expecting you. A shepherd friend sighted you early this morning and warned us of your imminent arrival. You are to be our guest. No arguments. You remind us of Andrea who like you lost his way ten years ago and arrived unannounced and has never left…"

I'm not surprised I thought. Lucky man. She continued. "Today is our Saint's Day. You saw the Choir entering the church for St Teresa's Mass. And, here they are this evening for a celebratory supper and you are to be their special guest. So no worries, enjoy your bath and come down in your own time."

The meal is all a hazy memory. I remember a thick broth followed by thinly sliced cold meats and cheeses, followed by a casserole….and pints of warm ale. I have no idea why but they all appeared very interested in my adventures and asked me endless questions. It was all very exhausting and I can't remember being taken to bed. It was a raucous and friendly evening…

I stayed for two more nights and earned my keep by helping Andrea chop wood, load his trailer and stack them around the Inn. Now that was quite a skill. It so happened the Inn had been in Francesca's family for six generations. For me it was a home from home. Their hospitality and kindness was natural and sincere, the food, simple country fare, and the decor resounded in history and comfort. One word, snug, describes the Inn. Of course, like all who stayed I fell in love with Francesca and Andrea and their children, and Wolfie. I was to return many times until the earthquake destroyed much of the village. Luckily, the Inn survived and by then the children had grown and left home, and their parents had leased the building whilst they sort new adventures in the City.

Postcards sent home

23

WHERE TO EAT AND DRINK

Selecting a café, inn or restaurant with rooms can make or break a romantic weekend. It may also determine where you decide to stay. Luckily, you have an amazing choice. The Cotswolds has an over supply of food emporia from the humble tearoom to the precious dining-pub. These have grown out of the demise of the common pub and in their place have come young, ambitious chefs to turn what was potentially an attractive building into a restaurant within (what was) a pub. To appease the locals, a couple of bar stools and a little bar area may remain, (and the skittle alley will be available for two nights a week). The Cotswolds has a fair number of traditional hostelries and at least three breweries: Donningtons, Hook Norton, and the Uley Brewery. Specialist cider houses have fallen by the wayside.

The English Country House hotel is well represented here too, and they all have prestigious restaurants and (often) a more laid-back brasserie or bistro for informal dining. Seek out the Lunch Deals.

Herewith, a representative selection of what follows in the following pages. If the pub/restaurant has rooms, this has been indicated with a B&B which will help you select a country pub with rooms.

Lords of the Manor ss

New Brewery Arts, Brewery Court, Cirencester. B&B. 01285 657181
newbreweryarts.org.uk

Quayles, Tetbury. 07974422272
quaylescornerhhouse.com

Quince & Clover, The Old Post Office, Great Tew. 01608 683225
quinceandclover.co.uk

Williams Food Hall & Oyster Bar, Nailsworth. 01453 852240
williamsfoodhall.co.uk

CAFÉ/BISTROS/DELIS

Bakery On The Water, Bourton-On-The-Water. 01451 822748 bakeryonthewater.co.uk

Broadway Deli, 16 High Street, Broadway. 01386 853040 broadwaydeli.co.uk

D'Ambrosi Fine Foods, Stow-On-The-Wold. 01451 833888 dambrosi.co.uk

The Old Prison Café, Northleach. 01451 860339 theoldprison.co.uk

Hampers Food & Wine Company, Oxford Street, Woodstock. 01993 811535 hampersfoodandwine.co.uk

Jolly Nice Farm Shop & Kitchen (Takeaway) Café, Frampton Mansell. 01285 760868 jollynicefarmshop.com

MBB Brasserie, Corn Hall, Cirencester. 01285 700900 mbbbrasserie.co.uk

Mrs Bumbles of Burford, 31 Lower High St. Burford. 01993 822209 bumblesofburford.co.uk

The Chequers, Churchill ss

WHERE TO EAT AND DRINK

Buckland Manor Hotel ss

ETHNIC/VEGETARIAN RESTAURANTS

Chef Imperial, 22 High Street, Woodstock.
01993 813591

Curry Corner, 133 Fairview Road, Cheltenham. 01242 528449 thecurrycorner.com

Joy Kitchen, 157 Southgate St., Gloucester.
01452 923120 joykitchen-gl.co.uk

La Galleria Ristorante Italiano, 2 Market Place, Woodstock. 01993 813781
lagalleriawoodstock.com

Mayflower Chinese Restaurant, 29 Sheep Street, Cirencester. 01285 642777

Oak Vegetarian Restaurant, 2 North Parade Passage. 01225 446059 oakrestaurant.co.uk

Prithvi, Bath Road, Cheltenham.
01242 226229 prithvirestaurant.com

Siam Thai, 1 Horse Street, Chipping Sodbury.
01454 850095 siamthai.org

FARM SHOPS WITH RESTAURANTS

Daylesford Organic Farmshop.
01608 731670 daylesford.com

The Organic Farm Shop, Burford Road, Cirencester. 01285 640441
theorganicfarmshop.co.uk

FOODIE HOSTELRIES/(GASTRO) PUBS

Gumstool Inn, Calcot Manor, Tetbury. B&B.
01666 890391 calcot.co

Bell at Sapperton. 01285 760298
bellsapperton.co.uk

Bell Inn, Langford. 01367 860249
thebelllangford.com

Boxing Hare, Swerford. 01608 683212
theboxinghare.co.uk

Butchers Arms, Eldersfield. 01452 840381
thebutcherarms.net

Churchill Arms, Paxford. B&B.
01386 593159 churchillarms.co

Five Alls (The), Filkins. B&B. 01367 860875
thefiveallsfilkins.co.uk

Horse & Groom, Charlton. 01666 823904
butcombe.com

The Chequers at Churchill. 01608 659393
lionearth.co.uk

The Halfway at Kineton. 07425 970507
thehalfwayatkineton.com

The Plough at Kingham. B&B. 01608 658327
thekinghamplough.co.uk

Kings Head Inn, Bledington. B&B.
01608 658365 thekingsheadinn.net

WHERE TO EAT AND DRINK

Olive Tree Restaurant, Queensberry Hotel ss

Lion Inn, 33 North Street, Winchcombe. B&B. 01242 603300 butcombe.com

Maytime Inn, Asthall. B&B. 01993 822068 themaytime.com

Plough Inn (The), Kelmscott. B&B. 01367 253543 theploughinnkelmscott.com

Royal Oak, Whatcote. 01295 688100 theroyaloakwhatcote.co.uk

Swan Inn, Swinbrook. B&B. 01993 823339 theswanswinbrook.co.uk

The Boot, Barnsley. B&B. 01285 740421 thebootbarnsley.co.uk

The Swan, Southrop. B&B. 01367 850205 thyme.co.uk

The Wheatsheaf Inn, Northleach. B&B. 01451 539889 cotswoldswheatsheaf.com

The Wild Rabbit, Kingham. B&B. 01608 658389 thewildrabbit.co.uk

LUNCH IN FORMAL SURROUNDINGS

Barnsley House (& garden visit), Nr Cirencester. 01285 740000 barnsleyhouse.com

Bath Priory Hotel, Weston Road Bath. 01225 331922. thebathpriory.co.uk

Buckland Manor, Nr Broadway. 01386 852626 bucklandmanor.co.uk

Calcot Hotel & Spa, Nr Tetbury. 01666 890391 calcot.co

Close Hotel, Long Street, Tetbury. 01666 502172 cotswold-inns-hotels.co.uk

Cotswold House Hotel & Spa, The Square, Chipping Campden. 01386 840330 cotswoldhouse.com

Lords of the Manor, Upper Slaughter. 01451 820243 lordsofthemanor.com

Lucknam Park Hotel & Spa, Colerne. 01225 742777 lucknampark.co.uk

Slaughters Manor Hotel. 01451 820456 slaughtersmanor.co.uk

The Painswick, Kemps Lane. Painswick. 01452 813688 thepainswick.co.uk

The Royal Crescent Hotel & Spa, 16 Royal Crescent, Bath. 01225 823333 royalcrescent.co.uk

RESTAURANT WITH ROOMS

Angel, 14 Witney Street, Burford. 01993 822714 theangelatburford.co.uk

Bower House, Market Place, Shipston-On-Stour. 01608 663333 bower.house

Feathered Nest, Nether Westcote. 01993 833030 thefeatherednestinn.co.uk

Russell's, Broadway. 01386 853555 russellsofbroadway.co.uk

The Rectory, Crudwell. 01666 577194 therectoryhotel.com

Three Ways House Hotel, Mickleton. 01386 438429 threewayshousehotel.com

Timbrell's Yard, 49 St Margaret's Street, Bradford-On-Avon. 01225 869492 timbrellsyard.com

WHERE TO EAT AND DRINK

Wesley House, Winchcombe. 01242 602366
wesleyhouse.co.uk

Wild Garlic & Wilder, 3 Cossack Square, Nailsworth. 01453 832615 wild-garlic.co.uk

TOWN RESTAURANTS

Purslane, Rodney Road, Cheltenham. 01242 321639 purslane-restaurant.co.uk

5 North Street, Winchcombe. 01242 604566
5northstreetrestaurant.co.uk

No. 131 The Promenade, Cheltenham. 01242 822939 no131.com

The Circus Restaurant, 34 Brock Street, Bath. 01225 466020
thecircusrestaurant.co.uk

The Old Butchers, Stow-on-the-Wold. 01451 831700 theoldbutchers.squarespace.com

Woods, 9-13 Alfred Street, Bath. 01225 314812 woodsrestaurant.com

TRADITIONAL PUBS (NOT ALL SERVE FOOD – BUT, MOST DO)

Back Lane Tavern, 11 Park Lane, Woodstock. 01993 810826 backlanetavern.co.uk

Bakers Arms, Broad Campden. 01386 840515 bakersarmscampden.co.uk

Bathurst Arms, North Cerney. 01285 831888 bathurstarms.co.uk

Bear Inn, Bisley. 01452 771153
bearinnbisley.com

The Wild Rabbit ss

Beehive, 1-3 Montpelier Villas, Cheltenham. 01242 702270 thebeehivemontpelier.com

Butcher's Arms, Sheepscombe. 01452 812113
butchers-arms.co.uk

Ebrington Arms, Ebrington. B&B.
01386 593223 theebringtonarms.co.uk

Falkland Arms, Great Tew. B&B.
01608 683653 falklandarms.co.uk

Fleece Inn, Bretforton. 01386 831173
thefleeceinn.co.uk

Fox at Oddington. 01451 767000
thefoxatoddington.com

George Inn, 4 West Street, Lacock. 01249 730263 georgeinnlacock.co.uk

Golden Heart, Birdlip. B&B. 01242 870261
thegoldenheart.co.uk

Lamb Inn, Sheep St. Burford. B&B.
01993 823155
cotswold-inns-hotels.co.uk/the-lamb-inn

Old Spot Inn, Hill Road, Dursley. 01453 542870 oldspotinn.co.uk

Plough Inn, Ford. 01386 584215
theploughinnford.co.uk

Morris Clown, High Street, Bampton. 01993 850217

Royal Oak, Ramsden. 01993 868213
royaloakramsden.com

Seven Tuns Inn, Chedworth. 01285 720630
seventuns.com

The Trout, Tadpole Bridge. B&B.
01367 870382 butcombe.com

The Volunteer, Chipping Campden. 01386 840688 thevolunteerinn.net

Weighbridge Inn, Longfords, Nailsworth. 01453 832520 weighbridgeinn.co.uk

Woodstock Arms, Market Street. 01993 811251 thewoodstockarms.com

Woolpack Inn, Slad. 01452 813429
thewoolpackslad.com

Yew Tree Inn, Conderton. 01386 725364
yewtreepub.com

THE GOLDEN FLEECE OF THE COTSWOLD SHEEP

Sheep have grazed on the Cotswold hills for more than 2,000 years - and the most famous breed was The Cotswold, whose lustrous, curly fleece was famous throughout Europe. Here is the story of that sheep - known as The Lion of the Cotswolds...

Today, there is not much more than a ton or two of Cotswold fleece-wool available each year. It is long-stapled (more than 6 inches), reasonably lustrous and of mid 40's quality (for comparison Merino is mid 60's plus, Lincoln about mid 30's). Until recently, Cotswold wool was for many years lumped in with other English lustre-wools - and used mainly for carpets and industrial cloths. During the early 1980's Cotswold Woollen Weavers recognised its potential and revived its use. In particular, the natural lustre and the clarity with which it accepts dye made the wool ideal for loose-twist worsted spinning, and weaving into soft-furnishing cloths - a range of dramatic block-weave throws and rugs.

Cotswold Woollen Weavers' activities have coincided with a renewed interest in the Cotswold breed, and is thus a good time for a re-appraisal of the breed. For too long, the historic pedigree of Cotswold wool has been ignored as irrelevant. But it was not always so. The Cotswolds are marked with the history of the Cotswold sheep and its fleece. But, it is a puzzling, clouded history. For, although the great Wool Churches stand four-square in many a Cotswold village, as solid testimony to the power and wealth of the medieval merchants who endowed them, not much can be said with certainty about the wool which the Cotswold sheep provided. There is certainly a lot of superstition: even a bogus derivation of the very word Cotswold (sheep cot on the wold, or open hillside) has been widely used to puff the influence of wool in the area.

Certainly wool has long been an important English commodity, and the Cotswolds an important source for it. 500 years ago wise men agreed that half the wealth of England rides on the back of the sheep - wool exports paid for Richard the Lionheart's ransom to the Saracens.

The Lord Chancellor sits in The House of Lords to this day on a sack stuffed with wool to show the preeminent position which the wool industry has played in this country's affairs. The medieval weavers of C12 Flanders happily sang: The best wool in Europe is Cotswold, and the best wool in England is Cotswold. But what sort of wool was it that they prized so highly?

The Medieval Cotswolds

There is evidence that the Romans brought sheep with them as they battled northwards, and perhaps they introduced them to the Cotswold hills around the important Roman settlement of Corinium, (Cirencester). They would have valued these sheep for their milk and for their fleece: shivering Southern European mercenary soldiers needed warm winter coats. There is further evidence, based mostly on scanty skeletal remains, that these Roman imports were the ancestors of the great flocks of Medieval Cotswolds - and indeed of all the English longwool breeds.

The temptation is to look at a Cotswold sheep today, to sink one's hand in its thick lustrous long-wool fleece, and think fondly of an unbroken pedigree stretching back 2,000 years to those early Roman farmers. The problem is that for most of the intervening years virtually nothing is known for sure. Shepherds reasonably enough have rarely thought it sensible to spend their time writing down descriptions of their flocks: the first book in English entirely about sheep was not published until 1749 (Ellis- The Shepherd's Sure Guide), and the first comprehensive resumé of English wool not until 1809 (Luccock - An Essay on Wool). But by then, the early C19, the heyday of the Cotswold sheep was over. And of course, woollen cloth gets worn out, and is attacked by moth and mould: there is very little extant medieval woollen cloth available for analysis.

During the Early Medieval centuries England was a relatively underpopulated country, with plenty of rolling hill-pasture to sustain vast land-hungry flocks of sheep kept for their fleece. Perhaps 500,000 sheep roamed the Cotswolds, and most of their wool was exported to Flanders and Lombardy; more densely populated countries which could not spare land for wool growing. Thousands upon thousands of packhorses laden with wool-bales wound their way down from the High Cotswold hills to The Thames. They crossed the river at Radcot and proceeded southwards to Southampton, or saw their loads shipped on barges to London. The continental weavers paid royally for the wool, the Cotswold merchants grew rich and built their churches, and the English crown paid its way with the taxes levied on the trade.

But was this Golden Fleece (the Cotswold sheep was long known as The Lion of the Cotswolds) the long, heavy, lashy wool that the modern Cotswold bears, or something shorter, softer and more like the Ryeland wool from Herefordshire which was equally important to the medieval weavers?

There are memorial brasses in Northleach church which show what look like newly shorn Cotswolds just like those which crop the grass today, and some commentators suggest the Cotswold was always

Cotswolds Lions

a big, longwoolled breed (Youatt, for instance, quotes that sage Gervase Markham to this effect). But others suggest that the wool was once much softer: Michael Drayton, writing at the end of the C16 suggests that Cotswold wool was very fine: it comes very near that of Spain, for from it a thread may be drawn as fine as silk.

This Spanish comparison is important, because one conundrum revolves around the export - widely noted by contemporary commentators - of Cotswold sheep to Spain, particularly by Edward IV but up to 1425 when the export was banned as part of the increasingly draconian network of laws to safeguard the interests of the burgeoning English wool-weaving industry. Spain was the home of the fine-woolled merino sheep, and it is inconceivable that English, and specifically Cotswold sheep, could have been so fine as to be worth cross-breeding with merinos. The most likely explanation is that Cotswolds were different from merinos: long-woolled enough to provide fleece to make alternative cloths.

Clattering Loom-shuttles

Until the late C19, and advanced mechanical innovation, it was not possible to spin worsted yarn from short fibre. The wool from which worsted yarn was spun had to be combed by hand to eliminate short hair (noils) and to align every fibre parallel to the direction of the yarn. Then tight, flat yarn could be spun and tough, sleek cloth could be woven: quite different from the spongy, less sophisticated cloths which could be woven from yarn woollen spun from shorter merino and down-breed fleece. Perhaps medieval Cotswold sheep were shorter and softer fleeced than they are today, but their wool was still lustrous and strong enough to be ideal for worsted spinning. If nothing else, Cotswold fleece could provide Spanish soldiers with tough, resilient serge uniforms, and nobles with flowing, draping cloaks to wear over their shirts of soft, fluffy merino.

During the C16 and C17s, the rising clatter of loom-shuttles in the valleys around Stroud presaged England's transition from raw-fleece exporter to major woollen cloth manufacturer. So complete was this change that the crown eventually forbade the export of fleece altogether, and it remained illegal until 1824. Although, gradually, vast amounts of wool began to be imported from the wide, open spaces of Australia and South Africa (ideal for extensive sheeprearing) but it was the pre-eminence of English combing wools (including Cotswold) which helped establish England's superiority as a woollen textile manufacturer.

To some extent this issue of the nature of Cotswold wool is one of semantics: as William Marshall wrote, after he rode the Cotswold hills at the end of the C18, the Cotswold is a breed which has been prevalent on these hills, [since] time immemorial: it has been improved, but has not changed. (During the Improving Years of the C18, the Cotswold certainly increased in size as shepherds learnt new husbandry techniques.) Or as Ezra Carman wrote disarmingly in 1892, as he strove to sum up the evidence of three hundred years of literature about Cotswold fleece: It is difficult to reconcile these opinions, nor indeed is it necessary; the Cotswolds beyond the memory of our day have long been a longwoolled race and valuable... for their wool.

So, superstitions and all, in this volatile world perhaps it is acceptable, even necessary that there are these noble, mythic links with the past. If this be so, then The Golden Fleece, which might have provided uniforms for the Roman legions, paid for the Crusades, clothed C18 Europe with West of England Broadcloth and today makes splendid block-weave rugs, is certainly an ideal candidate.

Richard Martin
Cotswold Woollen Weavers, Filkins

THE SOUTH WEST COTSWOLDS

For Architecture, Cultural Festivals, Luxurious Hedonism, Shopping Sprees, Walking the Cotswold Way...

Bath is arguably the most beautiful town in England. It is second to London in the number of visitors it attracts and is thus a fine place to eat, drink and be merry, and to shop and attend cultural events. The surrounding villages are accordingly affluent and well-heeled (expensive) places to live. Bath is expensive but you can find more reasonably priced accommodation outside the town limits and many of these are listed in this book.

There are pretty and attractive villages aplenty outside Bath. The most popular being Castle Combe and Lacock. Both grew out of the wool industry, and both have been so well maintained that they amount to showcase villages. Sadly, you won't witness a herd of cattle being walked through at dawn and dusk, only perhaps the drayman upsetting the balance of this new life.

THE SOUTH WEST COTSWOLDS

Cross the M4 and you encounter two towns of comparative interest: Malmesbury and Tetbury. Malmesbury was the home of Athelstan, the first King of All England. And, Tetbury is the home of Prince Charles, next in line for the throne of England, and its protectorates. But, if these two men and their burghs don't hold your interest, and you still have a spring in your step after tramping the streets of Bath. Look to the Cotswold Way, a long distance footpath that leads north to Chipping Campden. It follows the edge of the escarpment, passes through many pretty villages and gorgeous woodland and will reward you with fine views and hours of solitary reflection. And, if trees take your fancy you must visit Westonbirt Arboretum, an arboreal paradise, second to none.

Pulteney Bridge, Bath

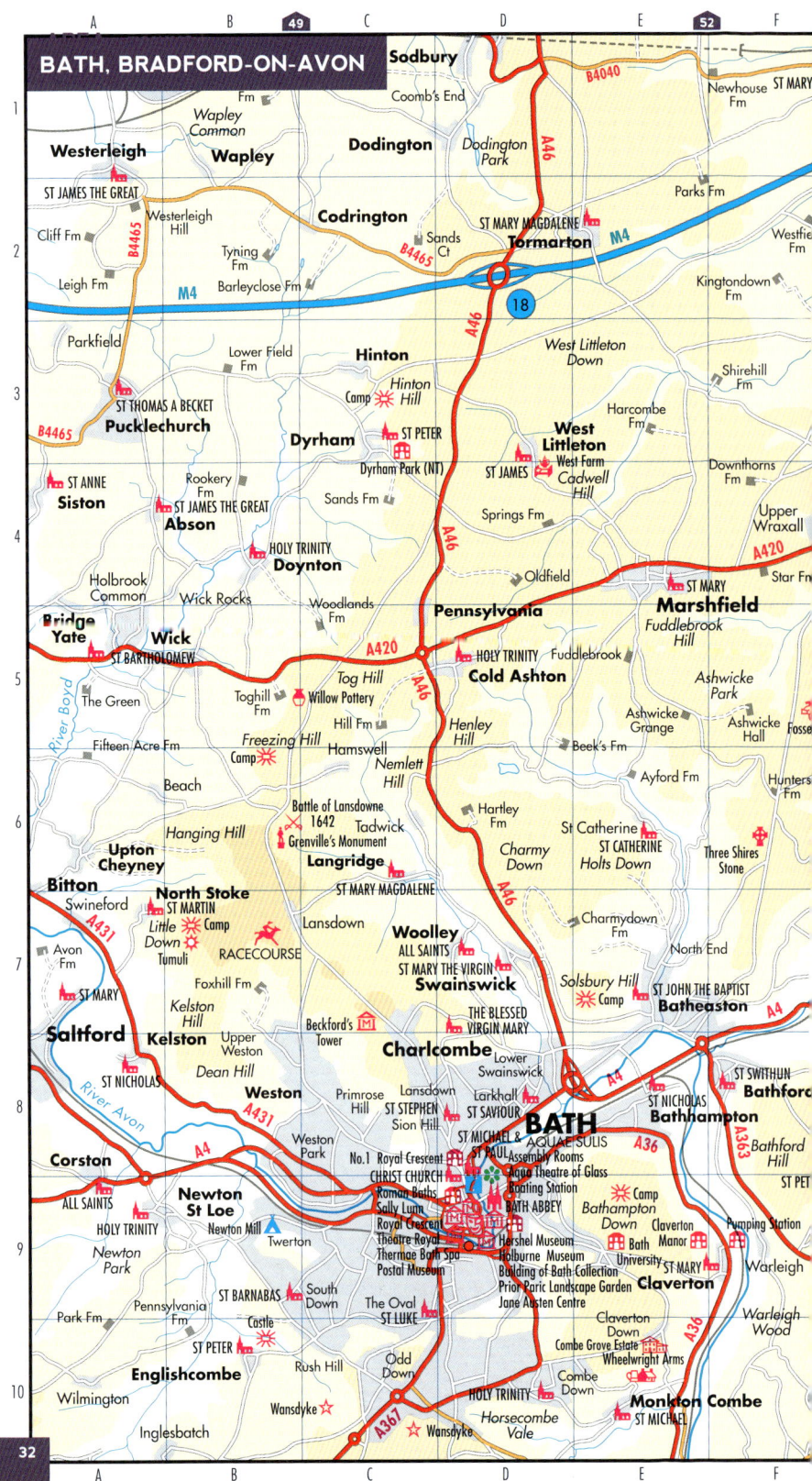

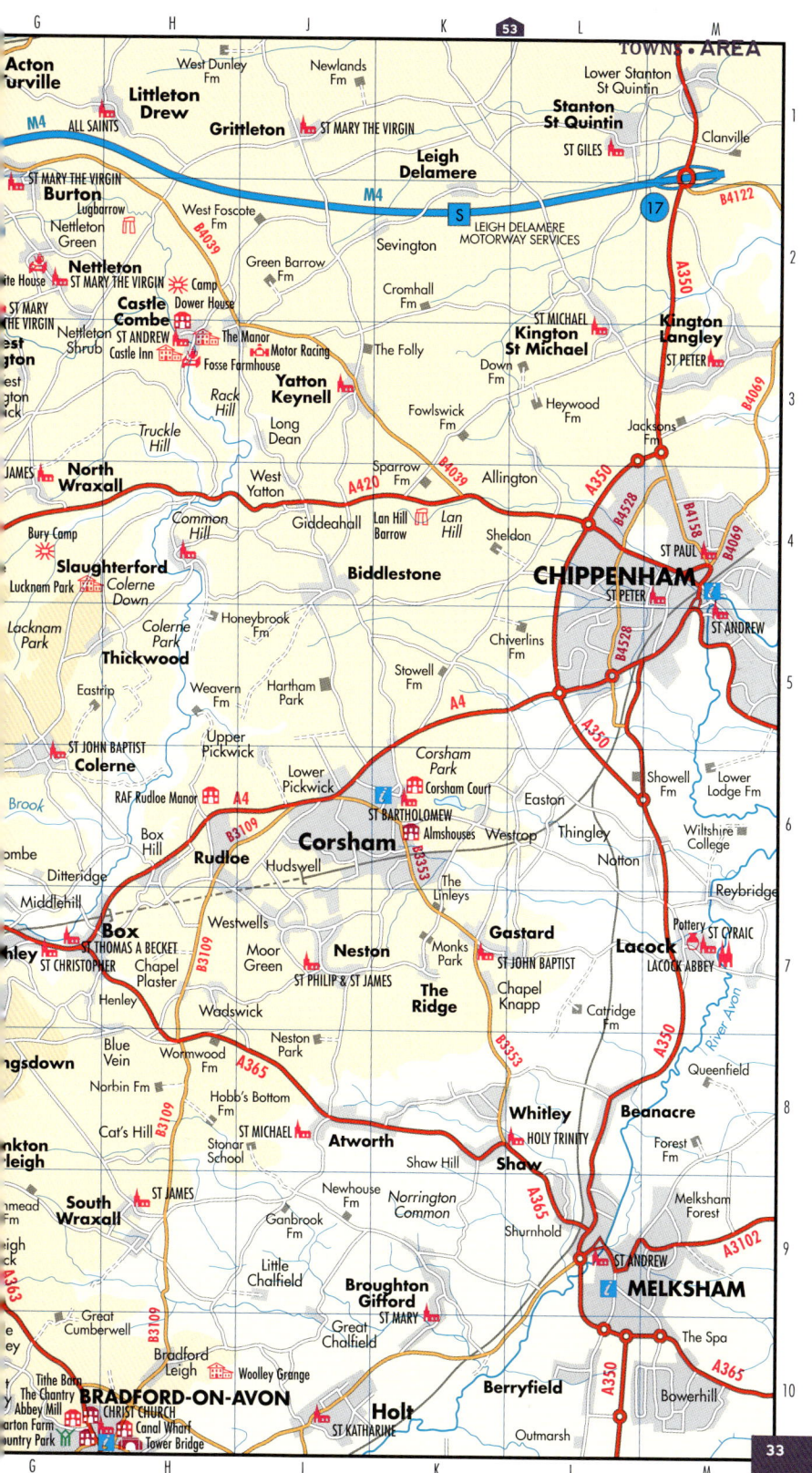

THE SOUTH WEST • Bath, Bradford-On-Avon, Castle Combe

BATH

Is Bath the most beautiful city in England? Many believe so, for, it is second only to London, in the number of visitors it attracts. It will captivate you today, as it has done so down the centuries, from the Romans to Jane Austen, to Robert Southey and the Romantic Poets, to the Rugby aficionados jostling to get into the Recreation Ground.

There is surely only one way to see Bath (apart from the top of an open double-decker bus, or from a hot-air balloon) and, that is to walk. So, prepare yourself, first with a good night's sleep, and second, with a comfortable pair of shoes, and a clear map. The day will be long and exhausting. Your eyes will be worn out with an overload of images, and your feet in need of a soothing bath. However, the next day you will be raring to go and see more of this visual feast and to revisit your favourite crescent. You have become a Bathophile. The Bath springs or hot waters were discovered by the mythical King Bladud (or Blaiddyd) in 863 BC, King of the Britons, and father of King Lear. The Celts venerated the site but it was the Romans in about 60-70 AD who developed the hot springs and built a wall around the 23 acre site naming it Aquae Sulis. The site held warm to hot to very cold baths, sweating rooms, massage areas and fitness rooms. It prospered for 400 years until the Romans withdrew from Britain in 410 AD. In 973 the Abbey was chosen as the setting for the coronation of King Edgar, and in 1157 it received the seat of a Bishopric. The city saw much prosperity in the Middle Ages due to the sale of Cotswold wool. The building of today's Abbey started in the C15. But, the heyday of Bath began over a 40- year period when three men of immense vision transformed the city from a populace of 3,000 into the Georgian city of 30,000 citizens. The three men, Beau Nash (Master of Ceremonies, manners and fashion), John Wood, (Architect), and Ralph Allen, (benefactor, financier and quarry owner who supplied the building materials). Today, Bath is an educational centre and host to many festivals: Cricket, Fashion, Literature, Music, to name, but a few. It is a bustling shopping centre with more than your average number of independent retailers. For those seeking

Golden Morning, The Circus, Bath

| 34 | 3500 BC | Neolithic farmers and herdsmen clear the forests | 3000 BC | Neolithic farmers and herdsmen clear the forests |

Bath, Bradford-On-Avon, Castle Combe • THE SOUTH WEST

York Street Arch & Bath Abbey

refreshment there appears to be a café, or bar, on every corner, and it boasts some of the West Country's finest restaurants. Listed and described below, are the most notable attractions to visit. For those arriving by car there are three Park & Rides, from the M4 there is the Race Course at Lansdown on the northern side of the City. In the City, 13 car parks, one is beneath the Podium Shopping Centre. Beware of bus lanes. More details below. E8) visitbath.co.uk

SPECIAL PLACES OF INTEREST...

Assembly Rooms (NT), Bennett Street. Designed in 1769 by John Wood, the Younger. These public rooms epitomise the elegance of fashion conscious life in Georgian society. These magnificent rooms were let out for parties and functions in the C18, as they are today. Café. Open daily 10-5. (D9) 01225 833977 nationaltrust.org.uk

Bath Abbey. The Church of St Peter and St Paul has seen three churches occupy this site: an Anglo-Saxon church in 757, and a Norman Cathedral in 1090, but, later in 1137 much was destroyed by fire. Today's building was founded in 1499, to replace the ruin damaged by fire. However, it had again to be rebuilt in 1611 following Henry VIII's Dissolution of the Monasteries. In simple architectural terms, it can be described as Perpendicular Gothic, and cruciform, in plan. The fan vaulting of the Nave is very fine and was designed by Robert and William Vertue, designers of Henry VII's chapel in Westminster Abbey. It was never finished until Gilbert Scott completed the original designs in the 1860s. Note, the Stairway to Heaven on the West Front: two ladders of carved angels are climbing towards Jesus Christ. Tower Tours. Open daily (Shop 10-4.30). (D9) 01225 422462 bathabbey.org

Bath Aqua Theatre of Glass, 105-107 Walcot Street. Demonstrations of glass blowing (from 10.30am) with a history of glass, stained glass, and museum. Gift shop. Open M-Sa 9.30-5, Su 10-5. (D9) 01225 428146 bathaquaglass.com

Bath Boating Station, Forrester Road. Try your hand at 'Wind in the Willows' on the River Avon. You can hire skiffs (rowing boats), punts and canoes (Canadian and kayaks) and navigate between Bathampton Weir and Pulteney Bridge. Boatman Restaurant. Self-catering units. Open daily 10-5.30. (D9) 01225 312900 bathboating.co.uk

| 3500 BC | Hetty Pegler's Tump and Belas Knapp long barrow, along with thousands of others are established across Britain | AD 43 | Romans invade Britain | 35 |

THE SOUTH WEST • Bath, Bradford-On-Avon, Castle Combe

Great Bath and Bath Abbey ss

Bath Rugby Club, Recreation Ground. Loyalty to this club hath no bounds. One of the West Country's premier rugby club has won glory in all competitions from the Heineken Cup to the English Premiership and European Challenge. Who can forget the sight of Jeremy Guscott, Stuart Barnes and Ben Clarke in full flow? (D9) 01225 325200
bathrugby.com

Beckford's Tower & Museum, Lansdown Road. Designed by Henry Goodridge in 1825 for the eccentric collector William Beckford, (1760-1844) to house his library of rare books, prints and paintings. For panoramic views over Bath, you must climb the spiral staircase of the 120ft neo-classical Tower. Open Mar to end Oct W/Es & BH Ms 11-4. (C7) 01225 422212
bath-preservation- trust.org.uk

Museum of Bath Architecture, The Paragon. A fascinating study of how Bath was transformed from a provincial town into the world-renowned Georgian city, thought of (at the time) as the finest city in Western Europe, and how classical design influenced the architects, builders and visionaries. Open Apr to Nov, M-F 1-5, W/Es & BHs 10-5. (D9) 01225 333895
museumofbatharchitecture.org.uk

Francis Gallery, 3 Fountain Buildings, Lansdown Road. Very much a gallery featuring contemporary art forms; paintings, sculptures, fabrics. Eclectic pieces that draw you in (forgive the pun), and may extract conversation, debate, sublimity. (D9) 01225 443220
francisgallery.co

Gallery Nine, 9b Margarets Buildings. The very best of jewellery, shell ceramics, sculptures in wood and engravings. Open Tu-Sa 10-5. 01225 319197
galleryninebath.com

Georgian Garden, Royal Victoria Park. A place to sit and meditate after pounding the streets amidst a simple, formal garden of variegated leaves and double-flowers. Open daily from 9. (D9)

Herschel Museum of Astronomy, 19 New King Street. A celebration of the many achievements of William and Caroline Herschel, distinguished astronomers and talented musicians whose research broached new knowledge of the solar system. In 1781 William discovered Uranus. Open daily 10-5. (D9) 01225 446865
herschelmuseum.org.uk

Holburne Museum of Art, Great Pulteney Street. A collection of fine, and decorative art, founded by Sir William Holburne in the C19. The paintings include landscapes by Guardi and Turner, portraits by Stubbs, Zoffany and Gainsborough. Café. Open daily 10-5, Su & BHs 11-5. (D9) 01225 388569
holburne.org

Jane Austen Centre, 40 Gay Street. Jane lived in Bath from 1801-1806 and the experience had a profound effect on her

| 36 | 44 | Celts build a shrine to the goddess Sulis | 60 | Romans name Bath, Aquae Sulis |

Bath, Bradford-On-Avon, Castle Combe • THE SOUTH WEST

writing. There are costume displays from TV's Persuasion and there are guided tours of Jane's Bath. Bookshop. Tearoom. Open Apr-Oct 9.45-5.30, Nov-Feb 10-4. (D9) 01225 443000 janeausten.co.uk

...and don't miss out on **Sydney Gardens** a favourite of Miss Austen.

Komedia, 22-23 Westgate Street. An arts venue with daytime café and evening bar. Comedy club, music from jazz to pop, and post-punk. Film. Closed M & Tu. 01225 489070 komedia.co.uk/bath

Little Theatre Cinema, St Michael's Place. Part of the Picturehouse chain of cinemas showing a mix of mainstream and art house films. Built in 1935, the cinema has retained the charm of the 30s, whilst being refurbished, with up-to-date technology and comfort. (D9) 0207326 2649 picturehouses.com

Magalleria, 5 Upper Borough Walls. Are you magazine crazy? Do you love to lie in bed reading mags all day, get off on the scents of rich print, the smooth texture of glossy paper? Specialist, independent titles galore. (D9) 01225 259602 store.magalleria.co.uk

Meticulous Ink, 134 Walcot Street. If you have a fascination for print, paper, typography and stationery this hive will enthuse you. Calligraphy and Letterpress workshops. Open daily M-Sa 10-5. (D9) 01225 333004 meticulousink.com

Museum of Bath at Work, Julian Road. Set in an C18 Real Tennis Court, the museum traces the development of Bath from the C17, to the present day, by illustrating engineering, printing, tourism and car making. Open daily Apr to end Oct 10.30-5. (D9) 01225 318348 bath-at-work.org.uk

Museum of East Asian Art, 12 Bennett Street. Founded by Brian McElney whose collection of fine ceramics, jades and bronzes from China, Japan, Korea and South East Asia date from 5,000 BC to the present day. Open summer W-F 11-5, Sa 10.30-5. (D9) 01225 464640 meaa.org.uk

No 1 Royal Crescent. Built between 1767 and 1774 by John Wood the Younger, to be the finest house in Bath. It was considered to be the very embodiment of C18 urban architecture, and was used to accommodate wealthy visitors and royalty. It portrays a vivid picture of Georgian Bath and you, too, can bathe in the brilliance of C18 life, by experiencing the Entrance Hall, Dining Room, Study, Drawing Room, Bedroom and Kitchen. Open Tu-Su 10-5.30. (D9) 01225 428126 no1royalcrescent.org.uk

Postal Museum, 27 Northgate Street. History of the postal system from ancient Egypt to today, and the men who developed Bath's system: Ralph Allen, John Palmer and Thomas Moore Musgrave. Wonderful display of the British postbox. Open M & Th 11-4, Tu, W & F 2-5. (D9) 01225 460333 bathpostalmuseum.org.uk

Prior Park Landscape Garden (NT). The brainchild of C18 entrepreneur Ralph Allen. Within an enchanting and wild wood, lies a Palladian bridge. The views of Bath from here are spectacular. Parking only for the disabled. Access is via a steep path from the railway station that passes by Widcombe's shops. Open daily 10-5 mid-Feb to 29 Oct and winter W/Es, 10-4. (D9) 01225 833977 nationaltrust.org.uk

Pulteney Bridge. Built by Robert Adam in 1773, for the entrepreneur Francis Pulteney, who planned to connect Bath with his new town, Bathwick. The plans were shelved, and this was sadly, Adam's only building in Bath. It was based on the Ponte Vecchio (Florence) and the Ponte di Rialto (Venice). (D9)

Roman Baths, Abbey Church Yard. The centre of this great city, and the centrifugal force of nature that created Bath. This is where the story began in 863 BC when King Bladud discovered the hot springs, whose rich mineral waters were to have magical healing powers. The Romans built a great temple around the spring, and dedicated it to the goddess, Sulis Minerva. What is extraordinary to fathom, is that the hot water erupts at 46 degrees centigrade, at a rate of 240,000 gallons (1,170,000 litres) per day. Where does it all go after this, you may well ask? The main features are: the Sacred Spring, the Roman Temple, the Roman Bath House and the Georgian Pump Room, a neo-classical salon where the hot spa water is available for consumption, along with morning coffee, lunch and afternoon teas. Open daily. (D9) 01225 477785 romanbaths.co.uk

Sally Lunn's Refreshment House & Museum, 4 North Parade Passage. The oldest

THE SOUTH WEST • Bath, Bradford-On-Avon, Castle Combe

Dyrham Park

house in Bath, and home of the original Bath bun. It houses a museum, as well as, providing coffee, lunch and cream teas. Open daily. (D9) 01225 461634 sallylunns.co.uk

The Circus. Originally named King's Circus, the vision and brilliance of John Wood the Elder, was built between 1754 and 1768. Sadly, he never saw his plans reach fruition. It was left to his son to complete the project. It was John Wood's intention to create a classical Palladian architectural landscape, inspired by Rome's Colosseum. The Circus is made up of 33 terraced houses. Thomas Gainsborough lived in No.17 from 1765-1774. In 1942 several were destroyed during the blitz. (D9)

The Royal Crescent. Built by John Wood the Younger between 1767 and 1774, and all houses were occupied by 1778. Today, the 30 original homes are split into flats, houses and an hotel, and many are privately owned. A society was founded in 1973 to protect the Crescent for future generations. Interestingly, it took the society 18 years to persuade the council to ban tourist buses and coaches from entering the crescent. (D9) royalcrescent.co.uk

Theatre Royal. A lively theatre with a busy Young People's Theatre, and locally sponsored events. It is one of the country's oldest theatres, first built by George Trim in 1705 with many guises, thereafter. The present building was renovated in 1982 and opened with "A Midsummer Night's Dream" starring Paul Scofield, Marsha Hunt and Jack Shepherd. The Vaults Restaurant. (D9) 01225 448844 theatreroyal.org.uk

Thermae Bath Spa. Combine the rich mineral waters of Bath with contemporary design, and the full range of spa treatments, and you have this haven of relaxation and hedonism. You can enjoy two-hour, four-hour or full day sessions, intermingled with the aromatic steam rooms and various massages on offer. Children under 16 are not permitted. Open daily from 9am. (D9) 01225 331234 thermaebathspa.com

Victoria Art Gallery, Bridge Street. Free admission provides a full programme of contemporary art, decorative art and British paintings by Sickert, Whistler, Zoffany and Gainsborough. Don't miss the hilarious caricatures depicting C18 Bath life. Open Tu-Su 10.30-5. (D9) 01225 477233 victoriagal.org.uk

EAT... DRINK...

Oak Vegetarian Restaurant, 2 North Parade Passage. Caters for vegetarians and vegans as well as all who love a tasty feast. Unpretentious and uncomplicated vegetarian food. Fine wines. Open for lunch 12-2.30 and dinner 5.30-9.30. 01225 446059 oakrestaurant.co.uk

Browns, Orange Grove. Browns does not offer an intimate dining experience, (100 seats) but the menu and ambience will be familiar to many who have a Browns in their locale, for sometimes, there is comfort in familiarity, especially when it tastes so good! Menu based on classic recognisable dishes. The building was once a police station and a Magistrates Court and retains the entrance doors suitable for horse-drawn Police vehicles! Open from 10 am. 01225 461199 browns-restaurants.co.uk

| 200 | Corinium (Cirencester) now the second largest town in Roman Britain | 577 | Native Britains beaten by Saxons (from Germania) at Battle of Dyrham (three British Kings killed in combat) |

Bath, Bradford-On-Avon, Castle Combe • THE SOUTH WEST

COFFEE/LIGHT BITES...

On every street corner and within every square and arcade you will be tempted to enter an eatery; from a specialist coffee shop to an organic deli to a full-scale restaurant. The choice is far and wide. Around the Abbey and Roman Baths, tourists flock. The locals tend to patronise the eateries north of Milsom Street or off it and in the squares, For Example: Kingsmead, and within the narrow lanes of Margaret Buildings and Bartlett Street. We list the independents. First head to the Royal Crescent. If **No 16** (hotel) doesn't take your fancy, pass by No 1 (historic building) and on your L is the walkway, Margaret's Buildings. Up on on your L, **The Green Bird Café at No 11**. A warm and friendly café open for breakfast, brunch and lunch. A visit here will set you up for the day in Bath. 01225 487846 greenbirdcafe.co.uk. Seeking inspiration? Head for **Berdoulat** at No. 8. A historic building since 1777 with goodies on 3-floors; An instore bakery and café, wine shop, herbs and spices, dried and fresh flowers, kitchen stuff and furniture. berdoulat.co.uk Moving onto and bearing L (north-east) through the (Kings) Circus, to **The Beckford Bottle Shop** at 5 Saville Row. Wine merchant and bistro serving small plates of charcuterie and large portions of intriguing conversation and hospitality. Bon Viveur! Open Tu-Sa 11-11. beckfordbottleshop.com You have a constitution of an Ox. Still hungry? Head down South Row to Bartlett Street into the Antiques Quarter, soon to find **Café Lucca** at No 1. An Italian experience of pleasures: pasta, salads, paninis. Indeed, considered a hip eatery and cake bakery. Very popular!

Onwards down Bartlett Street to The Paragon, a quick L for a reminder of your backpacking days and life on the trail, to the **Adventure Café.** Perhaps it's better to rough it than over sophisticate your pleasures? A cool place to hangout with your dog, bike and laptop. Food all-day. Great viewpoint. adventurecafebar.co.uk On leaving, R and L into Milsom Street for some shopping, exercise or culture vulturing. After which you may as well head for Kingsmead Square, to the **Society Café** in the corner. Popular with students, and locals and off the beaten track. Pasties and cakes, loose leaf teas, and artisan hot chocolates, and al fresco seating. society-café.com.

PUB-GRUB & ALES...

The choice is extensive. Heading the list, **The Star Inn, 23 The Vineyards**. A 16th century pub with oak panelled rooms. Rolls, bar snacks and choice of real ales. star-inn-bath.co.uk. Another authentic ale house is **The Old Green Tree at 12 Green Street.** Custom-made ales brewed for this cosy oak-panelled pub. Simple grub. Looking for more substantial food, head for **The Raven on Queen Street**. Hot pies, mash and sausages with gravy. A Free House with many ales. For some music and hippy-dom, **The Bell Inn on Walcot Street**. A co-operative owned by its 500+ customers. Free House with full range of beers and music thrice a week. Specialises in pizzas. Seeking to go a wee bit up-market? **The Marlborough Tavern** on Cavendish Road just north of the Royal Crescent is a popular dining pub with students and their families. An attractive Courtyard Garden, freshly prepared home cooked food and local ales is the draw. marlborough-tavern.com

COCKTAILS...

Canary Gin Bar, The Bath Distillery, 3 Queen Street. Words do sooth a parched throat, as does a G & T, added to whit an infusion of flavours - spices, botanicals, citrus fruit, herbs, aromatics. A cocktail of delights. Opens 5pm (Sa 3pm). Walk-In only. thebathgincompany.co.uk

The Dark Horse, 7A Kingsmead Square. A den of darkness, a stable of bottles awaite the starting flag. Bar food - cheeseboards, chorizo, pork pies...the full works. Opens 5pm, weekends 4pm. darkhorsebar.co.uk

THE SOUTH WEST • Bath, Bradford-On-Avon, Castle Combe

Royal Crescent, Bath

Hudson Steakhouse Bar & Grill, 14 London Street. A mix of steakhouse, and lively cocktail bar, all set in an old Edwardian pub. This apparent clash of genres results in a relaxed and surprisingly glamorous restaurant. Steaks come from grass-fed herds of Angus and Limousin Staffordshire cows slow-matured, for 28 days. Also fusion, seafood and classic dishes. 01225 332323 hudsonsteakhouse.co.uk

Olive Tree Restaurant, Queensberry Hotel, Russel Street. A sophisticated restaurant with modern art lining the walls, set in the basement of a luxury boutique hotel. Classy, high quality and modern British cuisine served with understated skill in a relaxed environment. Rarely does the quality of a hotel restaurant match the quality of the hotel itself. In this case, both get high marks. 01225 447928 olivetreebath.co.uk

The Circus Restaurant, 34 Brock Street. For a more formal coffee or lunch, or dining experience. Lunch may include fresh fish from Newlyn, or a Rib Eye steak, aged for 28 days. 01225 466020 thecircuscafeandrestaurant.co.uk

Woods, 9-13 Alfred Street. Woods has been owned by an Anglo-French couple and their children for 40-years. The Gallic in this paring shines through in the design of the place from the wicker chairs outside the front of the restaurant to the paraphernalia on the walls inside. Menus offer a range of gourmet European dishes. 01225 314812 woodsrestaurant.com

EAT...DRINK...SLEEEP...

The Bath Priory Hotel & Garden Spa, Weston Road. The Priory epitomises luxury and efficiency. Comfortable rooms with delightful garden views from the windows. The Restaurant is considered to be one of Bath's finest. Heated outdoor swimming pool. (D9) 01225 331922 thebathpriory.co.uk

Bathwick Gardens, 95 Sydney Place. A Regency townhouse B&B, the façade adorned with wrought iron balustrades. The interior is tastefully decorated with period touches. A self-catering 4-bed coach house situated at the bottom of the garden is also available. (D9) 01225 469435

Brindleys, 14 Pulteney Gardens. Boutique-style B&B provides luxurious bedrooms fitted with goose down duvets and pillows, bespoke fabrics, crisp white linens and quality bathroom fittings all within walking distance of the centre. 01225 310444 brindleysbath.co.uk

Dorian House, 1 Upper Oldfield Park. Think of the Dorian (Grey) that walks and not the image trapped on canvas when you think of Dorian House. For every inch of this B&B is gorgeous and full of period charm. From the bedrooms upstairs to the drawing room and gardens downstairs. (D9) 01225 426336 dorianhouse.co.uk

Dukes B&B Bath, Great Pulteney Street. In the heart of Bath sits this Grade I Palladian townhouse. Faithfully restored to high Georgian standards with a layer of contemporary comforts. Dukes has a pleasing ambience.

798 King Coenwulf of Mercia founds a monastery in Winchcombe
871 King Alfred lays out the town of Bath

Bath, Bradford-On-Avon, Castle Combe • THE SOUTH WEST

Bedrooms and Suites are dressed in period furnishings and fabrics. (D9) 01225 787960 dukesbath.co.uk

The Milsom, 24 Milsom Street. Represents 'restaurants with rooms' in the truest sense. This small stylish hotel has dispensed with a concierge and room service, and in their stead is a modern, pared-back elegance in concord with a Grade II listed building, set in the centre of this historic city. Relaxing and elegant simplicity. 01225 432233 themilsombath.com

15 Great Pulteney Street. Good design matters, and here there's a flourish of it in high detail: Dolls Houses, Georgian handbags, artworks on walls… together with sublime cocktails before bed, a classic breakfast to set you up for a day of shopping/cultural shenanigans. This boutique hotel and spa is different and comfortable, too. (D9) 01225 807015 guesthousehotels.co.uk

SPECIAL PLACES TO VISIT OUTSIDE BATH….

Claverton Church of St Mary. Norman church renovated in 1858. Ralph Allen, who financed the building of Georgian Bath, is buried here. Peel of bells. (E9)

Claverton Manor. An important Museum of Americana that displays furniture and decorative arts, and fosters anglo-american friendship. Fascinating collection of American furniture, decorative arts, silver, and textiles, taking you on a journey through American history. Important resource for students. Café and garden open from 10.30. Gift shop. Open mid-Mar to Dec Tu-Su & BHs: Garden 10-5, Deli 10-4.30 & Museum 11-4. (E9) 01225 460503 americanmuseum.org

Claverton Pumping Station. This attractive Grade II listed building is built of Bath stone, and is a feature on the Kennet and Avon Canal. From 1813-1952, it pumped gallons of water, per hour, from the river Avon into the canal 47 feet above. (F9) 01225 483001 claverton.org

Dyrham Park (NT). C17 William and Mary mansion house set in a deer park with elegant formal gardens. The house belonged to the family of Sir William Blathwayt's wife, Mary Wynter. Blathwayt was Secretary of War to William III (1671-1720). Sir William started to remodel the dilapidated Tudor mansion on site in 1692-1699. Victorian domestic quarters, Splendid collection of Dutch paintings. Film location for 'Remains of the Day' (1993). House Open Mar to Dec daily 11.30-4, tearoom 10.30-4.30 Park open all year 10-5. (C3) 0117 9372501 nationaltrust.org.uk

Grenville Monument (EH), Lansdowne Hill. This was built in 1720, in honour of Sir Bevil Grenville, who led his Cornish

Bath Priory ss

THE SOUTH WEST • Bath, Bradford-On-Avon, Castle Combe

Pikemen in the Battle of Lansdowne in 1643, during the English Civil War. Erected on the spot where he lay mortally wounded. He was taken to the Rectory at nearby Cold Ashton, where he died on the 5th July. He was buried on the 26th July at Kilkhampton, North Cornwall. (B6)

EAT...DRINK...SLEEP... OUTSIDE BATH...

Combe Grove Estate, Brassknocker Hill. An C18 manor house set in 70-acres of woodland. Fitness Club, Spa treatments and the pastoral location coupled with their one-week Metabolic Health Retreat will enliven your sensory glands to Indulge in some much-needed rest and wholesome foods. (E10)
01225 834644 combegrove.com

Lucknam Park Hotel & Spa, Colerne. Drive six miles from Bath, and you enter another era. This Palladian manor house built in 1720 was a family home until 1987 from whence it was transformed into a Country House Hotel restored to the elegance, and style, of the Georgian period. Set in 500 acres of listed parkland and gardens the hotel offers luxurious comfort in its 41-bedrooms including 13 suites. Fine dining in the Park Restaurant. More humble dining in the Brasserie. Spa, Equestrian Centre.
01225 742777
lucknampark.co.uk

Whatley Manor, Easton Grey. Set in a 12-acre traditional English country garden, Whatley Manor is a beautifully restored Cotswold manor house, made to feel more like a private home than a hotel. Bedrooms and suites are filled with contemporary, and antique furnishings to feed the senses. For those mixing business with pleasure, there is a boardroom and business centre including a 40-seat cinema. Spa.
01666 822888
whatleymanor.com

Wheelwrights Arms Hotel, Monkton Combe. A C18 carpenter's home and workshop converted into a public house in 1871. The workshop has been transformed into charming, light and airy B&B accommodation. (E10)
01225 722287
wheelwrightsarmsbath.com

BRADFORD-ON-AVON

Situated in the Avon Valley, and on an adjoining hillside, Bradford on Avon is the last Cotswold town in west Wiltshire, close to the borders of Somerset. The town centre is full of narrow streets lined with shops, as well as, impressive Roman and Norman architecture. It is dissected by the River Avon, and the Kennet and Avon Canal, which provide a glimpse into the mill-related past of the town. The surrounding hillside is scattered with weaver's cottage of all shapes, and sizes, built from Cotswold stone. A climb through the narrow passageways, between the houses, and up to St Mary's Tor, provides an excellent vantage point to view the town in its entirety, and beyond it, the shimmering Marlborough Downs, and the Westbury White Horse. It is no wonder that due to its proximity to Bath, and the beauty of the domestic architecture, it has become a less pricey place to live. (H10)

SPECIAL PLACES OF INTEREST...

Abbey Mill. Built in the mid-1800s, Abbey Mill has been used as a cloth mill, a rubber factory, offices, and has recently been transformed

Bradford-on-Avon Canal Lock

| 42 | 1000 | St Lawrence, Bradford-on-Avon is built | 1066 | The Norman Conquest heralds rebuilding of abbeys, castles and churches |

Bath, Bradford-On-Avon, Castle Combe • THE SOUTH WEST

Tithe Barn, Bradford-on-Avon

into 53-flats for age exclusive housing. Best viewed from across the river. (H10)

Barton Farm Country Park. A 36-acre park bounded by the River Avon on one side, and the Kennet and Avon Canal, on the other. The park offers something for everyone; from walking, rowing, and fishing, to relaxing with a picnic by the river. Sections of the park are managed specifically to encourage a wide range of wildlife. At the entrance to the park, the C14 farmhouse, granary and tithe barn of the original Barton Grange farm. Open all year, free of charge. (H10)

Canal Wharf & Lock. There are two wharfs on the Kennet and Avon Canal, both of which were busy commercial wharfs from 1810 to 1930. Lock Inn Cottage Café at the lower wharf. The larger wharf is the upper wharf by the lock. (H10)

Holy Trinity Church. The church is originally Norman and was extensively modified in the early 1300s, and throughout the following century. (H10) 01225 864444

Pack Horse Bridge. It spans the River Avon and was built in C14 to allow produce to be carried across the river by packhorses for storage in the tithe barn at Barton Grange farm. (H10)

Saxon Church. Near to Trinity Church is the Saxon church of St Laurence. This C7 building is all that remains of a monastery which once existed in the area. Throughout the C17 and C18 the Saxon church had various secular uses as, among other things, an ossuary, cottages and a free school for boys. Now protected by a trust. (H10)

The Chantry. Visible from the churchyard this striking building was once the home of a successful local clothier. (H10)

The Shambles. A crooked lane running between Silver Street and Market Street with a variety of shops. The name derives from the Anglo-Saxon word 'scamel,' meaning a bench on which goods were laid out for sale. (H10)

Tithe Barn. Formerly part of the estate of Shaftesbury Abbey, the C14 barn was used to collect 'tithes' or income in the form of produce, and livestock, for the Abbey. The barn is 51 metres (168ft) long and has a spectacular timber-cruck roof which is one of the largest stone roofs in Europe. Open all year 10.30 am to 1 pm. Free. (H10) 0370 333118

Town Bridge. The Town Bridge crosses the *broad ford* on the Avon which is likely to be the origin of the name Bradford on Avon. Originally built by the Normans, the bridge was very narrow and without parapets so a second bridge was built alongside to widen it - you can see the join if you look under the bridge. You can also still see two ribbed and pointed arches of the original Norman construction on the eastern

THE SOUTH WEST • Bath, Bradford-On-Avon, Castle Combe

Town Bridge, Bradford-on-Avon

LIGHT BITES...

Bridge Tea Rooms, 24a Bridge Street. Housed in a charmingly wonky former blacksmith's cottage dating from 1675, the tea room specialises in traditional afternoon tea and cakes served by waitresses in Victorian costume. Also, open for evening meals. (H10) 01225 865537
thebridgetearooms.co.uk

Weaving Shed, 3 Bridge Yard, Kingston Mills. Housed in an old weaving shed transformed into a fine contemporary build. Serves coffees, hot chocs and seriously good food. Brunch, lunch and dinner. Al fresco overlooking the Avon. (H10) 01225 866519
weaving-shed.co.uk

side. The tiny C17 building on the bridge was originally a chapel (see the early Christian symbol on the weather vane). Later it became a small prison or 'Blind House' where local drunks and troublemakers were left overnight to cool off. (H10)

Wiltshire Music Centre, Ashley Road. Hosts in excess of 90 concerts a year; classical, folk and jazz, many world-class artists in a 300-seat auditorium. Family shows and storytelling venues. 01225 860110
wiltshiremusic.org.uk

EAT...DRINK..SLEEP...

Castle Inn, Mount Pleasant. Revived from dilapidation and a failing reputation, this listed Georgian building is now a thriving freehouse pub with boutique bedrooms, stunning views and a large and sunny garden and terrace. (G10) 01225 309217
thecastleinnboa.co.uk

Timbrell's Yard, 49 St Margaret's Street. Great food and atmosphere, luxurious bedrooms with quirky pieces of decor, and all within a handsome riverside building overlooking the Avon. (G10) 01225 869492
timbrellsyard.com

Woolley Grange, Woolley Green. The original Luxury Family Hotel is set in a beautiful Jacobean Manor House standing in 14 acres of grounds on the outskirts of Bradford. All the comfort and sophistication parents might crave with all the activities and adventure a kid could want. (H10) 01225 864705
woolleygrangehotel.co.uk

CASTLE COMBE

One of the prettiest, and most visited villages in the south Cotswolds lies sheltered in a hidden valley surrounded by steep, wooded hills. In former times, a flourishing medieval wool centre, as evidenced by the weavers and clothiers cottages that descend from the Market Cross to By Brook, and the three-arch bridge. Its great claim to fame followed

44 | 1089 The nave of Gloucester Cathedral undergoes construction | 1107 Stow granted a charter by Henry 1

Bath, Bradford-On-Avon, Castle Combe • THE SOUTH WEST

its appearance in the 1966 film of 'Doctor Doolittle' starring Rex Harrison. The village remains a popular location for TV commercials, and period dramas, because of its rows of quaint cottages undisturbed by time, or any life. More recently, used in the film 'War Horse.' You rarely see children or families (who can't afford to live here), and the post office has closed as have most or all of the shops. There is parking at the top, and bottom end of the village. (H3) castle-combe.com

SPECIAL PLACES OF INTEREST…

Colham Farm Trail. The circular trail starts opposite the Dower House in Castle Combe and takes you through ancient woodland in Parsonage Wood and down into the By Brook valley where the meadow is a Site of Special Scientific Interest. Resident species include the green winged meadow orchid. (H3)

Dower House. The finest house in the village built in the C17. Note the beautiful shell-hooded doorway. (H3)

Motor Racing Circuit. Regular car and motorcycle race days take place at this circuit through the summer. One of the longest established tracks in the UK. Track Days for motorcyclists. (J3) 01249 782417
castlecombecircuit.co.uk

St Andrew's Church. Originally C13, the nave was added in the C14 and the tower completed in the C16. In the 1850's much of the church had to be rebuilt. Note the beautiful fan vaulting reminiscent of Bath Abbey. Also, the medieval faceless clock, one of the most ancient working clocks in the country. (H3)

EAT…DRINK…SLEEP…

Castle Inn Hotel. This is a pretty honey-coloured building set in the market place. Many features of the original C12 construction remain thanks to considerate restoration. The eleven bedrooms are individual in character. You can choose fine dining in the restaurant or more simple bar food in the bar itself. (H3) 01249 783030
exclusive.co.uk/the-castle-inn

Manor House Hotel. A manicured hotel within an C18 build, more at home in Surrey rather than a dingly dell in Wiltshire. Popular with corporate events and Americans seeking the English Style. All surrounded by 365 acres of gardens, woodland and an 18-hole golf course. (H3) 01249 782206
exclusive.co.uk/the-manor-house

White Hart, Market Place. C14 pub at the heart of the village with a sunny conservatory and patio gardens to the rear. (H3) 01249 782295

SLEEP…OUTSIDE CASTLE COMBE…

Fosse Farm B&B. Set conveniently close to the north-west corner of the village's circular walk. Caron's home is furnished in English vintage and French Brocante. Your hostess is a resource of local knowledge and warm hospitality. Dogs and children welcome. Self-catering, too. (H3) 01249 782286
fossefarmhouse.com

West Farm B&B, West Littleton. The family-run working farm is a substantial climber-covered red-roofed building. Ensuite bedrooms are bright and airy. (D3) 01225 891249

The Bridge, Castle Combe

THE SOUTH WEST • Bath, Bradford-On-Avon, Castle Combe

Almshouses, Corsham

CORSHAM

Not to be missed! A really attractive town of Cotswold stone and lime-washed houses dominated by the Methuen-Campbell's home, Corsham Court. Make sure you have time to walk the High Street and admire the exterior of the noted Alshouses. Recently used for the Truro scenes in the Poldark TV series. For refreshments seek out The Methuen Arms. (J6)

SPECIAL PLACES OF INTEREST...

Corsham Court. Home of the Methuen-Campbells since the C15 - the current inhabitants are 8th generation. The building dates back to 978 when it was a summer palace for the Kings of Wessex. Major alterations were undertaken in the C16 and C18s, with the house being converted to an E-plan in 1582. In C19, however, major dry rot problems were found which set back the family's finances. The gardens were laid out by Capability Brown. The current mansion has a superb collection of paintings by Joshua Reynolds, Van Dyke and Phillipo Lippi among others, as well as Chippendale furniture.

Open summer, late Mar to 30 Sept daily except M & F 2-5.30, winter 1 Oct to late Mar W/Es 2-4.30 (closed Dec). (K6)
01249 701610
corsham-court.co.uk

RAF Rudloe Manor (now know as JSU Corsham). This was a Royal Air Force station above an MOD underground tunnel complex which, during WWII, was the Central Ammunitions Depot for the UK and the world's largest underground factory. A Beaverbrook aircraft engine factory was also created here as a fallback should the factories in Bristol be damaged by bombing - but it was never used. The labyrinth of caverns supplied 2,250,000 square feet (209,000 m2) of space, divided into many smaller chambers and including 14 miles of conveyor belts. There was cause for much rumour and conspiracy theories during its time, and until very recently, most of Corsham's inhabitants were unaware of the tunnel complex, some parts of which are still classified. Nowadays, a wine merchant rents out some areas for wine storage, and amateur cavers often explore (and gaffiti) the tunnels. (H6)

LACOCK

This is a show village owned and protected by the National Trust. You could be forgiven for thinking you were on a film set. Not surprisingly, it is a favourite for location scouts. Pride and Prejudice, Cranford and Wolfman are just some of the TV/Film projects produced here. The houses are lime-washed and half- timbered, and many date from the C13. There are some old inns and tearooms, and gift shops awaiting your custom. (M7)

SPECIAL PLACES OF INTEREST...

Lacock Abbey (NT). Founded in 1232 by Lady Ela, the Countess of Salisbury as a nunnery for the Augustinian order. The abbey prospered from the wool trade in the Middle Ages but its religious foundation came to a sad end following the Dissolution of the Monasteries. It was converted into a country house around 1540 and eventually passed into the Talbot family. In the C19, William Fox-Talbot lived here, and began experimenting with photography. In 1835 he invented the negative-positive

---

46 | 1121 Founding of St Leonard's Augustinian Priory, Selsey | 1176 Death of 'Fair Rosamund Clifford' mistress to Henry 11

Bath, Bradford-On-Avon, Castle Combe • THE SOUTH WEST

Lacock Abbey

process. His achievements can be seen in the museum. The gardens are a great attraction especially the Victorian woodland and Fox-Talbot's botanic garden. Abbey & Museum open daily Mar to Oct from 10 am. Winter see website. (M7) 01249 730459
<u>nationaltrust.org.uk</u>

Lacock Pottery, 1 The Tanyard. Coloured glazes cover the stoneware pieces. The B&B is set in the old workhouse. A most impressive building overlooking the church. (M7) 01249 730266

EAT…DRINK…SLEEP…

George Inn, 4 West Street. The George Inn dates back to 1361. Its interior is so evocative of 'Ye Olde Worlde' that you would be forgiven for imagining that the man at the bar is Cromwell and that the dogwheel by the huge open fireplace is still being turned by a specially bred dog known as a turnspit. B&B with two bedrooms. 01249 730263
<u>georgeinnlacock.co.uk</u>

Old Rectory, Cantax Hill. Built in 1866, this Victorian Gothic house has an impressive entrance hall with original Victorian tiles and stained glass windows. The bedrooms are elegant with large windows and guests have use of the drawing room, dining room and garden including orchard and croquet lawn. 01249 730335
<u>oldrectorylacock.co.uk</u>

Sign of the Angel, Church Street. C15 coaching inn (restaurant with rooms) of great character; wood fires, flagstone floors and fine cuisine combine to make this a magnetic destination. Upstairs, a cosy wood-panelled lounge. Crooked

Corsham Court

| 1227 | Northleach is founded as a new market town by the Abbot of Gloucester | 1232 | Lacock Abbey founded by Ela, Countess of Salisbury | 47 |

THE SOUTH WEST • Bath, Bradford-On-Avon, Castle Combe

corridors and low doorways lead into the snug bedrooms which are furnished with dark, carved, period furniture. One has an enormous carved bed that once belonged to Isambard Kingdom Brunel. 01249 730230 signoftheangel.co.uk

CHIPPING SODBURY

An ancient medieval town that has escaped the hectic intrusions of tourism, and with its close neighbour Yate (which provides the commerce) has become a quality place to live and work. The wide main street formerly held sheep fairs and market fairs. For Light Bites; coffee and cakes, the smart Hamptons Deli, for a taste of the Mediterranean, La Passione is popular, but the most highly recommended eatery is **Siam Thai** at the bottom of the High Street on 01454 850095. Forgive their English, just enjoy their food if you can find them. They spell their address 1 Horse Street on their menu and 1 Hose Street on their business card! (D9)

SLEEP...

The Moda House, 1 High Street. Enjoy B&B with an international flavour if you can pull yourself away from the photo-covered walls, you will settle easily into the comforts of this idiosyncratic C18 home. Nine comfy bedrooms. Relaxed sitting room and snugs, ideal for families. Wifi. (D9) 01454 312135 modahouse.co.uk

SPECIAL PLACES OF INTEREST IN CHIPPING SODBURY...

Jack Russell Gallery, 41 High Street. Jack was Gloucestershire's and England's wicketkeeper, and (saviour) batsmen, for many years in the late 1980s and 90s. He started painting cricket scenes in the West Indies, in 1990, and has since built an international reputation. His paintings cover diverse subjects; cricket, landscape, the legal profession, portraits and wildlife. Originals and prints for sale. Open M-F 9.30-1. (D9) 01454 329583 jackrussell.co.uk

OUTSIDE CHIPPING SODBURY...

Brackenbury Ditches. An unexcavated Iron Age earthwork in an impregnable position on the Cotswold Way. The ramparts and entrance are vaguely visible from the south side. Good viewpoint. (E3)

Kingswood Abbey Gatehouse. Almost sole remnant of Abbey built in the C16 for the Cistercian Order. Of interest, the richly decorated mullioned window. Open daily 9-5 to view. 0370 333 1181 (E4)

Tortworth Chestnut. An enormous sweet chestnut tree. Age is unknown, but reckoned to be about 1,000 years old. The tree sits in St Leonard's churchyard and continues to gather legends. Follow the signs to the Farm shop, and continue down the lane for a further 200 yards. (C4)

Tyndale Monument. Built by the people of Berkeley in 1866 to honour the memory of their famous son, and martyr, William Tyndale, 1490-1536. Tyndale translated the Old and New Testaments which was considered, at the time, a heretical offence, and he was summarily executed for his transgressions. His work became the foundation of the King James Version of the Bible. The monument rises to 111 feet and has an inner spiral staircase which ascends to a stupendous viewpoint. Open as advertised. (E2)

Cricket-On-College-Field, Jack Russell Gallery ss

| 1246 | Hailes Abbey founded by the Earl of Cornwall, son of King John | 1253 | Lady Berkeley obtains a grant for Wotton's market and fair |

CHIPPING SODBURY

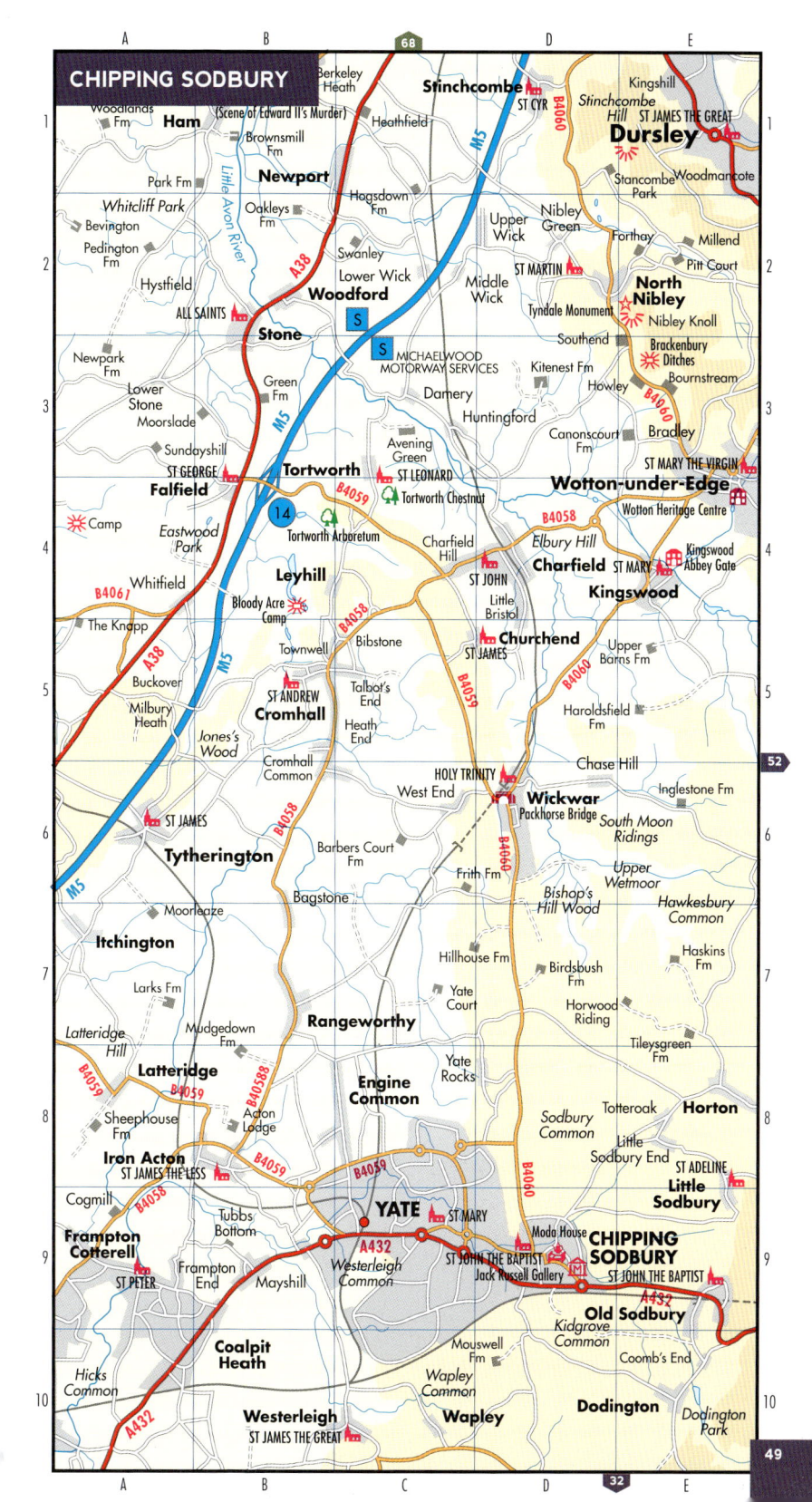

COTSWOLD COTTAGES

Arlington Row, Bibury

Broad Campden

Cottage Garden, Guiting Power

Gothic Door, Windrush

Three Cottages, Calmsden

Entering Lower Slaughter

TETBURY, MALMESBURY, WOTTON-UNDER-EDGE

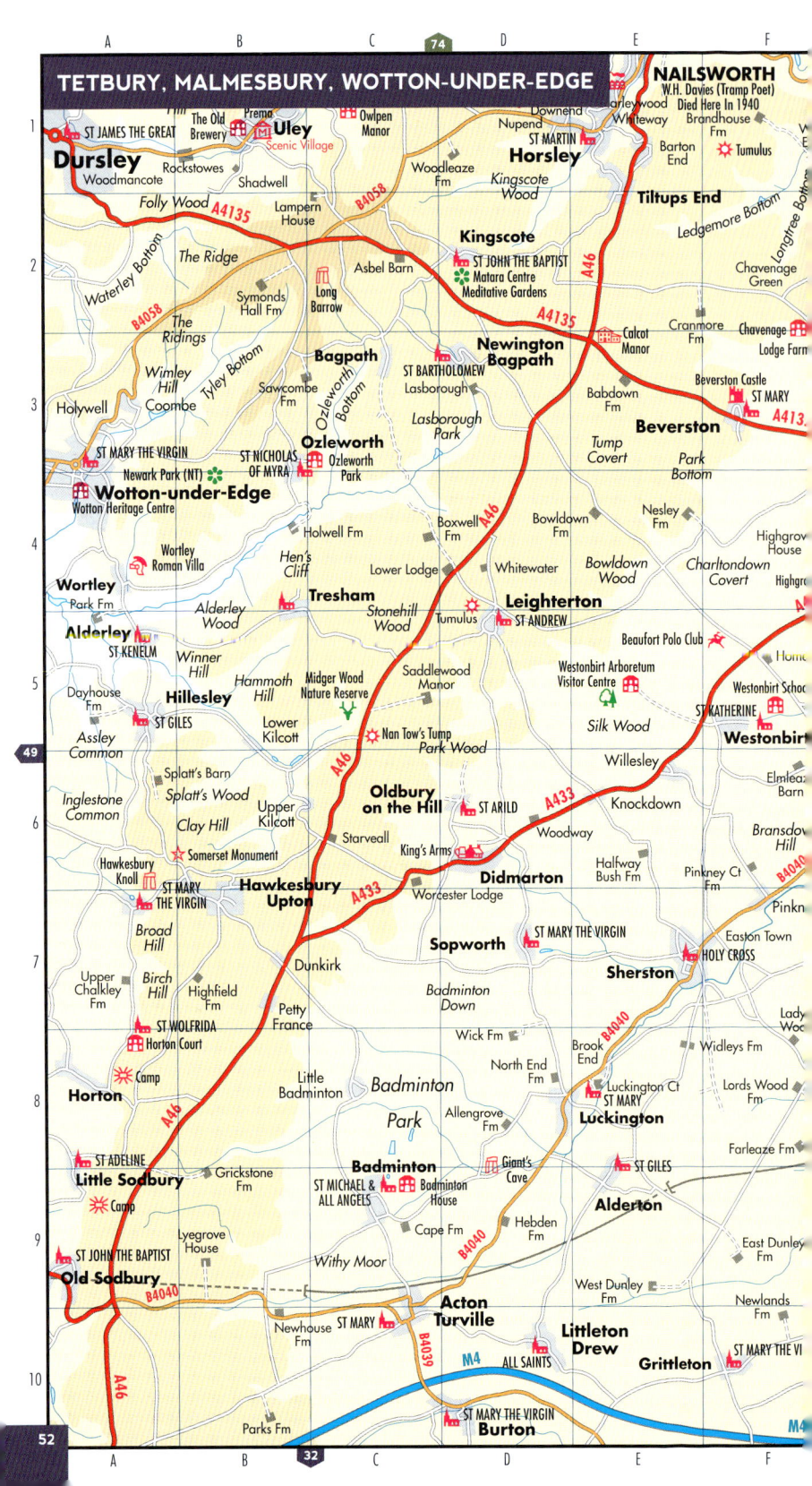

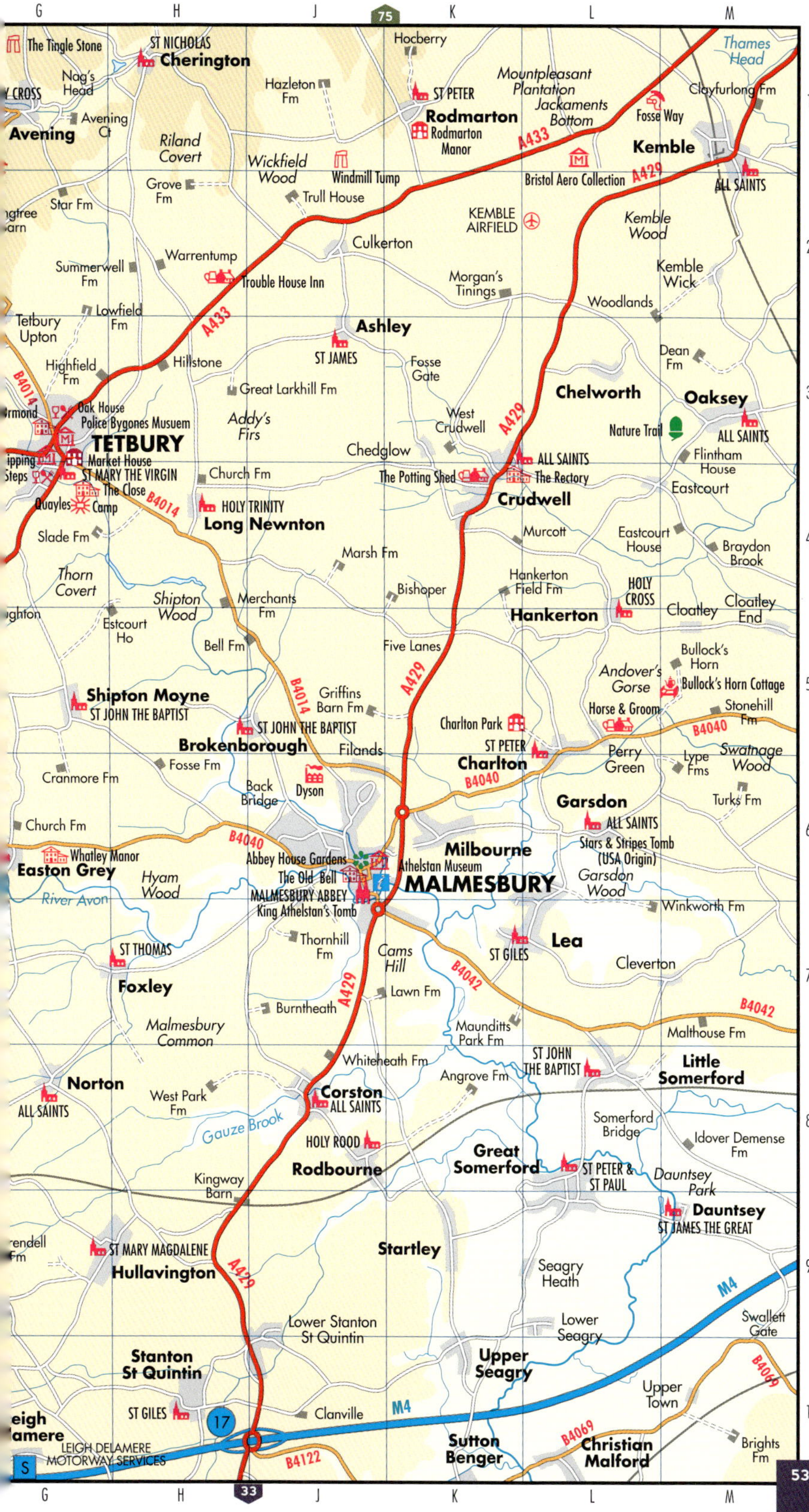

G
H
J
75
K
L
M
The Tingle Stone
ST NICHOLAS
Cherington
Hocberry
Thames Head
Nag's Head
Hazleton Fm
ST PETER
Mountpleasant Plantation
Jackaments Bottom
Clayfurlong Fm
1
CROSS
Avening Ct
Avening
Rodmarton
Rodmarton Manor
A433
Fosse Way
Kemble
Riland Covert
Wickfield Wood
Windmill Tump
Bristol Aero Collection
A429
ALL SAINTS
Grove Fm
Trull House
Star Fm
KEMBLE AIRFIELD
Kemble Wood
Culkerton
2
Warrentump
Summerwell Fm
Trouble House Inn
Morgan's Tinings
Kemble Wick
Lowfield Fm
Woodlands
Tetbury Upton
A433
Ashley
ST JAMES
Dean Fm
Highfield Fm
Hillstone
Fosse Gate
B4014
Great Larkhill Fm
Chelworth
Oaksey
3
Oak House
Police Bygones Museum
Addy's Firs
West Crudwell
A429
Nature Trail
ALL SAINTS
TETBURY
Market House
Chedglow
ALL SAINTS
Flintham House
ST MARY THE VIRGIN
Church Fm
The Potting Shed
The Rectory
Eastcourt
The Close
Quayles
Camp
B4014
HOLY TRINITY
Crudwell
Long Newnton
Slade Fm
Murcott
Eastcourt House
4
Braydon Brook
Marsh Fm
Thorn Covert
Hankerton Field Fm
Bishoper
Shipton Wood
Merchants Fm
HOLY CROSS
Cloatley
Cloatley End
Estcourt Ho
Hankerton
Bell Fm
Five Lanes
Bullock's Horn
Andover's Gorse
Bullock's Horn Cottage
5
A429
Shipton Moyne
ST JOHN THE BAPTIST
Griffins Barn Fm
B4014
Horse & Groom
Stonehill Fm
ST JOHN THE BAPTIST
Charlton Park
B4040
Brokenborough
Filands
ST PETER
Perry Green
Lype Fms
Swatnage Wood
Fosse Fm
Charlton
Cranmore Fm
B4040
Back Bridge
Dyson
Garsdon
Turks Fm
Church Fm
ALL SAINTS
6
B4040
Stars & Stripes Tomb (USA Origin)
Whatley Manor
Abbey House Gardens
Athelstan Museum
Milbourne
Easton Grey
Hyam Wood
The Old Bell
MALMESBURY
Garsdon Wood
River Avon
MALMESBURY ABBEY
King Athelstan's Tomb
Winkworth Fm
Thornhill Fm
ST THOMAS
Cams Hill
ST GILES
Lea
B4042
Cleverton
7
Foxley
Lawn Fm
A429
Burntheath
B4042
Malmesbury Common
Maunditts Park Fm
Malthouse Fm
Whiteheath Fm
ST JOHN THE BAPTIST
Little Somerford
Norton
Angrove Fm
ALL SAINTS
West Park Fm
Corston
ALL SAINTS
8
Somerford Bridge
Gauze Brook
Idover Demense Fm
HOLY ROOD
Great Somerford
ST PETER & ST PAUL
Dauntsey Park
Rodbourne
Kingway Barn
Dauntsey
ST JAMES THE GREAT
rendell Fm
ST MARY MAGDALENE
Startley
9
Hullavington
A429
Seagry Heath
M4
Lower Stanton St Quintin
Lower Seagry
Swallett Gate
Stanton St Quintin
Upper Seagry
B4069
Upper Town
10
ST GILES
17
Clanville
M4
eigh amere
LEIGH DELAMERE MOTORWAY SERVICES
Sutton Benger
B4069
Christian Malford
Brights Fm
S
B4122
G
H
33
J
K
L
M

THE SOUTH WEST • Tetbury, Malmesbury, Wotton-Under-Edge

Market House, Tetbury

TETBURY

A market town with a fine church, St. Mary's. The town's more recent claim to fame has been due to its proximity to Highgrove, King Charles' home at Doughton. The opening of his Highgrove shop brought an influx of new visitors to the town, with coach outings bringing the traffic to a standstill. How this helps the rest of the town's merchants, one can only surmise?

Today, it is the Cotswold's major centre for antiques. It has, also, had much welcome investment in the shape of new shops, galleries, and places to eat and drink. Nearby is Gatcombe Park, the home of Anne, The Princess Royal. The Woolsack Races on May Bank Holiday are fun to watch, and do cause great merriment to the bystanders, but not the participants who are forced to carry the heavy woolsack. (G3)

SPECIAL PLACES OF INTEREST...

Beverston Church of St Mary. Saxon sculptures. Norman additions. Three pointed arches on south arcade are of interest. Screen with some C15 work. (F3)

Beverston Castle. A substantial ruin incorporated into a C17 house. King Harold stayed here in 1051. It was besieged by King Stephen in 1145. The Berkeleys lorded over it, and added a gatehouse. The gardens have an impressive collection of orchids, and are open for the National Garden Scheme. (F3)

Chavenage. A haunted Elizabethan manor house that has remained virtually unchanged for 400 years. A replica of a bygone age. It contains two complete tapestry rooms, furniture and relics of the Civil War. Guided tours by the family. Specialises in weddings and corporate events. Location for much of the recent Poldark TV series. Cofffee shop. Open East Su & M, also May to Sept Th & Su 2-5.(F3) 01666 502329
chavenage.com

Parish Church of St Mary the Virgin. The Early Gothic revivalism gives the interior a sparse ambience. There are some box pews of interest. The whole is surrounded by an enclosed cloister housing some ancient tombs of knights and

---

54 | 1265 | Simon de Montfort, along with 18 barons, 160 knights and 4000 men-at-arms are slain at the Battle of Evesham | 1270 | A phial of Christ's blood is presented to Hailes Abbey which becomes a major destination for pilgrims

Tetbury, Malmesbury, Wotton-Under-Edge • THE SOUTH WEST

local dignitaries. It is best viewed from afar, across the fields on the south side of town. (G3)

Market House. A substantial building of c.1655 supported by thick Tuscan pillars. It dominates the Market Place of this affluent little town, and is often the venue for Saturday markets. (G3)

Matara Centre Meditative Gardens, Kingscote Park. Labyrinths, ponds, sculptures, Shinto woodlands, meadows and a Meditative Walled Garden. A place of calm and healing. Specialises in weddings with accommodation on hand. Open daily Apr-Sept, garden tours W at 2pm. (D2) 01453 861050 matara.co.uk

Nan Tow's Tump. A Long barrow. 9ft high and 100ft in diameter crowned with trees. Believed to contain skeleton of Nan Tow, a local Witch buried upright. (C5)

Westonbirt, The National Arboretum. If you believe trees to be the most beautiful

Ross Poldark, Chavenage ss

Master Bedroom, Chavenage ss

| 1300 | Gloucester Abbey owns a herd of 10,000 sheep | 1327 | Edward II murdered at Berkeley Castle and buried in Gloucester Cathedral |

THE SOUTH WEST • Tetbury, Malmesbury, Wotton-Under-Edge

Gold-Yellow Acer Tree, Westonbirt Arboretum

LIGHT BITES...

Café 53, Long Street. Breakfast from 9 in this hidden away café with a med-style flavour. Lunch 12-4. Open M-Sa 9-4, Su 10-4. (G3) 01666 502020 cafe53.co.uk

Cross Long Street to **Lola & Co** a Spanish deli of infinitessimal class and delicacies. Your taste buds will be on fire: toasties, coffees, hot chocs, cheeses and Tapas. Open daily. (G3) 01666 504000 lolaandco.co.uk

Moving up toward the Market Hall: **Quayles, 1 Long Street.** Café, bar & bistro shop ideal for resting and watching the passers-by. (G3) 07976 412248 quayles.co.uk

Perhaps, you seek a Full English Breakfast and other morsels for pleasure? Try **The Blue Zucchini** at 7 Church St., 01666 505852 where your Hostess will spoil you.

things in creation, then a visit to this arboreal wonderland must be at the top of your agenda. Here, in this paradise garden, you will find 600 acres of magnificent trees and shrubs from around the world. With no less than 15,000 tree specimens of 2,500 species of trees and a good 17 miles of footpaths ahead, you will need comfy footwear. Needless to say, it is quite a sight in Spring and Autumn, and popular too. Oak Hall Visitor Centre, giftshop and courtyard café. Plant centre. Open daily 9-dusk. (E5) 0300 067 4890 forestry.gov.uk/westonbirt

Westonbirt School. Girls independent school. Grade 1 listed house. Former home of Robert Stayner Holford (1808-1892), the founder of the Westonbirt Arboretum.

EAT...DRINK...SLEEP

Calcot Manor Hotel & Spa. A leisure complex combining an English country house hotel furnished in contemporary, up-to-the-minute designs, that flow with ease into the C14 Cistercian barns, and all ideally suited for a family, business or leisurely stay. Adjacent, you have Calcot Spa for health, beauty and relaxation, for

pampering the Self. And if, after all this hedonism you need some simple refreshment, a glass of ale, or some nourishment, then skip next door to the Gumstool Inn. Location is ideal for exploring the southern Cotswolds and Bath. (E3) 01666 890391 calcot.co

Close Hotel, Long Street. A traditional Cotswold hotel that's been transformed into the present day with contemporary furnishings and decor. Lunch can be exceptional value and a comfortable chair awaits you in their lovely garden whilst you

| 56 | 1350 | England's exports of wool amounts to about 30,000 bales per annum with estimated sheep population exceeding 6,000,000 | 1380 | Building of William Grevel's House in Chipping Campden |

Tetbury, Malmesbury, Wotton-Under-Edge • THE SOUTH WEST

Brecciarolis 63, Badminton

look forward to your afternoon tea. (G3) 01666 502272
cotswold-inns-hotels.co.uk/the-close-hotel

Oak House No1 Hotel, The Chipping. An extravaganza of sumptuous decadence and wild decor were you can realise your fantasies (of Arabian Nights?) and have that crazy weekend you have always dreamed of. What you get is that personal touch so missing from many hospitality units. Full techie stuff on offer; Wifi etc., 01666 505741 (G3) oakhouseno1.com

The Ormond, 23 Long Street. A former coaching inn that's (again) been completely revamped into a modern small hotel furnished with colour and panache. Restaurant, bar, lounge and courtyard for al fresco refreshments. (G3) 01666 505690
theormondtetbury.co.uk

The Kings Arm's, Didmarton. C17 coaching inn on the edge of the Badminton Estate. Specialises in dishes of seasonal game and English lamb. B&B. (D6) 01454 238245
butcombe.com

SPECIAL PLACES OF INTEREST...

Badminton. Known throughout the world as the venue for the Badminton Horse Trials, and the home of the Dukes of Beaufort. The buildings are of a soft Cotswold stone or with lime washed exterior. (C9)

Badminton House. The home of the Dukes of Beaufort, and venue for the annual Badminton Horse Trials. The Estate was bought by the Worcesters in 1682. It was the 3rd Duke who was responsible for the house as we see it today. First, he invited James Gibbs to set about remodelling the East and West wings, then William Kent finished the North Front in the Palladian style. Fox hunting has been a great passion of the Beauforts. Their early forebears hunted all the way to London and back. Publishing was another passion. From 1885 to 1902 they devised The Badminton Library of Sports & Pastimes - an aristocratic leather bound series of books that was more like a combination of Punch, and your High Street cricket, or football magazine, albeit, a little more high brow. And, of course, the game of Badminton was re-introduced here in 1873 following its Indian origins. The House is closed to the public. The closest you'll get is to visit during the Three Day Horse Trials. (C9)
badminton-horse.co.uk
badmintonestate.com

Highgrove Royal Gardens. The (unofficial) home of His Majesty The King and the Queen Consort. The gardens are open to the public for guided tours on selected dates between April and September each year. There are various tours to choose from: Garden Tours, Champagne Tours, Tours with Supper, Group and Private Tours to be booked in advance. (F4) highgrovegardens.com

THE SOUTH WEST • Tetbury, Malmesbury, Wotton-Under-Edge

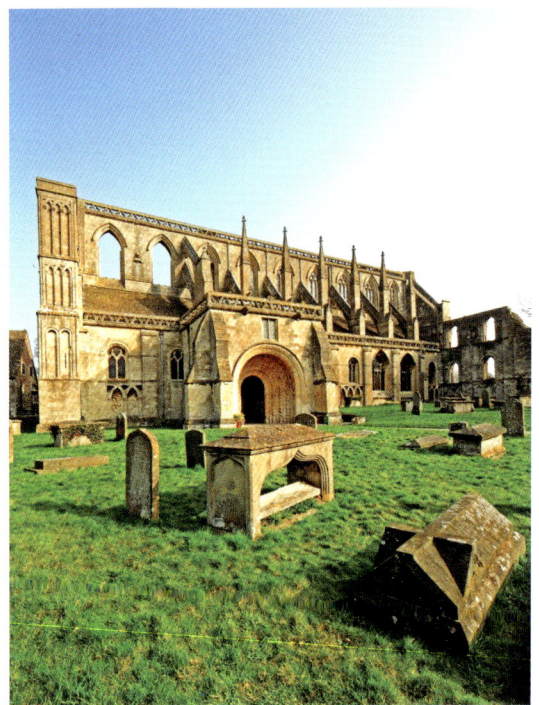

Malmesbury Abbey & Churchyard

MALMESBURY

Claims to be the oldest borough in England (although Barnstaple, in North Devon may dispute this) - established in 880 AD. Military strategists have described its hilltop location as the best naturally defended inland position of all ancient settlements. No wonder then that King Athelstan, the first King of all England, chose it as his home. Set on the edge of the Cotswold escarpment, it is a cheaper place to stay than the more central towns. Its spirit though lies with the Wiltshire landscape. Dyson, the innovative design company of vacuum cleaners, is the major employer and has brought some much needed zest, style and money to this isolated town. However, James Dyson was not the first inventor to work in the town. You must go back to the free-spirited monk, Eilmer, in the C11, who designed and built his own hang glider (see Malmesbury Abbey for details). (J6)

SPECIAL PLACES OF INTEREST...

Abbey House Manor Gardens. The former home of the Naked Gardeners. There are bulbs galore, especially the 70,000 tulips in Spring and a massive range of 2,200 different roses, herbaceous borders, specimen trees and shrubs. Future uncertain - open as locally advertised. (J6)
01666 822212
abbeyhousegardens.co.uk

Athelstan Museum, Cross Hayes. Wonderful collection of Roman and Saxon coins, as well as bicycles, fire engines, Tom Girtin drawings and a Turner original of Malmesbury. Open Tu-Sa 10.30-4.30, Su 11.30-3.30. (J6) 01666 829258
athelstanmuseum.org.uk

Charlton Park. Palatial mansion built in 1607. Home to the Earls of Suffolk since the C16. There are 4,500 acres of arable and woodland with trout fishing and game shooting on hand. It is also the venue for WOMAD, the World of Music, Arts & Dance festival, with its own park and camp facility. (L5) 01666 822146
charltonparkestate.com

Dyson, Tetbury Hill. The firm established by James Dyson: a temple of innovation and engineering design, and world leader in the manufacture of vacuum cleaners and hand dryers. Dyson is the market leader in the USA. The first vacuum cleaner took 5 years and 5,127 prototypes to develop. (J6) dyson.co.uk

Malmesbury Abbey Church of St Peter & St Paul. Founded as a Benedictine Monastery in 676 AD by the saintly and scholarly Brother Aldhelm. King Athelstan was buried here in 941 AD. By the C11 the monastery held the second largest library in Europe and was a place of learning and pilgrimage. The Abbey was built and completed by 1180. The tall spire rose to 431 feet (131m) and was to be seen for miles around. However, in 1500 it collapsed destroying the Nave and the Transept. A few years later, in 1550, the West Tower also collapsed. What you see today is less than half of the original structure. Yet, it still remains a formidable church, and a sight to behold. It was also a place of great inspiration, for in 1010, the monk Eilmer of

Tetbury, Malmesbury, Wotton-Under-Edge • THE SOUTH WEST

Dyson, Malmesbury

Malmesbury became the first man to fly by jumping off the roof of the Tower, and fly his hang glider 200 yards before crashing and breaking both his legs - Leonardo da Vinci was to design a similar machine 350 years later! Open daily. (J6) 01666 826666
malmesburyabbey.com

Market Cross. Built in 1490 to shelter the poor and despondent from the rain. (J6)

The Old Bell Hotel, Abbey Row. England's oldest purpose built hotel dating back to 1220. A fine place to stay if you seek whimsical and wakey interior design coupled with luxurious comfort and historic charm. Dine in the formal Abbey Row, or the less formal Tyger Bar. (J6) 01666 822344
oldbellhotel.co.uk

EAT..DRINK...SLEEP

Bullocks Horn Cottage, Charlton. Log fires in winter and in summer dine outside in the cool shade of the arbour or by candlelight in the conservatory. 01666 577600
bullockshorn.co.uk

The Horse and Groom Inn, The Street, Charlton. All the charm of a true country inn in a beautiful setting. Great food and stylish bedrooms and even an outside bar for those warm summer nights! (L5) 01666 823904 butcombe.com

The Potting Shed, Crudwell. A light and airy Inn with a contemporary flavour in its architectural form. Lunch is considered by my Peers to be exceptional. 01666 577833
thepottingshedpub.com

The Rectory, Crudwell. A lovely C16 house that has been transformed into a small, comfortable country house hotel with 18-bedrooms. Three acres with Victorian walled garden, croquet lawn and heated, outdoor swimming pool. Beauty and Health therapies on hand. (K4) 01666 577194
therectoryhotel.com

Old Bell Hotel, Malmesbury

| 1401 | Death of William Grevel, Chipping Campden's great beneficiary | 1417 | Stratford's Guildhall and Grammar School built |

THE SOUTH WEST • Tetbury, Malmesbury, Wotton-Under-Edge

Church of St Nicholas of Myra, Ozleworth

WOTTON-UNDER-EDGE

As the name suggests, Wotton hangs on the southern edge of the Cotswold escarpment. To the north and north-west of Wotton you have rolling hills and deep valleys blessed for walking. Enchanting countryside rarely praised. In its long history, the Berkeley family have dominated the town with varying success. King John's mercenaries devastated the Berkeley's property in the C11. Later, the simmering dispute between the de Lisles and the Berkeleys was sorted out in the latter's favour at the Battle at Nibley Green in 1470. The Berkeleys were generous patrons; Katherine Lady Berkeley established one of the country's first grammar schools here in 1384. Weaving and cloth making grew from cottage industries in the C13. Wotton is a quiet market town with some splendid C17 and C18 buildings. Isaac Pitman, 1813-97, who invented shorthand lived on Orchard Street. The Ram Inn is probably the town's oldest building, but, it is to St Mary the Virgin that all historians will be drawn. (A4)

SPECIAL PLACES OF INTEREST...

Newark Park, Ozleworth (NT). Former Tudor hunting lodge with an eclectic art collection. Countryside walks. Plant sales. Open daily mid-Feb to Oct & early Nov to mid-Dec W/Es, Garden from 10, House from 11. (B4) 01453 842644 nationaltrust.org.uk

Ozleworth Park. C18 house with rose garden and spacious lawns. Home to an affluent shoot and the start of a fine walk down to Ozleworth Bottom. Next door, the Church of St Nicholas with its C12 hexagonal tower, rare weathercock and C13 font. (B3)

St Mary the Virgin, Wotton-under-Edge. The first church on this site was probably destroyed by King John's mercenaries in the C11. The present structure was consecrated in 1283. Its Perpendicular tower, one of the county's finest has corner buttresses crowned with crocketed pinnacles. The marble tomb and the C15 brasses of Thomas, Lord Berkeley and his wife are outstanding. Note the C16 stained glass. Edward Barnsley in the Gimson tradition (Arts & Crafts Movement) designed the new altar and reredos on the north wall. The organ originally came from St. Martin in the Fields and had been a gift from George 1. George Handel played on it. Yet, despite all of this the church still lacks the beauty of Burford, or Chipping Campden, and cannot be described as one of the notable "Wool" churches. (A3)

The Bottoms: Waterley Bottom, Tyley Bottom and Ozleworth Bottom. Deep combes (valleys) of rare, and solitary beauty, rich in wild flowers and bird life. And, all can be viewed from countless footpaths. Strange to believe, but in the C17 and C18 Waterley operated 15 fulling mills (to cleanse and thicken cloth) within a radius of 5-miles. Keep your dogs on a lead due to the pheasants and shoot.(B3)

Wortley Roman Villa. Believed to be in existence from the C1 to C4. It was accidentally discovered in 1981 when an archaeological dig by the University of Keele unveiled Roman and Saxon coins, painted wall plaster, pottery and a damaged hypocaust. Much is now on display in Stroud Museum. (A4)

Wotton Heritage Centre, The Chipping. Run by the local Historical Society. Museum and research room. Open daily except W, Th & Su 10.30-3.30 (A4) 01453 521541 wottonheritage.com

Tetbury, Malmesbury, Wotton-Under-Edge • THE SOUTH WEST

North Nibley Walk

Windy Red Acers, Westonbirt Arboretum

| 1451 | William Fiennes marries into the Wykeham family of Broughton Castle starting the Fiennes lineage for 550-years | 1457 | New Inn, Gloucester is built to house pilgrims |

COTSWOLD HOSTELRIES

The Lamb Inn, Burford ss

The Trout, Tadpole Bridge ss

The Kings Arms, Didmarton ss

Falkland Arms, Great Tew

Skittle Alley, Seven Tuns, Chedworth

The Angel, Burford ss

PUB SIGNS

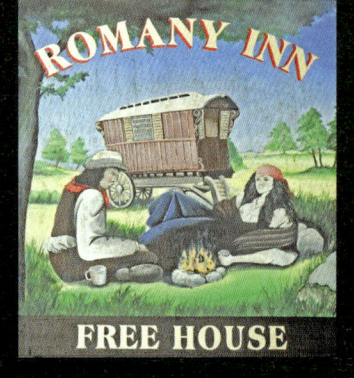

The SMOKING DOG

FREE HOUSE
The Hunt on CAT & CUSTARD POT Day

ROMANY INN
FREE HOUSE

FREE HOUSE

RAM INN
WOODCHESTER

ELIZABETH QVEEN OF ENGLAND
1558 — 1603

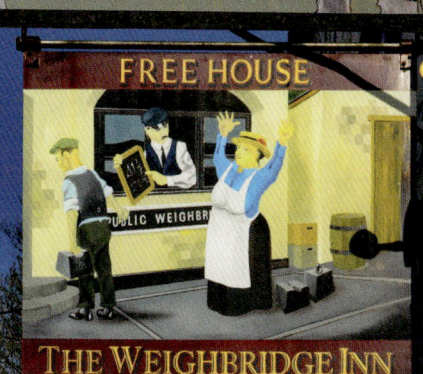

FREE HOUSE
THE WEIGHBRIDGE INN

THE SOUTH COTSWOLDS

For art and bohemia, 'Wool' churches, river valleys, roman remains, gastro-pubs, hunting and polo, industrial archaeology, gardens, idyllic villages, rolling hills and woodland…

You are now in the heart of the Cotswold experience. From the deep-sided valleys surrounding Stroud to the gentler slopes of the southern Wolds drained by the rivers Churn, Coln and Windrush. Out of these valleys have sprung hamlets with matching stone…made up of the manor house beside the church surrounded by cottages covered in roses and clematis.

The property developer has been busy in this Cotswold landscape. Rarely do you spy an old barn or hayloft that has not been converted into a domestic dwelling. Never has the picture-postcard village looked so perfect.

The Roman influence is notable in the fast-flowing A-roads that pass by Cirencester: Fosse Way, Ermin Way and Akeman Street where you can imagine the auxiliary cavalry units charging up and down these thoroughfares. A visit to the Corinium Museum will connect you to Hadrian and Caesar and you will learn that the conquering Romans built Corinium Dobunnorum (Cirencester) into the second largest Roman settlement in Britain with a populace of 12,000 inhabitants.

Sherborne Brook in summer

THE SOUTH COTSWOLDS

A few miles east of Cirencester lies the medieval town of Fairford, home to perhaps the finest stained glass in the Cotswolds.

In the Stroud area there is much to interest the industrial archaeologist. Tours are organised to the woollen mills where you can see for yourself the looms in action.

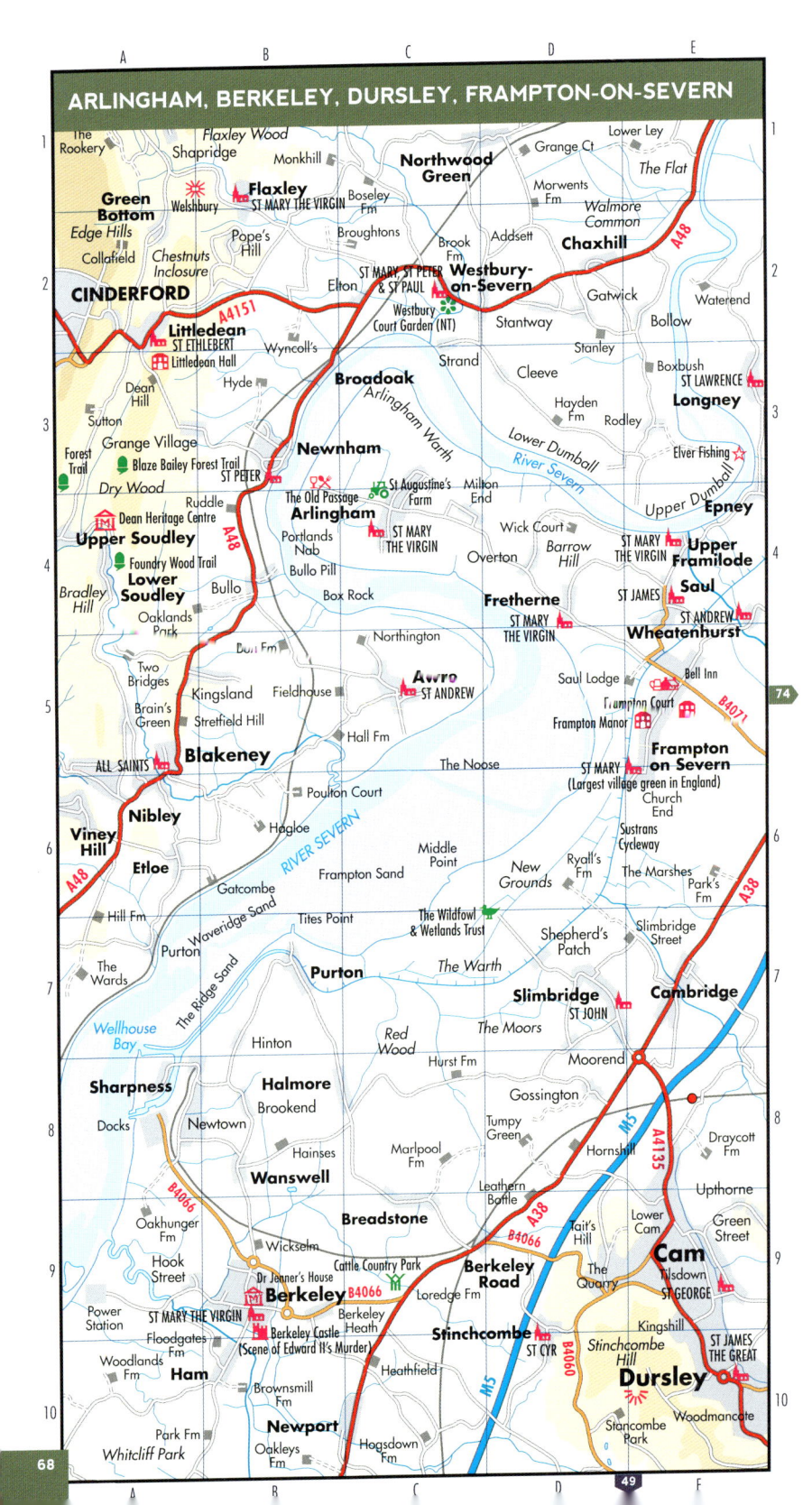

ARLINGHAM, BERKELEY, DURSLEY, FRAMPTON-ON-SEVERN

Arlingham, Berkeley, Dursley, Frampton-on-Severn • **THE SOUTH COTSWOLDS**

Berkeley Castle

ARLINGHAM PENINSULA

This is one of Gloucestershire's hidden gems that lies tucked away between a sweeping bend in the River Severn's southern course. Centuries of floods and silt have made this peninsula into rich agricultural land. You can enjoy all of this by following one, or all, of the four circular walks that start from a map board beside the Red Lion Inn on Arlingham's High Street. All walks have kissing gates and bridges, and can be muddy. So take your pick of either, the Hare Walk, Gloucester Cattle Walk, Salmon Walk, and or, the Skylark Walk, before or after, luncheon. All walks take about 2.5 hours, and are between 4.5 to 5 miles in length. (C3)

St Augustine's Farm. Working farm where you can stroke and feed the animals, and buy free range eggs. Open F-M in school holidays, Term Time F & Sa, 10-4. (C3) 01452 740720
staugustinesfarm.co.uk

BERKELEY

An attractive small town with wide streets that lies at the centre of the Vale of Berkeley. It has been in the midst of English history for over 1,000 years, all vividly displayed in its three outstanding attractions: Berkeley Castle, the Edward Jenner Museum and St Mary's Church. For some refreshment, there is the Berkeley Arms Hotel with coffee lounge, bars and a restaurant. (B9) 01453 811177
hotelinberkeley.co.uk

SPECIAL PLACES TO VISIT...

Berkeley Castle. Home of the Berkeley family for the last 850 years. It remains a splendidly preserved Norman fortress with an enclosing curtain wall. Scene of Edward II's murder in 1327. Lovely terraced gardens. Butterfly House. Open April to early Nov Su-W 11-5. (B9) 01453 810303 berkeley-castle.com

Cattle Country Adventure Farm Park. A full panoply of kids activities; Farmyard, play area, pets corner, splash pool, climbing net, assault courses, and much more. Open daily East-Oct from 10. (C9) 01453 810510
cattlecountry.co.uk

Dr Jenner's House, Museum & Garden. A Queen Anne House with traditional and modern displays that celebrate the life of Edward Jenner, the surgeon who discovered a vaccine for smallpox. Open Apr to Sept, Su-W 11-4, (B9) 01453 810631 jennermuseum.com

Parish Church of St Mary's. One of Gloucestershire's most historic and interesting churches with a mass of features: Ring of ten bells, Norman doorway, C12 font, C13 chancel, C13-15 murals, C15 rood screen, C16 brass, Berkeley family tombs from the C15, and life-size effigies in alabaster, Jenner family vault and separate Gothic tower built in 1753. (B9)
stmarys-berkeley.co.uk

1457 Founding of Burford's Almshouses   1465   St Peter's, Winchcombe is rebuilt in the Perpendicular style employing some 500 men   69

THE SOUTH COTSWOLDS • Arlingham, Berkeley, Dursley, Frampton-on-Severn

Berkeley Tombs, Church of St Mary's, Berkeley

DURSLEY

This ancient market town, nestling in a wooded valley, on the very edge of the Cotswold escarpment, modestly hides its innovative, and industrial past. The Market House is a magnificent building that was funded by the Estcourt family of Shipton Moyne in 1738. It has a hipped tile roof and white-washed stone columns. There are some splendid Georgian town houses on the northern fringes of the town. Industry and enterprise are synonymous with Dursley's heritage: from the manufacture of C15 woollen cloth to the mighty C19 diesel, paraffin and petrol engines built by the engineering firm of R A Lister who also employed the failed inventor and genius, Mikael Pedersen. Pedersen invented the centrifugal cream separator (cream and whey from milk) and the Dursley Pedersen Bicycle, a machine of classic design and rare beauty. Architectural innovation carries on with the new Library in May Lane and the splendid new school on the Berkeley Road. Let's hope Dursley is another Cotswold town (like its neighbours, Nailsworth and Tetbury) that is on the up.

For some much-needed refreshment try "the pub of a thousand local's" - **The Old Spot Inn on Hill Road**. The pub of the late, much missed, Old Ric (Sainty). One of CAMRA's favourites and if you are drawn to fine watering holes, then rest your heels here, awhile. (E10) 01453 542870 oldspotinn.co.uk

Stinchcombe Common. Superb viewpoint over the Vale of Berkeley and River Severn. Walks. Golf courses. (D10)

FRAMPTON-ON-SEVERN

An enchanting, straggling village with one of the largest village greens in England. Cricket is played here in summer on Saturday afternoons - so beware of men dressed in shimmering white garb chasing projectiles. It is a haven of wild flowers, bird life and insects due to the absence of ploughing, spraying or cultivation for the past 250 years. Two inns beside The Green: **The Bell** and **The Three Horseshoes.** (E5)

Elver Fishing. The elver is a baby eel which arrives here in Spring after a two-year journey from the Sargasso Sea. They are fished with nets at Epney on the Severn and considered to be a culinary delicacy (if par-boiled and fried in bacon fat), and are reputed to be aphrodisiac, in effect. The elvers mature in isolated ponds then return across the Atlantic to spawn. In days of old, Easter Monday would herald an elver eating contest and the winner would then be allowed to rest in a quiet bedchamber with their beloved, sic. (E5)

SPECIAL PLACES TO VISIT...

Frampton Court. A Grade I Vanbrugh House, garden and family home. Fine panelling, original furniture and porcelain,1732. Superb Gothic C18 garden building, The Orangery for self-catering accommodation (sleeps 8). Fine landscaping with park, lake and ornamental canal. Home of the 'The Frampton Flora' a famous wild flower painting. C16 Wool Barn for hire. Country fair in September. Available for B&B & House Parties. (E5) 01452 740698 framptoncourtestate.co.uk

Frampton Manor. Grade I timber-framed medieval Manor House with walled garden and barn. C12 Birthplace of 'Fair Rosamund' Clifford, mistress to Henry II. House and garden open by written appointment, for groups of 10, or more. (E5) Tours: 01452 740268.

| 1490 | St Mary's Church, Fairford is almost completely rebuilt by John Tame, wool-merchant | 1499 | Bishop Oliver King begins construction of Bath Abbey |

Arlingham, Berkeley, Dursley, Frampton-on-Severn • **THE SOUTH COTSWOLDS**

Frampton Manor Garden ss

Orangery, Frampton Court ss

Tapestry & 4-Poster Room, Frampton Court ss

| 1500 | Stroud now the centre of the Cotswold cloth industry | 1515 | Design of Cirencester St John the Baptist's 'wine glass' pulpit |

THE SOUTH COTSWOLDS • Arlingham, Berkeley, Dursley, Frampton-on-Severn

EAT...DRINK...

The Bell Inn, The Green. A full range of ales and fresh fish and seasonal game to whet your appetite. Up-graded with contemporary furnishings to tempt you to stay awhile in this pretty village within walking distance of a maze of footpaths. (E5) 01452 740346
quality-inns.co.uk

SPECIAL PLACES TO VISIT...

Wildfowl & Wetlands Trust, Slimbridge. Founded by the late Sir Peter Scott in 1946, and home to the world's largest collection of flamingos, swans, geese and ducks - with over 35,000 wildfowl in winter. In historic terms, it is most probably the birthplace of modern conservation. Restaurant. Shop. Picnic areas. Free wheelchairs for the disabled. Open daily Apr to Oct 9.30-5.30, Nov-Mar 9.30-5. (C7) 01453 891900 wwt.org.uk

AND, ACROSS THE RIVER...

Littledean Hall. One of the oldest houses in Britain dating from C11. Archaeological site of Roman Temple. Lovely ancient trees and bluebells in Spring. Open as locally advertised. (A3)
littledeanhall.co.uk

Westbury Court Garden (NT). C17 Dutch water garden laid out between 1696 and 1705. Designed with canals, yew hedge and vegetable plots. Open East to Oct W-Su & BH Ms 10-5 & daily July & Aug 10-5. (C2) 01452 760461
nationaltrust.org.uk

Flamingos, Wildfowl & Wetlands Trust, Slimbridge

Littledean Hall

| 72 | 1529 | John Shakespeare (William's father) moves the family from Snitterfield to Stratford | 1535 | The Dissolution of the Monasteries sees the destruction of the monastic estates at Cirencester, Hailes, Gloucester & Winchcomb |

Arlingham, Berkeley, Dursley, Frampton-on-Severn • **THE SOUTH COTSWOLDS**

Canvas For Creativity, Painswick ss

| 1536 | William Tyndale, the first translator of the Bible is burnt at the stake for heresy | 1540 | Newark Park is designed by Sir Nicholas Poyntz |

156

68

A
B
C
D
E
F
1
2
3
4
5
6
7
8
9
10
GLOUCESTER
GLEVUM
Tredworth
Saintbridge
Abbeydale
Linden
Podsmead
Tuffley
Matson House
Robins Wood Hill
Matson
Wheatridge
Gloucestershire Wildlife Trust
Robins Wood Hill Country Park
ST LEONARD
Upton St Leonard
Lower Tuffley
Whaddon
Moorend
Quedgeley
Court Fm
Naas Fm
ST SWITHUN
Brookthorpe
Brentlands
Spoonbed Hill
Painswick Beacon
Chambers Fm
Bacchus
Hudinknoll Hill
Rococo Garden
Scenic Village
Painswick
The Painswick
ST MARY THE VIRGIN
The Falcon
Churchyard Yew Trees
Queen of the Cotswolds
Harescombe
ST JOHN THE BAPTIST
Edge
Haresfield Hill
Haresfield Beacon
Ring Hill
Scottsquar Hill
Sheephouse
ST JOHN THE BAPTIST
Pitchcombe
Painswick Valley
Whiteshill
Wick Street
HOLY TRINITY
Slad
Laurie Lee (Cider with Rosie)
ST PAUL
Bread Street
Uplands
ALL SAINTS
Paganhill
STROUD
ST LAWRENCE
Cainscross
Museum in the Park
HOLY TRINITY
Tinto
Rodborough Common
Bowbridge
ST MARY MAGDALENE
Lightpill
Butter Row
Kings Court
Rooksmoor
Stroud Brewery
Thrupp
Far Thrupp
Bagpath
Quarhouse
Brimscombe
Houndscroft
St Chloe
Whitfield's Tump
Littleworth
Burleigh
Amberley Inn
Minchinhampton Common
Amberley
HOLY TRINITY
Market House
Pinfarthings
Egypt Mill Hotel
Olive Tree
Box
Bubblewell
Hobbs House
Weigh Bridge Inn
Ball's Green
Forwood
ST GEORGE
NAILSWORTH
W.H. Davies (Tramp Poet) Died Here In 1940
Gigg Mill
Ruskin Mill
Harleywood
Whiteway
Brandhouse Fm
Barton End
Tumulus
Tiltups End
Wild Garlic
Williams Kitchen Deli
Dunkirk Mill
Forestgreen
Windsoredge
Inchbrook
Atcombe Ct
Woodchester Park
Woodchester Mansion
Easter Park Fm
Lynch Knoll
Bowlas Wood
Field Fm
Wallow Green
Tickmorend
Downend
Nupend
ST MARTIN
Horsley
Kingscote Wood
Woodleaze Fm
Woodchester
The Ram
ST MARY
Pen Hill
Bown Hill
Orpheus Pavement
Selsey Common
Middleyard
ALL SAINTS
King's Stanley
Selsey
Ebley
Dudbridge
Ryeford
Stanley Mill
ST GEORGE
Stanley Wood
Stonehouse
Doverow Hill
Cashes Green
Westrip
Puckshole
Randwick
ST JOHN THE BAPTIST
Maiden Hill
Ruscombe
Lansdown Pottery
Stroud Green
Standish Park Fm
Arlebrook
Vinegar Hill
Standish
ST NICHOLAS
Almonry (rems)
Court Hill
Pidgemore Fm
Nupend
Nastend
Oldend
ST CYR
Bridgend
Stanley Downton
Grey Cottage
Leonard Stanley
ST SWITHUN
St Leonard's Priory (rems)
Estate Barn
Frocester
ST ANDREW
Eastington
Millend
Churchend
ST MICHAEL & ALL ANGELS
Alkerton
Cress Green
Middle Street
Wicksters Bridge
Downton Fms
Elmcote
Lapley Fm
Coaley
ST BARTHOLOMEW
Silver Street
Hamshill
Upthorne
Green Street
Far Green
Coaley Peak
Frocester Hill
Long Barrow
Sandford's Knoll
Nympsfield
ST BARTHOLOMEW
Hetty Pegler's Tump
West Hill
Crawley
Woodcock Fm
Owlpen Manor
Uley
Scenic Village
Prema
ST GILES
Camp
Uley Bury
The Old Brewery
Lampern House
Shadwell
Cam
ST GEORGE
Ashmead Green
Comley Wood
Cam Long Down
Downham Hill
Dursley
ST JAMES THE GREAT
Rockstowes
Woodmancote
Whitminster
ST ANDREW
Westend
Stroudwater Navigation
Fromebridge
Apple Tree Park
Claypits
Wheatenhurst
ST ANDREW
Packthorne Fm
Moreton Valence
ST STEPHEN
Putloe
Parkend
Little Haresfield
Haresfield
ST PETER
Colethrop
Epney
Parkend Bridge
Harwicke Court
Elver Fishing
Lynch Fm
Hardwicke
ST NICHOLAS
Four Mile Elm
Longney
ST LAWRENCE
Madam's End Fm
Monk's Hill
Hockley Hill
Velthouse Fm
Wicksgreen
Bridgemacote
Kenton Green
Sustrans Cycleway
Stonebench
ST JAMES
ST JOHN THE BAPTIST
Elmore
Farley's End
Elmore Court
Windmill Hill
Corn Ham
Lower Rea
Rea
Back
River Severn
A38
A4173
A46
A419
A4135
B4008
B4066
B4058
B4070
B4071
B4073
M5
12
13

52

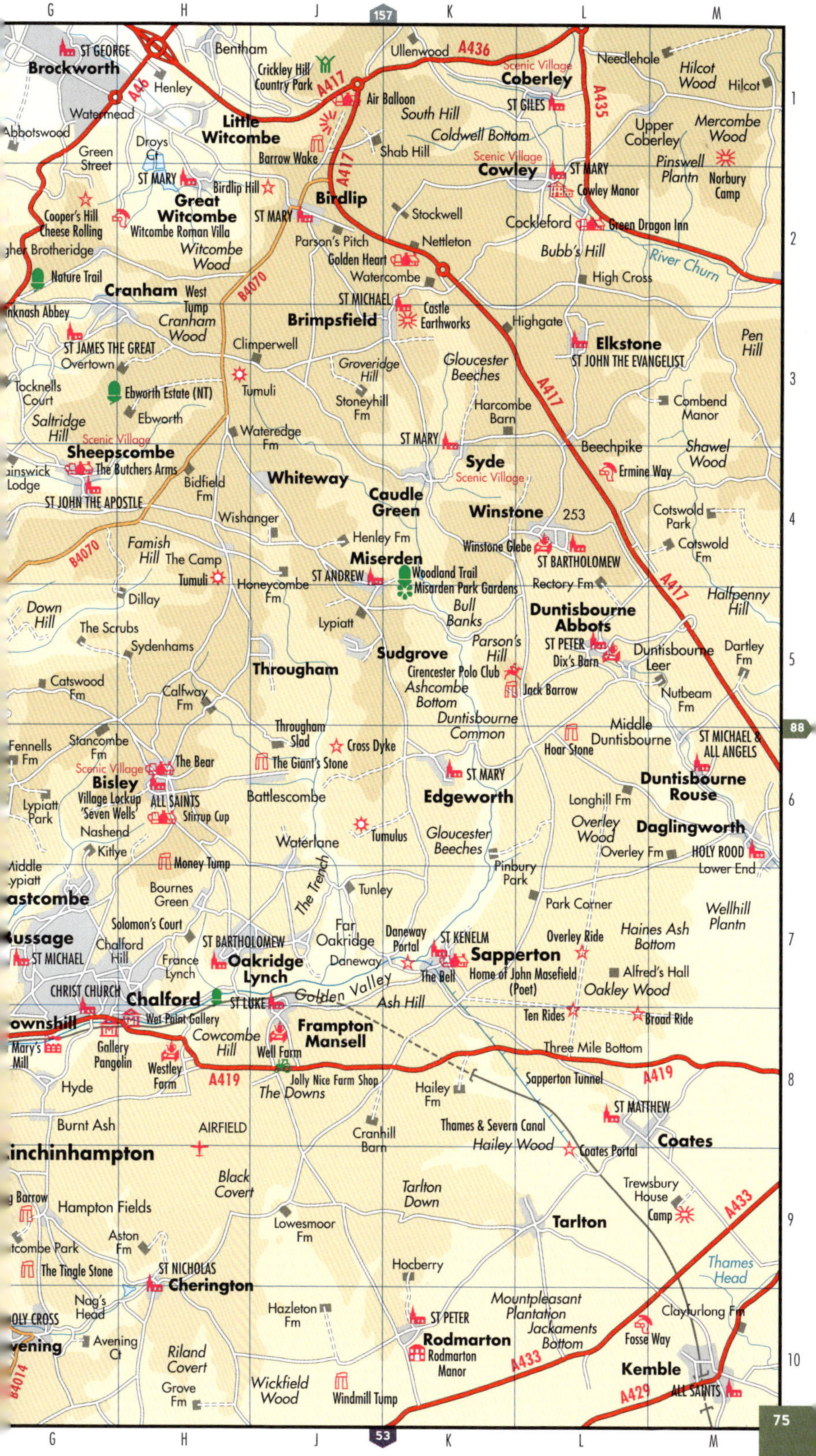
G
H
J
157
K
L
M
ST GEORGE
Brockworth
Bentham
Crickley Hill Country Park
A417
Air Balloon
Ullenwood
A436
Scenic Village
Coberley
Needlehole
Hilcot Wood
Hilcot
A46
Henley
Watermead
Abbotswood
Little Witcombe
South Hill
ST GILES
A435
Upper Coberley
Mercombe Wood
Droys Ct
Green Street
Barrow Wake
Shab Hill
Coldwell Bottom
Scenic Village
Cowley
ST MARY
Pinswell Plantn
Norbury Camp
ST MARY
Birdlip Hill
Birdlip
Cowley Manor
Great Witcombe
Cooper's Hill Cheese Rolling
Witcombe Roman Villa
ST MARY
Stockwell
Cockleford
Green Dragon Inn
Brotheridge
Parson's Pitch
Nettleton
Witcombe Wood
Golden Heart
Bubb's Hill
River Churn
Nature Trail
Watercombe
High Cross
Cranham
West Tump
B4070
ST MICHAEL
Castle Earthworks
Prinknash Abbey
Cranham Wood
Brimpsfield
Highgate
Elkstone
ST JAMES THE GREAT
Climperwell
ST JOHN THE EVANGELIST
Pen Hill
Overtown
Groveridge Hill
Gloucester Beeches
Tocknells Court
Tumuli
Ebworth Estate (NT)
Stoneyhill Fm
A417
Combend Manor
Saltridge Hill
Ebworth
Harcombe Barn
Scenic Village
Wateredge Fm
ST MARY
Beechpike
Shawel Wood
Sheepscombe
The Butchers Arms
Syde
Ermine Way
Painswick Lodge
Bidfield Fm
Whiteway
Scenic Village
ST JOHN THE APOSTLE
Caudle Green
Winstone
253
Cotswold Park
Wishanger
B4070
Famish Hill
Henley Fm
Cotswold Fm
The Camp
Miserden
Winstone Glebe
ST BARTHOLOMEW
Tumuli
ST ANDREW
Woodland Trail
Honeycombe Fm
Misarden Park Gardens
Rectory Fm
A417
Halfpenny Hill
Dillay
Bull Banks
Duntisbourne Abbots
Down Hill
Lypiatt
The Scrubs
Parson's Hill
ST PETER
Duntisbourne Leer
Dartley Fm
Sydenhams
Sudgrove
Dix's Barn
Througham
Cirencester Polo Club
Catswood Fm
Ashcombe Bottom
Jack Barrow
Nutbeam Fm
Calfway Fm
Duntisbourne Common
Middle Duntisbourne
Througham Slad
88
ST MICHAEL & ALL ANGELS
Fennells Fm
Stancombe Fm
Cross Dyke
Hoar Stone
The Bear
Scenic Village
The Giant's Stone
ST MARY
Bisley
Duntisbourne Rouse
Village Lockup
Edgeworth
Lypiatt Park
'Seven Wells'
ALL SAINTS
Battlescombe
Longhill Fm
Stirrup Cup
Overley Wood
Daglingworth
Nashend
Tumulus
Gloucester Beeches
Waterlane
Overley Fm
HOLY ROOD
Kitlye
Lower End
Middle Lypiatt
Money Tump
Pinbury Park
The Trench
Tunley
Eastcombe
Bournes Green
Park Corner
Wellhill Plantn
Solomon's Court
Far Oakridge
Daneway Portal
Haines Ash Bottom
Bussage
Chalford Hill
ST BARTHOLOMEW
ST KENELM
Overley Ride
ST MICHAEL
France Lynch
Oakridge Lynch
Daneway
Sapperton
Alfred's Hall
The Bell
Home of John Masefield (Poet)
CHRIST CHURCH
Golden Valley
Oakley Wood
Chalford
ST LUKE
Ash Hill
Ten Rides
Broad Ride
Brownshill
Wet Paint Gallery
Frampton Mansell
Cowcombe Hill
St Mary's Mill
Gallery Pangolin
Well Farm
Three Mile Bottom
Westley Farm
A419
Sapperton Tunnel
A419
Jolly Nice Farm Shop
Hyde
The Downs
Hailey Fm
ST MATTHEW
Burnt Ash
AIRFIELD
Cranhill Barn
Thames & Severn Canal
Coates
Minchinhampton
Hailey Wood
Coates Portal
Black Covert
Tarlton Down
Trewsbury House
Long Barrow
Hampton Fields
Camp
A433
Lowesmoor Fm
Tarlton
Aston Fm
Gatcombe Park
Thames Head
The Tingle Stone
ST NICHOLAS
Cherington
Hocberry
Nag's Head
Mountpleasant Plantation
HOLY CROSS
Hazleton Fm
ST PETER
Clayfurlong Fm
Jackaments Bottom
Rodmarton
Avening
Avening Ct
Fosse Way
Rodmarton Manor
A433
Riland Covert
Kemble
B4014
A429
ALL SAINTS
Wickfield Wood
Grove Fm
Windmill Tump
53
1
2
3
4
5
6
7
8
9
10

THE SOUTH COTSWOLDS • Stroud, Nailsworth, Painswick

Dusk on Saltridge Wood, Sheepscombe

STROUD

This is not a pretty, pretty, almost too perfect, Cotswold town. No. Stroud was as close to the grime of the industrial revolution as any other town in the Gloucestershire Cotswolds. It has few architectural gems. However, its attraction lies in its energy and artistic ambitions. There has been a liberal, bohemian attitude at play here since the group of Tolstoyan Anarchists settled at Whiteways in 1898. There is a lively community of writers and artists living in the surrounding valleys. Many will have read Laurie Lee's "Cider With Rosie" about his early life in the Slad Valley but artists Michael Cardew, Lyn Chadwick and Norman Jewson settled here, too. And Damien Hirst has a business making up his prints and artworks in nearby Chalford. So, supposedly the claim that it is the Arts and Crafts centre of the Cotswolds is justified. A busy café culture pervades, too. The weaving industry all began in a couple of cottages up the hill in Bisley. This moved into the town where 150 mills were soon in action using the water-powered valleys. But, as the C19 progressed much of this cloth making moved north to the West Riding of Yorkshire. The surrounding valleys provide wonderful walks through combes and woodland that are so very different from the Central Wolds. Look out for the Subscription Rooms built around 1833. (F6)

LIGHT BITES...

Head for the **Stroud Bookshop** at the top of the High Street. Behind you is **Woodruffs** for an All-Day Breakfast, coffees, brunch, lunch, cakes, vegan and vegetarian. Open M-Sa 8-5, Su 9.30-3.

Or, cross the street into Witheys Yard, to **Yard Café & Kitchen** where they also serve all-day breakfasts, toasted tea cakes and homemade cakes. For lunch; soups and Specials, spinach and lasagne, all with al fresco seating.

In need of a glass of bubbly or wine? You have passed the **Stroud Wine Company** where you are welcome to sample the latest vintage. Or, cross to Church Street, to **The Retreat,** a wine bar which opens at noon until 12pm. This Bar has a loyal following who are regularly fed bubble and squeak, wild boar chilli and hot chicken sarnies, their all-time favourites. You'll be greeted with a warm welcome, red walls and a woodburner - the beers go down a treat, too. 01453 750208 retreatstroud.com

If you seek an all-day breakfast of Eggs Benedict, and the like, turn R out of the bookshop into Union Street to **JRool Bistro**, open Tu-F from 12-10pm and Sa 9-10pm The menu changes fortnightly. Its all meat and fresh veg, and fresh fish. 01453 767123 jrool.co.uk

Looking for something different? At the top of town **The Loganberry Take-Away and Coffee-Shop**. Home-made fresh food and hanging plants for sale.

| 1540 | Winchcombe becomes a tobacco growing area | 1542 | The Crown sells Hailes Abbey to an agent who demolishes it |

Stroud, Nailsworth, Painswick • **THE SOUTH COTSWOLDS**

SPECIAL PLACES TO VISIT...

Gallery Pangolin, Chalford. Specialists in modern and contemporary sculptures that have been cast in their foundry, and also sculptors' drawings. Open M-F 10-6, Sa 10-1. (H8) 01453 889765
gallery-pangolin.com

Lansdown Pottery, Hill Farm, Whiteshill. A small group of potters work here developing their own different styles. Please call before your visit. (E5) 01453 298567
lansdownpottery.co.uk

Museum In The Park, Stratford Park. Innovative and colourful displays and changing exhibitions ranging from Dinosaurs to the Uley Roman Temple to the world's first lawnmower and contemporary sculpture. A Must-See for all Cotswold enthusiasts. Beautiful garden to the rear. Open Summer Tu-F 10-4.30, W/Es & BHs 11-4.30. (E6) 01453 763394
museuminthepark.org.uk

Stroud Brewery, London Road, Brimscombe. Established in 2006 to brew craft beers. Bar open for Brunch, Pizzas & Tours. Complex opening hours so please check website. (F8) 01453 887122
stroudbrewery.co.uk

Stroud Valley Cycle Trail. A flattish route ideal for family cycling takes you along the Nailsworth valley, a former railway track. Start from the Kings Stanley car park, cross the A46, to Dudbridge Roundabout and follow the trail to Egypt Mill. (D7)

Woodchester Roman Villa, Church Lane. This huge villa was excavated by Lysons in 1993 and revealed 64 rooms including the Orpheus Pavement. Today, there is little to see. The pavement lies buried and plans to uncover it lie dormant. (E7)

MINCHINHAMPTON

A large village noted for the Market House, Holy Trinity and rows of weavers' cottages. The Parish Church of the Holy Trinity has an unusual Coronet Tower and some richly ornate monuments. A living and working village, off the tourist route, and better for it. The wide, open spaces have room for three golf courses. So pack your clubs. (F9)

FARMERS' MARKET

This is held every Saturday from 9am to 2pm. There are over 85 stalls, much of which are organic, and they change weekly, so there are regulars and guests to keep it fresh, like the produce. It is considered one of the best in the country, and must not be missed if you are in the area, come Saturday. There are buskers and entertainers to keep the kids happy, and the local ale flows from the bars. Parking is the only handicap. Be prepared to walk. 01453 758060 madeinstroud.co.uk Made In Stroud shop open M-Sa 9-5.30.

Jolly Nice Farm Shop & Kitchen (Drive Through) Café. Rarely have I eaten a more scrumptious burger! Farm Shop & Butchery, Harriet's Ice Cream Parlour, Bakery and plants for sale. Eat out or inside. Open daily 8-7 (-8 summer) (J8) 01285 760868
jollynicefarmshop.com

Market House. Impressive building built in 1698 with stone columns and row of wooden pillars. (F8)

Minchinhampton Common (NT). A wide, open space, popular with dog walkers, riding horses, golfers, and the ancient Saxons final resting place - see the Long Barrows and Earthworks. (F8)

1547 — Katherine Parr, widow of Henry VIII, marries Sir Edward Seymour and settles at Sudeley Castle

1548 — Katherine Parr dies in childbirth

THE SOUTH COTSWOLDS • Stroud, Nailsworth, Painswick

The Painswick, Painswick ss

NAILSWORTH

In the last few years this little town has come alive! Transformed into a thriving, bustling shopping centre with bakery, restaurants, tearooms, arts and craft shops. An eclectic mix of Cotswold domestic and industrial architecture is to be seen dotted about the hillside overlooking a wooded valley. Its position is convenient as a centre for visiting Bath, and the southern Cotswolds. (E9)

SPECIAL PLACES TO VISIT...

Dunkirk Mill Centre. A mill with machinery driven by the largest working water wheel in Gloucestershire. Displays on the finishing processes of fulling, teasel raising and cross cutting. Access is via the Cycle Track by Egypt Mill. Open Apr to Sept on odd W/Es 2-4. (E9) 01453 766123 stroudtextiletrust.org.uk

Gigg Mill, Old Bristol Road. Historic mill with weaving shed containing ancient and modern looms. Visits must be pre-booked. (E9) stroudtextiletrust.org.uk

Ruskin Mill. A thriving arts, craft and education centre set in a restored 1820s woollen mill. (E9) 01453 837500 rmet.org

PAINSWICK

Its local description as *'The Queen of the Cotswolds'* is fully justified. The houses and cottages are built from a grey, almost white, limestone, in marked contrast to Broadway and Chipping Campden, and some of the buildings have an almost Palladian, statuesque quality about them.

Look out for the Court House and **The Painswick** (Hotel). Wander down the pretty

LIGHT BITES...

From the X-roads, head East. Beside the stream on your L is **Hobbs House, 4 George Street.** Busy bakery and deli serving coffee, cakes, panninis and sandwiches. You can eat upstairs, or outside overlooking the stream. (E9) 01453 839396 hobbshousebakery.co.uk

Around the corner, opposite the Morrisons entrance is the **Olive Tree, 28 George Street.** Just the place to sit and wile away lazy days in the sunshine, or perhaps, to write the next Harry Potter. Breakfasts, coffee, lunch and suppers. Daily Specials can be Fish Pie, Ratatouille Crumble or Rump Steak. Open M-Sa from 8.30am. (E9) 01453 834802 theolivetree-nailsworth.com

Returning to the X-roads to Fountain Street (the Bath Road) is **William's Food Hall & Oyster Bar, 3 Fountain Street.** In need of a lunch time sandwich, or seafood (delivery Thursdays) to take home and bake. This deli has been spoiling the locals for so long they have probably forgotten how lucky they are to have it. Restaurant opens for breakfast and coffee. Open Tu-Sa. (E9) 01453 832240 williamsfoodhall.co.uk

Continue up this street where there are all manor of interesting independent shops and galleries, to **No.28 Café**. It has the best coffee in town, and opens for breakfast at 8.30-5. Its artisan and rustic, and serves homemade cakes. Artworks line the walls. For the famous 2 in 1 pie, and a pint of ale, you must drive eastwards out of Nailsworth towards Avening to the **Weigh Bridge Inn, Longfords.** Home of the famous 2 in 1 pie. Half of the bowl contains the filling of your choice: steak and mushroom, chicken, ham and leek, pork, bacon and celery... the other half is brimming with home made cauliflower cheese. Freehouse with log fires and cosy corners to sample fine ales. (E9) 01453 832520 weighbridgeinn.co.uk

And now, for something substantial: **Wild Garlic, 3 Cossack Square.** Cosy ambience, fresh organic produce, making friends, modern British food cooked by the former head chef of nearby Calcot Manor. What more could you wish for? Perhaps, a bright and colourful bedroom to rest, and digest your food. (E9) 01453 832615 wild-garlic.co.uk

| 78 | 1552 | Westwoods Grammar School, Northleach founded | 1555 | Bishop Hooper (of Gloucester) is burnt at the stake |

Stroud, Nailsworth, Painswick • **THE SOUTH COTSWOLDS**

Sculptured Yew Trees, Painswick

side streets but above all you must and it's tricky to ignore, visit the churchyard, famous for the legendary 99 yew trees. The 100th yew tree has been planted, time and again, but has never survived. Painswick is one of the gems of the southern Cotswolds, and is a worthy base from which to explore this region. It is also connected to a network of footpaths including the Cotswold Way, so you can arrive by car, or taxi, and then just walk for the rest of your stay.

SPECIAL PLACES TO VISIT...

Painswick Beacon. Fine viewpoint. Footpaths. Parking. (F3)

Parish Church of St Mary. It is the soaring spire that will first captivate you, then as you enter, it will be the line of yew trees and then, as you wander around the churchyard, the tombs or monuments carved with their intricate figures. But, do look up and admire the gold clock. The spire has been struck by lightning on many occasions, in 1763 and 1883. The 100th yew tree always fades away. So much, for hope. (F4)

Prinknash Abbey Park. Benedictine Monastery with C14 and C15 origins set amidst an idyllic, rolling landscape. Monastery Chapel opens 8-7.45pm. Monastery garden with possible Tudor origins. Café and grounds open daily. (G2) 01452 812455
prinknashabbey.org.uk

Rococo Garden. A beautiful C18 Rococo garden set in 6-acres, dating from a period of flamboyant and romantic garden design, nestles in a hidden Cotswold valley. Maze. Be sure you visit in February for the display of magical snowdrops. Open daily mid-Jan to Sept, 10.30-5. New Nursery, Restaurant and Gift Shop. (F4) 01452 813204
rococogarden.org.uk

EAT...DRINK...SLEEP...

Wild Garlic Rooms & Wilder (Fine Dining), Cossack Square. It started as a bistro with rooms. With its success been able to develop Wilder (01453 835483) around the corner on Market Street for fine dining (an 8-course surprise tasting menu) open on Wednesday to Saturday evenings 7-close (Taxis at 10.15). Five comfortable bedrooms. Nailsworth is becoming an arty and foodie centre perfect for a visit to Bath and a grand location for the south Cotswolds. (E9) 01453 832615 wild-garlic.co.uk

Painswick Rococo Garden

1558   Bath becomes a popular spa   1564   William Shakespeare baptized   79

THE SOUTH COTSWOLDS • Stroud, Nailsworth, Painswick

The Falcon, New Street. In grand position overlooking the Churchyard. Tasty British seasonal food, local ales, bedrooms with high ceilings, comfy beds and en-suite facilities makes for a fine unpretentious combination. 01452 814222 (F4)
thefalconpainswick.com

The Painswick, Kemps Lane. Palladian-style Cotswold rectory that has been transformed, again, but this time (thankfully) back into a comfortable country house hotel with contemporary furnishings, feastings of lovely food and various hedonistic treatments. Without exception, one of the Cotswolds most stylish retreats. (F4)
01452 813688
thepainswick.co.uk

St Michaels Bistro/ Restaurant & B&B, Victoria Street. This is where I stop for coffee and brunch when in Painswick. Overlooking the Churchyard the location is a delight and in summer you can sit outside watching the passersby. Bistro open Tu-Su from 10 am. 01452 203306, B&B 01452 812712
stmichaelsbistro.co.uk

St Anne's B&B, Gloucester Street. A listed, C18 former wool merchant's house with a relaxed family atmosphere. Within easy walking distance of pubs and restaurants. (F4) 01452 812879
st-annes-painswick.co.uk

VILLAGES OF INTEREST...

Bisley. Home of the novelist, Jilly Cooper, and the sculptor, the late Lynn Chadwick. Noted for the Well Dressing on Ascension Day and its rows of beautiful stone cottages. Two pubs. Village stores. (H6)

Duntisbournes. A group of hamlets dotted along a beautiful wooded valley. Duntisbourne Abbot stands at the head of the valley. The Dunt Brook flows through each hamlet. The road to Duntisbourne Leer lies beneath a stream. Middle Duntisbourne and Duntisbourne Rouse are two farming hamlets, the latter famous for its idyllic Saxon Church. (L5)

Sapperton. In a splendid position overlooking woodland and the Golden Valley. Home of the William Morris protégés, Ernest Gimson and, Sydney and Ernest Barnsley of the Cotswold Arts and Crafts Movement, creators of beautiful furniture who also built their own cottages in the village. Their fame rose after completing restorative work at nearby Pinsbury Park which became during World War II, home to the Poet Laureate, John Masefield. Ernest Gimson died young at 59 and is buried in the churchyard. The area is rich in industrial heritage, woodland and circular walks. The dining pub, **The Bell**, is on hand to refresh you. (K7)

Sheepscombe. A straggling village surrounded by beautiful woodland, rolling pastures and green hills. The view down the valley looking

View of Lower Slad

| 80 | 1570 | The 'Great Rebuilding' of England begins | 1576 | Chavenage developed into a substantial manor |

Stroud, Nailsworth, Painswick • **THE SOUTH COTSWOLDS**

Fields from The Woolpack, Slad

Laurie Lee 1914 – 1997

Author, Film Maker, Musician, Novelist, Playwright, Poet, Screenwriter, Travel Writer. Born in Stroud and brought up in the village of Slad, Laurie is remembered for his autobiographical trilogy Cider With Rosie (1959), As I Walked Out One Midsummer Morning (1969), and A Moment of War (1991). Cider With Rosie established him as a brilliant and original writer of descriptive prose, an achingly evocative chronicle of village life before the advent of the motor car and an English countryside lost in time. It has been made into countless TV films and has sold in excess of six million copies worldwide. Laurie was a slow, ponderous writer who debated over every syllable and word. The sentence had to have a musical rhythm. He was most proud of his poetry. His first volume, The Sun My Monument was published in 1944. His last Selected Poems in 1983. Valerie Grove wrote a wonderful biography The Well-Loved Stranger in 1999. He lies buried in Slad's Churchyard overlooking his beloved Woolpack Inn.

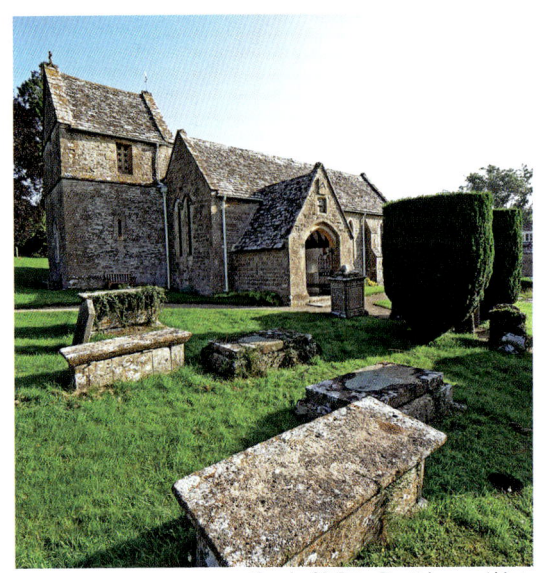

THE SOUTH COTSWOLDS • Stroud, Nailsworth, Painswick

Church of St Peter, Duntisbourne Abbots

towards Painswick church is a beauty. It is the ancestral home of Laurie Lee whose parents moved to Slad. He maintained a connection with the village by purchasing a field for the cricket club, so named Laurie Lee Field. A network of footpaths leads through woodland to Painswick, Cranham and Slad. (G4)

Slad. One of the Stroud villages where cloth was spun in the little cottages before it all moved to South Riding, Yorkshire. Hundreds flock here to walk in the shadow of Laurie Lee's "Cider With Rosie" and to sample the brew still available in the Woolpack Inn. If you have recently read the book, which captures an England long forgotten, you will recognise the woods and valleys, so described. You may wish to make your way to Bulls Cross, the hanging place, and now the start-off point for a circular walk. Laurie Lee lies buried in the churchyard, opposite the Woolpack. (F5)

Uley. A long, attractive village with some fine Georgian houses, and famous as a centre of the cloth industry in the C17 and C18s. In 1608 three Uley clothiers represented 29 local weavers of broadcloth, and also, the 13 weavers from Owlpen. The site of a Roman settlement, too. (B10)

SPECIAL PLACES OF INTEREST...

Cotswold Canals. The Stroudwater Navigation was opened in 1779 linking Stroud to the River Severn, to serve the cloth industry of the Stroud Valleys. The Thames and Severn Canal was built to link the Stroudwater to the River Thames via the Sapperton Tunnel. The towpath is open and the best places to see the restored canal are at Eastington, near Stonehouse and at both portals of the Sapperton Tunnel, and west of the Spine Road in the Cotswold Water Park. The restoration work is on-going and is actively creating freshwater habitats where wildflowers abound, notably Lilies of the Valley. (L8) 01453 752568
cotswoldcanals.org.uk

Frocester Court's Medieval Estate Barn. This is an enormous barn, built between 1284 and 1306. It remains the second largest in England, and is one of the best preserved with a massive oak roof, and is used every day by the farmer who owns it. For conducted tours (of 5 or more) phone: 01453 823250. (B7)

Misarden Park Gardens. The home of the Wills family, of tobacco fame has shrubs, a traditional rose garden, perennial borders, extensive yew topiary, magnolia Goulangeana and spring bulbs amidst a picturesque woodland setting. Rill and Summerhouse. The Elizabethan mansion has mullion windows and was extended by Waterhouses in the C19 and by Lutyens who added a new wing between 1920-21. Sculptures Galore! Airbnb at Miserden Park Flat. The gardens are open in Spring/Summer W-Su 10-5. Glasshouse Café W-Su & BHs 10-5. (K5) 01285 821303
miserden.org

Owlpen Manor. An iconic group of picturesque Cotswold buildings: Manor House, Tithe Barn, Church, Mill and Court House. Water Garden and terrace. The Tudor manor dates from 1450-1616, but the whole estate has 900 years of history to tell. Holiday cottages for hire. Events. (C10) 01453 860261 owlpen.com

Prema, Uley. Independent rural arts centre shows new work by emerging artists in their converted Bethesda chapel. Open W-Sa 9-5. Vestry

| 82 | 1587 | Endymion Porter born at The Manor, Aston-sub-Edge patron of the poets Robert Herrick and Ben Jonson | 1590 | Elizabeth 1 grants Bath city status |

Stroud, Nailsworth, Painswick • THE SOUTH COTSWOLDS

café open W-Sa 9-4. (B10) 01453 860703 prema.org.uk

Rodmarton Manor, Cirencester. This is a unique building built by Ernest Barnsley and his Cotswold group of craftsmen for the Biddulph family from 1909 to 1929. It displays Cotswold "Arts and Crafts" furniture, metalwork and wall hangings. The 8-acre garden is a series of outdoor rooms and is a marvel throughout the year. Refreshments. Open Feb for the snowdrops, then May to Sept W, Sa & BHs 2-5. (K10) 01285 841442 rodmarton-manor.co.uk

St Mary's Mill, Chalford. An 1820 mill housing a large water wheel and a powerful Tangye steam engine. Open for 'Open Days' on 01453 766273 (H8) stroudtextiletrust.org.uk

The Old Brewery, Uley. The mill owner, Samuel Price built this brewery in 1833 to assuage his workers thirst. It was restored in 1984 and has since won many awards for their Old Spot, Pigs Ear and Uley Bitter. It is not open to prying visitors, only the trade. You can sample their wares in **The Old Crown Inn** at the top of the village, or in various hostelries around the Cotswolds. (B10)

Whiteway Colony. Founded in 1898 by a group of Tolstoyan Anarchists made up of liberal minded teachers and clerks from Croydon who found land they could buy for £7 an acre and who built small, wooden houses. They grew their own vegetables, buried their own dead and invited musicians and intellectuals to visit them. The men wore shorts and beards, the women, smocks. They housed a number of Republican refugees from the Spanish Civil War which

later had a profound effect on Laurie Lee's education and travels. Today, many of their descendants still live here from whom you can buy fresh honey and vegetables. (J4)

Woodchester Mansion. Be prepared for a good 1-mile walk from the car park down to this unfinished masterpiece of Victorian stone masonry set in a secret Cotswold valley. The restoration project is on-going and ambitious. Bat Experiences. Guided tours. Open F, W/Es & BH Ms, Apr-Oct 11-5. (C8) 01453 861541 woodchestermansion.org.uk

CHURCHES TO VISIT...

Coates. Norman. Perpendicular tower. Brasses. Best viewed from across the fields. (L8)

Coberley. C15 Gargoyles. Enter through farm gates. (L1)

Daglingworth. Saxon carvings. (M6)

Duntisbourne Rouse. Small Saxon. Saddleback Tower. Norman additions. Lovely situation. (M6)

Edgeworth. Early Saxon with some Norman additions: nave, chancel and south door. A restored C13 porch and C14 stained glass. Look for the cross in the churchyard with medieval base and mutilated head. (K6)

Elkstone. Famous Norman Cotswold church known for its Tympanum and claimed to be the highest in the Cotswolds. (L3)

Miserden. Late Saxon in origin, with a Norman font and windows. Some C16 tombs in churchyard. Sadly much was destroyed by the amateur architect, the Reverend W H Lowder, in 1886. Note the War

Memorial by Lutyens, and the beech, and yew trees. (J4)

Sapperton. Noted for its monuments, oak panelling supplied from the Manor House and woodcarvings, its hundreds of crocuses in Spring, and not forgetting, its superb position overlooking the Golden Valley. (K7)

Selsey. Spectacular position set high on the Cotswold escarpment. Stained glass by pre- Raphaelites, Edward Burne-Jones and William Morris. (D7)

Uley. In a spectacular position overlooking the valley. Noted for the Norman font, fine roof and stained glass. (B10)

SPECIAL PLACES OF NATURAL INTEREST...

Cam Long Down. A humpbacked ridge of oolitic limestone that once seen, is never forgotten. From the top, it's a good viewpoint crossed by the Cotswold Way, surrounded by beech woods and bracken. (A9)

Chalford Valley Nature Trail. Passes beside the River Frome and the Thames & Severn Canal. Parking near Round House by the Industrial Estate. (H8)

Coaley Peak. On the edge of the Cotswold escarpment, affording fine views. Picnic area. Ice cream van. (B8)

Cooper's Hill. 137 acres of common land in which to roam wild, crossed by nature trails. Start from the car park at Fiddler's Elbow. The scene of the Cheese-Rolling ceremony on Whit Monday at 6pm - a large cheese (originally representing the Sun in a Pagan ceremony) is chased down the hill. Only for the fittest, and craziest at

THE SOUTH COTSWOLDS • Stroud, Nailsworth, Painswick

heart, for limbs have known to be fractured here on many occasions. Scene of an Iron Age fort. (G2)

Cranham Woods. Bluebells and white garlic bloom in Spring and a web of footpaths are spread throughout this tangled woodland. Best approached from Birdlip in early summer when the foliage is green and new. (H3)

Ebworth Estate (NT). Woodland walks through beech woods rich in wildlife managed by English Nature. No parking facilities. (H3) 01452 814213

Frocester Hill. A superb viewpoint rising to 778 feet provides superb views over the Severn Estuary, Welsh Hills and Forest of Dean. (C8)

Gloucestershire Wildlife Trust, Robinswood Hill Country Park. Visitor Centre, exhibition and giftshop. Open daily 7.30-4.30 (E2) 01452 38333
gloucestershirewildlifetrust.co.uk

Golden Valley. Runs from Sapperton to Chalford, and is especially fine with the arrival of the Autumnal colours of beech, ash and oak. (G8)

Haresfield Beacon & Standish Wood (NT). High open grassland at 700 feet that was a natural fort held by Iron Age and Roman settlements. Delightful when the bluebells and primroses bloom in the Spring. (D4)

Rodborough Common (NT). 800 acres of open space provides great walks and views across the Stroud Valleys. (E7)

ANCIENT MONUMENTS TO VISIT...

Barrow Wake. Deep scarp edge. Favourite viewpoint.
Roman pottery found at the bottom of scarp. Car park. (J1)

Ermin Way. Roman road linking Cirencester with Gloucester and Kingsholm; two encampments on the edge of Roman civilisation that was built and manned by troops. This undulating road still leaves a marked pattern across the landscape. (L4)

Hetty Pegler's Tump Uley Tumulus. Neolithic Long Barrow 120ft x 22ft, 4 chambers, 38 skeletons found in C19. Torch and Wellington boots needed. (B9)

Uley Bury Iron Age Hill Fort. This is the Cotswolds most famous Iron Age site. The deep ramparts provide superb views across the Severn Vale, Welsh Hills, Dursley and Owlpen Woods. It's an enclosed area of about 32 acres and is used for arable crops. Of more interest, it has an easy circular walk possible for large wheeled buggies and pushchairs. (B9)

EAT...DRINK...SLEEP... IN A HOSTELRY...

Amberley Inn. This old hostelry overlooks the five Stroud valleys. The kitchen provides meals fostered from local Cotswold ingredients. 13 pretty bedrooms. (E8)
01453 872565
theamberleyinn.co.uk

Bear at Bisley (B&B). Bisley's oldest pub is traditional, friendly and the bar is well stocked with a range of traditional ales. Pub-grub. Bedrooms with showers. (H6)
01452 771153 bearinbisley.com

Bell at Sapperton (B&B). Popular dining pub given to natural stonewalls, polished flagstone floors where the winter log fires provide a comfortable ambience. Local beers. Al fresco in summer. Read the hilarious AA Gill review. Luxurious bedrooms. (K7) 01285 760298
bellsapperton.co.uk

Black Horse Inn, Cranham. A popular pub with walkers. The food is nourishing and good value and the real ales go down a treat. Unpretentious and cosy. Once, a family favourite with the Frickers, especially their sausages and cauliflower cheese! Opens at midday. (H3) 01452 812217

Butcher's Arms, Sheepscombe. The Butchers Arms has an unlikely national claim to fame - the much photographed carved sign of a

Cowley Manor ss

84 | 1611 The King James Version of the Bible incorporates much of Tyndale's work | 1612 Robert Dover holds the first Cotswold Olympicks at Chipping Campden

Stroud, Nailsworth, Painswick • **THE SOUTH COTSWOLDS**

View from Coaley Peak, The Cotswold Way

butcher sipping a pint of beer with a pig tied to his leg. 'Pie and a Pint' meal deal. Average pub-grub. (G4) 01452 812113
butchers-arms.co.uk

Golden Heart, Birdlip. Centuries-old coaching inn serving a range of local ales, and food from sandwiches to good pub-grub. Garden with pastoral views. B&B. (K2) 01242 870261
thegoldenheart.co.uk

Stirrup Cup, Bisley. An old favourite that has been transformed with contemporary furnishings and season British food to cater for the Cotswold Blow Ins. Skittle Alley. (H6) 01452 770007
thestirrupcup.com

Woolpack Inn, Slad. Traditional Cotswold pub with exceptional food simply cooked and home to a cup of Rosie's cider and the spirit of Laurie Lee. Newspapers, a pastoral view, Beer Fest, cricketers… bliss. (F5) 01452 813429
thewoolpackslad.com

EAT…DRINK…SLEEP…

Apple Tree Park, Eastington. Camping and caravan site with 100 pitches in 6-acres, a mile from the A38. (B6) 01452 742362
appletreepark.co.uk

Cowley Manor. A chic and stylish country hotel set in 55-acres of glorious gardens with four lakes and a Victorian cascade. Once more, a new chapter unfolds in the history of this Manor; expect luxurious bedrooms, hedonism aplenty and professional expertise. (L2) 01242 870900
cowleymanorexperimental.com

Dix's Barn B&B, Duntisbourne Abbots. This converted barn overlooks the Area of Outstanding Natural Beauty. Fishing and riding nearby. 01285 821249

Fireside Glamping, Westley Farm, Chalford. 80-acre hill farm of ancient woodlands, flower-rich hay meadows, and steep banks of limestone grassland with three traditional stone (self-catering) cottages spread over the hillside. For the more adventurous try one of their Turkoman style yurt tents situated in the diddlydumps. 01285 760262
westleyfarm.co.uk

Grey Cottage B&B, Bath Road, Leonard Stanley. Comfortable C19 cottage with lots of personal details. Dinners by arrangement. No dogs. No Children U-10. (C7) 01453 822515
grey-cottage.co.uk

The Daneway (Camping). Traditional country pub converted to a dining pub. Wadworth ales a bonus. 100-yards from the pub is a basic camping field set in a tranquil wooded valley, open all year. Toilet and washing facilities beside the pub. 01285 760297 thedaneway.pub

Well Farm B&B, Frampton Mansell. Charming building set in 20-acres of fields and garden in a peaceful location with stunning views. (J8) 07713 399613 well-farm.co.uk

| 1612 | Chipping Campden's Almshouses built by Sir Balptist Hicks | 1613 | Sir Baptist Hicks' Chipping Campden mansion burnt down by Royalist troops to prevent capture by Parliamentary forces |

THE COTSWOLD HORSE

Andoversford Point to Point

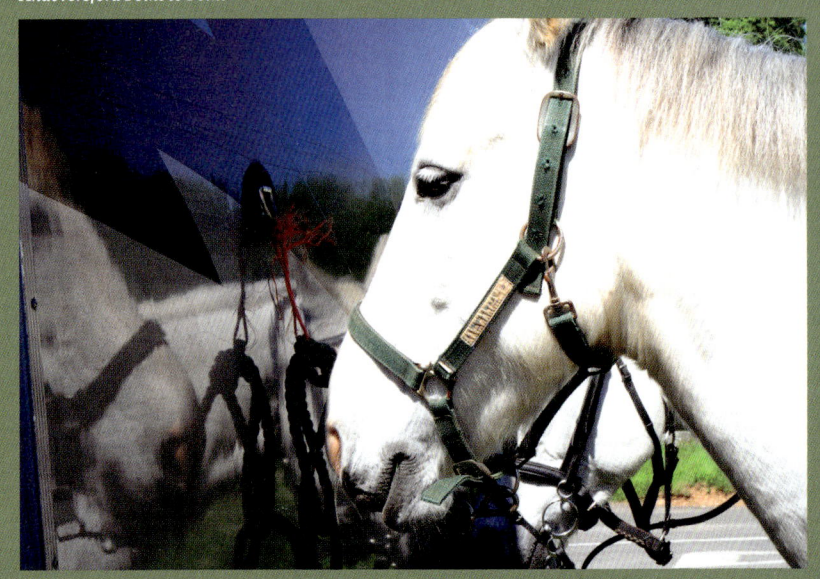

Grey Twin, Cirencester Park

Beaufort, Polo Club, Westonbirt

The horse, Equus ferus caballus, has evolved over 45 to 55 million years. They began to be domesticated about 4,000 BC and by 2,000 BC their use had spread across much of Europe, Central Asia and the Middle East. The only wild horse still in existence is the Przewalski, of Mongolian origin and now a protected species.

To many who live in the Cotswolds the horse is synonymous with their lifestyle. Whether it be hunting with hounds, training hunters for racing, point-to-pointing, playing polo, running a livery stable or just owning a horse for the simple pleasure of exercise, and because you adore these beautiful creatures. You can't travel very far in the Cotswolds without coming across a horse being ridden down a country lane or seeing ponies chasing each other around a field. The Cotswold countryside is criss-crossed with hundreds of miles of bridleways. For starters, you could try the Sabrina Way, a 44-mile (70km) route from Forthampton to Great Barrington. For details of more routes log on to: ride-uk.org.uk. For those wishing to join this merry band there are many riding stables just itching to teach you.

The Cotswold calendar is choc-a-bloc with events: from Cheltenham's National Hunt festival in March, to the Badminton Horse Trials in May, to the Gatcombe Park festival in August. In between are point-to-points, pony club meets and hunts. A few useful websites below to appease your appetite:

RIDING STABLES:

Bourton Vale Equestrian Centre, Bourton-On-The-Water. 07910 138465
bourtonvaleequestrian.co.uk

The Vines, Stanton. 01386 584250
cotswoldsriding.co.uk

TRAINERS' STABLES:

Adlestrop Stables, Moreton-in-Marsh. 01608 658710

Down Farm, Slad. 01452 814267

Jackdaws Castle, Temple Guiting. 01386 584209

Grange Hill Farm, Naunton.

CLUBS:

Beaufort Polo Club, Down Farm, Westonbirt. 01666 880510
beaufortpoloclub.com

Cirencester Park Polo Club, Cirencester. 01285 653225 cirencesterpolo.co.uk

Edgeworth Polo Club, Fieldbarn, Stroud. 01285 821695 edgeworthpoloclub.com

BIBURY, CIRENCESTER, FAIRFORD. NORTHLEACH

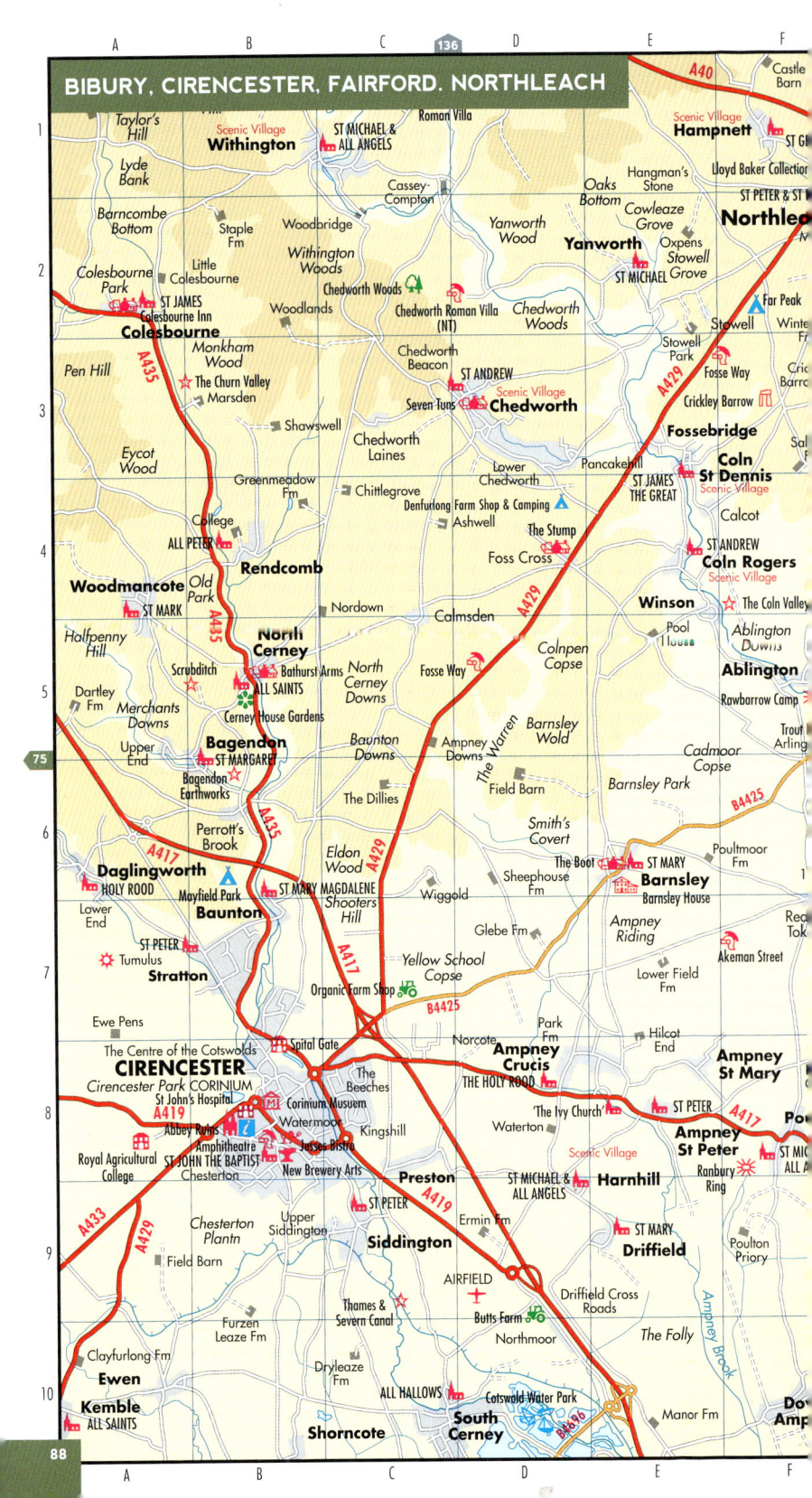

137

G H J K L M

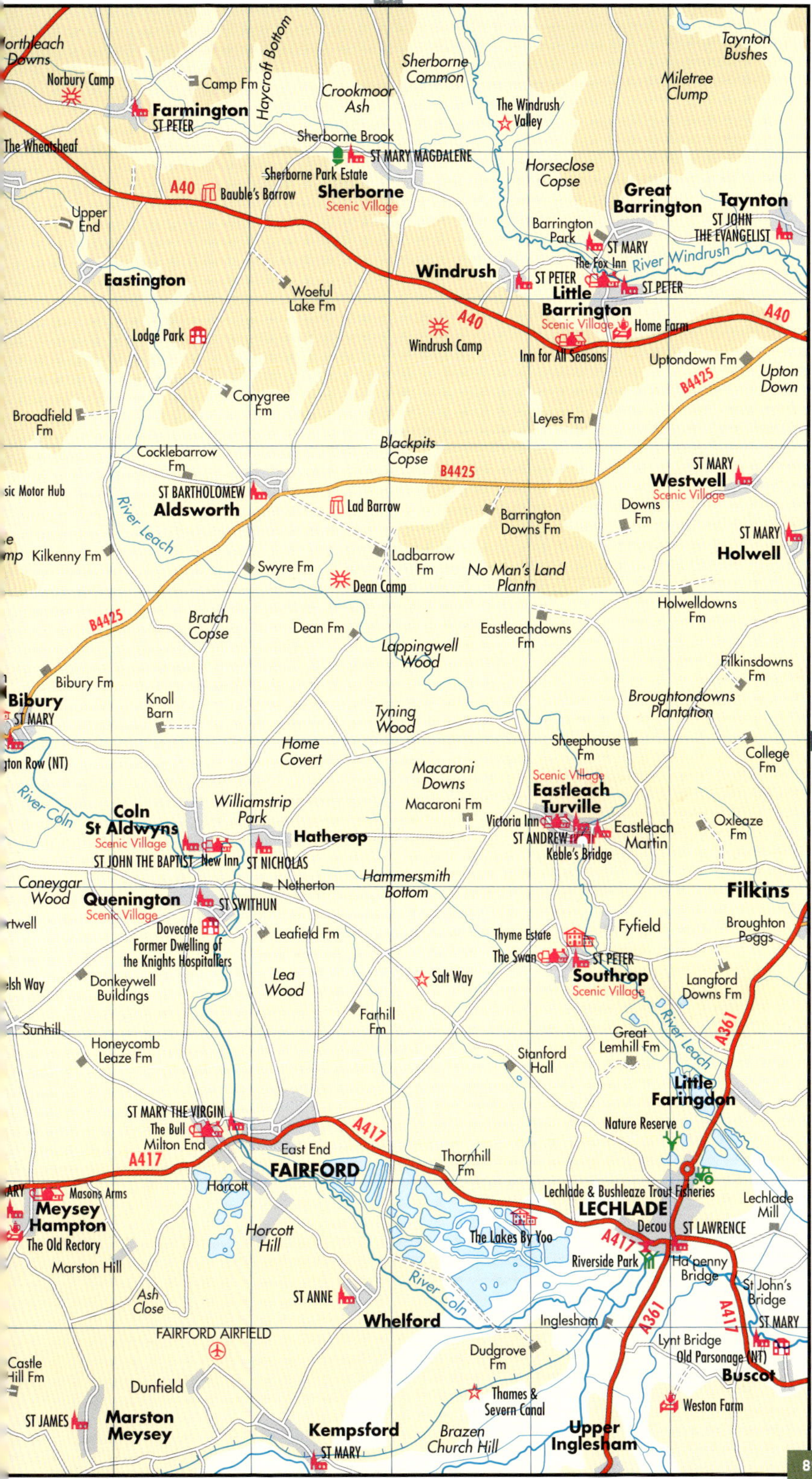

1 2 3 4 5 6 7 8 9 10

114

G H J K L M

BIBURY

Arlington Row in Summer

Geese On Song, River Coln

Tombs, St Mary's Churchyard

Wild Purple Garden

THE SOUTH COTSWOLDS • Bibury, Cirencester, Fairford. Northleach

Bibury Trout Farm

BIBURY

William Morris described Bibury as one of the prettiest villages in England, and few would argue with him. It attracts the crowds, and is thus the stop-off point for many coach tours. It is a honey-pot village made up of rose-covered cottages set behind idyllic kitchen gardens, and all, overlook the sleepy River Coln inhabited by swans, trout and duckling. During the C17 Bibury was notorious as a buccaneering centre for gambling and horse racing. (G5)

SPECIAL PLACES OF INTEREST...

Arlington Row (NT). These iconic cottages were originally monastic wool barns. However, in the C17 they were converted into weavers' homes. Now domestic dwellings, they overlook Rack Isle, a four-acre water meadow where cloth was once hung out to dry. (G5)

Bibury Trout Farm. This working trout farm lies in a beautiful setting beside the River Coln. You can feed the fish, or try your hand at fly fishing in the Beginner's Fishery (hours vary). There are fresh and prepared trout on sale, as well as plants and shrubs. Gift shop. Light refreshments. Open daily Mar-Sept 9-5 (-6 July/Aug), Oct-Feb 9-4. (F5) 01285 740215
biburytroutfarm.co.uk

Church of St Mary. If you seek refuge from the hurly burly of Bibury's tourists walk along the banks of the River Coln, and you'll soon find the entrance to this pretty church. With evidence of Saxon remains, Norman font, and superb sculptured table tombs. (G5)

Classic Motor Hub, Bibury Airfield. This is more than just a car showroom. It's a motorist's dream destination in the heart of the Cotswolds. The Hub holds regular motoring events throughout the year and is open by prior arrangement on weekdays for those seeking a classic, vintage or high-performance car. They also offer car storage, a workshop and transportation services. The cafe/shop is open daily. (G4) 01242 384092
classicmotorhub.com

EAT...DRINK...SLEEP...

Arlington Mill. A beautiful, historic C17 watermill beside the River Coln. Formerly a Countryside Museum. Today it has been converted into a luxurious holiday let for 12 guests. Much of the original industrial architecture is brilliantly displayed. (F5)
manorcottages.co.uk

New Inn, Coln St Aldwyn. Charming C16 ivy-clad inn delivers a combination of hotel, inn and restaurant. Efficient service, affordable cuisine, and contemporary-style bedrooms. (H6) 01285 750651
thenewinncoln.co.uk

The Swan Hotel. Few hotels have such a fabulous location as this. Overlooking the trout stream that is the River Coln. Photographed by every Bibury visitor. It is an iconic site. Swan Brasserie. Fishing rights. 22-luxurious bedrooms. (G5) 01285 740695
cotswold-inns-hotels.co.uk

CIRENCESTER

One of the finest and most affluent towns in the Cotswolds lies Cirencester surrounded by a plethora of attractive villages whose populace (often second home owners) tend to shop, and hob-knob in Ciren (as the locals call it). The smart shops, and bars, reflect the riches of its patrons. As the Roman town Corinium, it became the

---

92 | 1616 Death of William Shakespeare | 1620 Lygon Arms developed from small manor house into larger building

Bibury, Cirencester, Fairford. Northleach • **THE SOUTH COTSWOLDS**

second largest Roman town (after London) in Britain. Its strategic position at the confluence of the major routes (the Fosse Way, Ermin Way and Akeman Street) combined with the vast rolling sheep pastures brought great wealth in the Middle Ages. The history of Cirencester, and the Cotswolds, is ably documented at the impressive Corinium Museum. On the outskirts of the town stands the Royal Agricultural University famous for producing generations of estate managers and farmers from all classes of society. All the best eating places appear to be on Black Jack Street. Monday, Friday & Saturday are market days. July Carnival. Outdoor Lido. (B8)

SPECIAL PLACES OF INTEREST...

Cirencester Abbey. Only the Abbey grounds remain. A peaceful enclave behind the Parish Church of St John the Baptist. Open daily. (B8)

Cirencester Park. Belongs to the Bathurst family, who once generously opened their grounds for many years, giving you the opportunity to walk in 3,000 acres of landscaped parkland, and along a five-mile avenue of horse chestnuts, and hardwoods that were planted in the early C18. There is now a charge! The C18 mansion is home to Lord Apsley, and is closed to the public. If you like hobnobbing with celebrities, you have the opportunity to do so by watching polo on most Sundays at 3pm, from May to September, see: cirencesterpolo.co.uk or 01285 653225. The park opens daily all year from 8am to 5pm. Separate entrance to the cricket and tennis clubs on the Stroud road. (A8) bathurstestate.co.uk

Corinium Museum. An impressive collection of Roman remains clearly displayed to relate the development of the Cotswolds, from earliest times, with special reference to the Roman period. Open daily all year M-Sa 10-5, Su 2-5. Relish Tearoom & Kitchen. (B8) 01285 655611 coriniummuseum.org

New Brewery Arts, Brewery Court. The centre for contemporary craft in the Cotswolds. Craft shop selling 150+ British makers' work; Exhibitions; Galleries; Studios including glass, ceramics, textiles, furniture; Workshops and Courses; Café; Stylish Accommodation at The Barrel Store with 14 rooms accommodating up to 43 guests. Open M-Sa 9-5, Tu 10-5 - closed BHs. (B8) 01285 657181 newbreweryarts.org.uk

Parish Church of St John the Baptist. A fine mix of the C14 and C15, the largest of the 'Wool' churches, and the easiest to recognize with its three-storied, fan-vaulted porch. The porch, formerly the Town Hall, overshadows the Market Place. C15 'wine glass' pulpit, Ann Boleyn Cup, and many fine brasses. Guided tours. Open daily from 10. (B8) 01285 659317 cirenparish.co.uk

St John's Hospital. Founded by Henry II, later absorbed by the Abbey. Next door, Almshouses dated 1826. (B8)

The Organic Farm Shop, Burford Road. Their dictum: 'Eating organic is eating from the Earth, back to nature void of pesticides. All growing freely without insecticides,' is their passion and raison d'être. Café. Organic campsite. Cafe/shop open Tu-Sa from 9, Su from 10, Cafe M 9-12 drinks. (C7) 01285 640441 theorganicfarmshop.co.uk

JUST OUTSIDE CIRENCESTER..

Akeman Street. Roman road built to provide communications between military units and their forts. Best seen near Coln St Aldwyn and Quenington. (E7)

Grayson Perry, New Brewery Arts, Cirencester ss

1627 Market Hall, Chipping Campden built by Sir Baptist Hicks (Lord Campden)   1629 Death of Sir Baptist Hicks, City merchant

CIRENCESTER

Parish Church of St John the Baptist

CIRENCESTER

Cirencester

THE SOUTH COTSWOLDS • Bibury, Cirencester, Fairford. Northleach

LIGHT BITES...SPECIAL BITES...

If you like your coffee stop, or brunch to have some cultural affinity, then visit the café at the **New Brewery Arts,** or opposite, on the other side of the square, **Waterstones** have their own café serving light snacks, from 7.30-5.30. But, more choice can be found on **Black Jack Street** that runs from Park Street beside the **Corinium Museum**, to Gosditch Street opposite the side of the Parish Church. **Jack's** serves the best coffee (according to my Octavian (bookshop) spies), and amazing homemade cakes. You can sit, al fresco, or if you desire ale, pub-grub, it's a few yards to **The Golden Cross**, an appetite for a pastry, bread, sausage roll, next door is **Knead**. But, for a more formal affair the **Cote Brasserie** for breakfast, brunch or a substantial lunch. Not satisfied? Then turn R into the Market Place, and enter the Corn Hall to **MMB Brasserie.** Herewith, a popular food emporia open from 8.00 for breakfast, lunch and afternoon teas. It's got Ciren's Ladies of Means in a frenzy of excitement, all rushing in for their champagne cocktails and made-up TV dinners. (B8) 01285 700900 mmbbrasserie.co.uk.

However, if you seek a treat or wish to impress your other (or better) half then to **Henry's Seafood Bar & Grill** must you canter to. Just to the left side of the Parish Church on Gosditch Street. It's all very cool, relaxed and swish. With a smidgeon of the Cornish vibe and taste. Open Tu-Su. 07498 444170 henryscotswolds.co.uk

Bagendon Earthworks (Dykes). Remains of the Dobunni tribes' headquarters which was the capital of the Cotswolds in the C1 AD. The settlement was abandoned ten years after the Roman Conquest. Iron Age silver coins excavated here. (B6)

Butts Farm (& Farm Shop). Rare breeds, sheep, fowl, pigs and cattle in 30 acres of meadowland. Tractor safari. Picnics. Pets corner. Farm opens Apr to Oct half-term W-Su 10.30-5 Farm shop open W-Sa 9.-5.30, Su 10-3. (D9) 01285 862224
buttsfarmsrarebreeds.co.uk

Cerney House Gardens. Just look around and you will surmise that this garden has been created by persons of immense enthusiasm, passion and experimentation. And, you have a garden of maturity, with old roses and herbaceous borders that sit well beside the walled kitchen-flower garden. You may purchase plants from their expansive plant collections. Teas. Open daily all year 10-7. (B5) 01285 831300
cerneygardens.com

EAT...DRINK...SLEEP...

Barnsley House. The former home of the garden expert, the late Rosemary Verey. A chic hotel and spa offering discreet and friendly service, great food and state-of-the-art technology. A visit to this extraordinary garden may cost you lunch, but it will be a worthwhile, and memorable experience. Make sure you visit the vegetable garden. Cinema club. (E6) 01285 740000
barnsleyhouse.com

Kings Head Hotel & Spa, 24 Market Place. Sumptuous chic, elegance, quirkiness and informality set in a rambling 14th century Inn overlaid on a Roman build. Add a vibrant enthusiasm for the guests comforts and dietary needs. Cinema & Music Nights. Cirencester has a winner! 01285 70090
kingshead-hotel.co.uk

Butts Farm ss

| 1630 | The Gatehouse, Stanway House is built by Timothy Strong, master-mason | 1633 | Building of Bibury Court by Sir Thomas Sackville |

Bibury, Cirencester, Fairford, Northleach • **THE SOUTH COTSWOLDS**

Mosaic, Corinium Museum

Carving of Roman Figures, Corinium Museum

| 1642 | Battle of Edgehill | 1642 | Lord Chandos turns Sudeley Castle into a Royalist fortress |

THE SOUTH COTSWOLDS • Bibury, Cirencester, Fairford. Northleach

EASTLEACH

The twin hamlets of Eastleach Turville and Eastleach Martin face each other across the River Leach. The ancient clapper bridge (Keble's Bridge) connects the two. In Spring, hundreds of daffodils grow on both banks, and hidden behind the trees is the Norman Church of St Michael and St Martin. Across the river the tiny church of St Andrews. Rustic village hostelry, the **Victoria Inn**. (L6)

Keble's Bridge. This was most likely built by the Keble family whose descendant, John Keble, was curate here in 1815. He founded the Oxford Movement, and is know for his volume of religious verse The Christian Year. (L6)

Church of St Michael & St Martin. Founded by Richard Fitzpons, one of William the Conqueror's knights. It has a C14 north transept, decorated windows, and a memorable exterior, beside the river fronted by daffodils in spring. It closed for services in 1982. (L6)

Church of St Andrews. Hidden beneath the trees, this shy, tiny church, has a more interesting interior than its neighbour. Note, the splendid C14 saddleback tower of a Transitional, and Early English, period style. A Norman doorway c.1130 with a carved Tympanum of Christ. (L6)

Macaroni Downs. Quite a sight. These rolling sheep pastures were once the location for Regency derring-do, gambling and horse racing. Now just munched by sheep, cattle and ridden through by mountain bikers. (K6)

Keble's Bridge, Eastleach

Salar, Cirencester Park

| 98 | 1643 | Gloucester and Painswick are under siege during Civil War | 1644 | King Charles 1 seeks refuge in Moreton-in-Marsh |

Laburnam Walk, Barnsley House

THE SOUTH COTSWOLDS • Bibury, Cirencester, Fairford. Northleach

Church of St Michael & St Martin, Eastleach

Macaroni Downs Bikers

| 100 | 1644 | Sudeley Castle is partially demolished during siege | 1646 | Battle of Stow the final (and bloodiest) battle of the Civil War |

Bibury, Cirencester, Fairford. Northleach • THE SOUTH COTSWOLDS

FAIRFORD

An attractive market town on the tranquil River Coln, noted for the fine 'Wool' Church with its C15 stained glass windows. Mill. C6 Saxon cemetery. Venue for the annual, Royal International Air Tattoo. For a coffee and pastry try the **Lynwood & Co Café.** Opens at 8am, 2 High Street. (J8)

SPECIAL PLACES OF INTEREST...

Jake Sutton Clockmaker, 10 High Street. What a find! A maker of bespoke Regulators, the quintessential Grandfather Clock in a contemporary and rare design. Open by appointment. (J8) 01285 712500
jsuttonclockmaker.com

Parish Church of St Mary the Virgin. One of the Cotswolds "must-visit" destinations. It is the perfect, late C15 Perpendicular church, world-famous for the outstanding 28 stained glass windows depicting scenes from Genesis to the Last Judgement. Of further interest, the carved misericords and recumbent brasses. Note the stone cat, a memorial to Tiddles who fell off the church roof. Open 11.30-5 (4 winter) for visits and guided tours. (J8) 01285 712611

EAT...DRINK...SLEEP...

Bathurst Arms B&B, North Cerney. Always a favourite with students from the RAC, and families on long summer evenings sitting beside the Churn. (B5) 01285 831888
bathurstarms.co.uk

The Boot, Barnsley. A warren of little rooms serving ambitious pub food and local beers. Child/dog friendly. Luxurious B&B. Part of Barnsley House opposite, so expect a professional touch. (E6) 01285 740421
thebootbarnsley.co.uk

The Bull, Fairford. This has had a total revamp by the owners of late. It's a fascinating build with nooks, crannies and bottled up spirits. Expect English seasonal food and comfortable surroundings. What happened to the famous pub sign? (H8) 01285 712535
thebullhotelfairford.co.uk

The Fox Inn, The Barringtons. This has had a revamp but has not lost its olde-world charm. Expect top-class pub-grub. Stylish bedrooms for B&B. Garden overlooks the River Windrush. 01451 844385
thefoxatbarrington.com

The Masons Arms, Meysey Hampton. A strong community spirit and a drive to succeed delivers an aura of hospitality, charm and freshness, in the architectural decor and sumptuous food. B&B. (G9) 01285 850164
masonsmeysey.com

Montreal House, Nr Barnsley. A beautiful Cotswold cottage hidden away down a country lane (to rent) with 5 double-bedrooms and 4 bathrooms. (E5) 01285 707785
montrealhouse.co.uk

Seven Tuns, Chedworth. This ancient inn has been given a recent make-over. One hopes that it still can hold to long evenings of vivid conversation, dominoes and bountiful pints of golden ale. Live music and quiz nights. (D3) 01285 720630
seventuns.com

The Stump, Foss Cross. Here we have Baz & Fred's fashionable pub selling pizzas and more pizzas, and local ales, plus, 5-double rooms. A winning combination. Out back Russell's Barn for all your private events. (D4) 01285 720288
thestump.co.uk

Thyme Estate, Southrop. A "Spa" destination that has created a village of hedonism for the wealthy and style-minded. There is **The Swan**, a dining pub, a Cookery School, luxury B&B, Private Dining, cottages to hire for individuals and house parties. The food is provided by the kitchen garden and farm belonging to the Thyme and Southrop Manor Estate. 01367 850174 (K7)
thyme.co.uk

Jake Sutton Clockmaker ss

| 1647 | Thomas Cromwell and Ireton visit Chavenage to persuade Colonel Nathaniel Stephens to vote for Charles I's impeachment | 1649 | The Burford Levellers, a cornet and two corporals, are court-martialled and shot against the church wall |

ST MARY THE VIRGIN, FAIRFORD

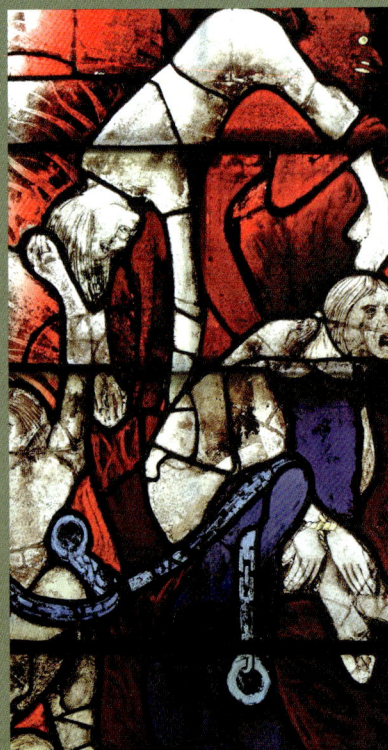

103

THE SOUTH COTSWOLDS • Bibury, Cirencester, Fairford. Northleach

Church of St Peter & St Paul, Northleach

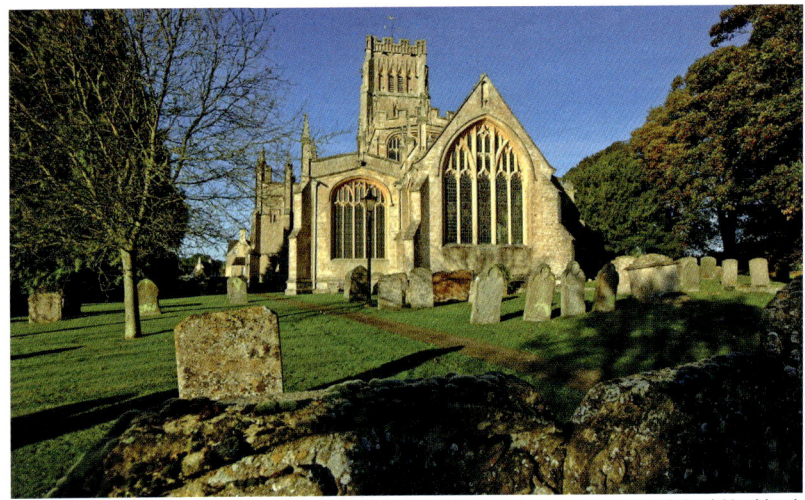

NORTHLEACH

An attractive Cotswold village noted for its exceptional Church and Market Place. Often overlooked, because the A40 now bypasses the village which at first left it out on a limb. However, the village elders have done much to restore the lifeblood of this little community. It is worth a special journey to admire the village's prize possesions. (F2)

SPECIAL PLACES OF INTEREST...

Lloyd Baker Countryside Collection. Fascinating medley of agricultural implements: carts and bygone machinery. Free entry via the **Old Prison Café**. (F1)

Parish Church of St Peter & St Paul. A C15 masterpice for the South Porch has been described as the most lovely in all England: Tall pinnacles and statue filled niches. From afar, the church appears to hover above the town. Brasses of wealthy wool barons. Guided tours: 01451 861132. (F2)

EAT...DRINK...SLEEP...

Far Peak Camping. A simple, rustic campsite centred conveniently in the centre of the Cotswolds and all within walking distance of Northleach's amenities. Glamping, bike hire, climbing tower and café. (F2) 01285 700370 farpeakcamping.co.uk

The Wheatsheaf, Northleach. A dining pub that pulled in many a visitor to Northleach. Indeed, a friendly C17 coaching inn that invited long hours beside the log fires and lazy mornings lounging in their comfy beds. Lunch and suppers were to be recommended. Now that it's part of the Youngs Brewery chain will it still have the same draw? (G2) 01451 539889 cotswoldswheatsheaf.com

LIGHT BITES...

Entering from the Cheltenham road, on your left at the traffic-lights resides the Old Prison, and inside the **Old Prison Café**, for home-made cakes, soups and wifi. Comfortable and ideal for meeting up with colleagues and friends. Plenty of parking, too. Open daily 9-4. (F1)

Enter the Market Square and head straight for **The Ox House** housing a wine merchant, wine bar and coffee shop. Brunch and light lunches available, and out back you have the garden room and **The Curious Wine Cellar** with comfy sofas and log fires, wifi, where you can watch the cricket and rugby, or snooze off their fine wines. Open daily from 9. (G2) 01451 860650 curiousaboutwine.com

For the more sober minded, the **Black Cat Café**, in the top left corner opens at 9 for breakfast, coffee and gluten free bread/cakes. Three cosy rooms with log burners and the morning papers. Cyclists, walkers, young mums, dog & child friendly. Open M-F from 9. (G2) 01451 861101

| 104 | 1689 | Nailsworth's Quaker Meeting House built | 1692 | Rebuilding of Dyrham Park |

Bibury, Cirencester, Fairford. Northleach • **THE SOUTH COTSWOLDS**

River Coln, Chedworth Woods

Mosaic of Spring, Chedworth Roman Villa

| 1694 | Hetty Pegler (owner of field surrounding the burial mound) dies | 1703 | A gale blows in the West Window of Fairford's stained glass |

THE SOUTH COTSWOLDS • Bibury, Cirencester, Fairford. Northleach

River Coln at Dawn, Yanworth

SPECIAL PLACES OF INTEREST...OUTSIDE NORTHLEACH...

Chedworth Roman Villa (NT). Discovered in 1864 by a local gamekeeper and later excavated between 1864 and 1866 revealing remains of a Romano-British villa containing mosaics, baths and hypocausts. Family trails. Museum. Open daily mid-Feb to late-Nov, from 10 am. (D2) 01242 890156
nationaltrust.org.uk

Chedworth Woods. A network of footpaths that criss-cross through tangled woodland close to the Roman Villa.(C2)

Churn Valley. A memorable route from Seven Springs to Cirencester follows one of England's most scenic drives. The variety of the trees, and the sunken river valley, are a sight, to behold. Beware, this is a fast road and accidents are frequent. (A2)

Coln Valley. Charming valley with typically quaint Cotswold villages: Calcot, Coln Rogers, Coln St Dennis, Winson and Ablington. (E4)

CHURCHES OF INTEREST...

Ampney Crucis. C14 wall paintings. Saxon, Early Norman, and Perpendicular features. Life-size effigies. Jacobean pews. (D8)

Ampney St Mary. Wall paintings from the C12 to the C15. Norman font with chevron moulding. Isolated in field. Rarely open. (E8)

Baunton. C14 wall painting of St Christopher. Remains of rood screen. Tudor doorway. (B7)

Bagendon. In fabulous, central position in small hamlet. Stained glass. Norman arcade. (B5)

Chedworth. Norman origins. C15 'wine glass' pulpit. Gargoyles. 'Wool' church. (D3)

Coln St Dennis. Picturesque. Massive Norman tower. (E3)

Eastleach Martin. Norman. Hipped roof. Beautiful place. Daffodils in spring. (L6)

North Cerney. Saddle-back tower. Rood loft. C15 stained glass. (B5)

Rendcomb. Perpendicular. Norman font. (B4)

Southrop. Norman nave. C12 font. (K7)

Stowell. Doom painting. Norman. (E2)

LECHLADE

A pleasant market town bejewelled with many fine C18 and C19 buildings. C15 'Wool' Church with fine Priest's Door. A busy boating and fishing centre given that it is the highest navigable point of the River Thames where you can hire a rowing boat and a swan (boat) to muck about in. Marina. Try the **New Wave Brasserie & Bar** for fresh fish, crustacea and cocktails. (L9)
newwavebrasserie.com

Decou, High Street. A studio and shop showcases talented

106 | 1704 John Wood (architect) the Elder born | 1705 Richard "Beau" Nash becomes Bath's Master of Ceremonies

Bibury, Cirencester, Fairford. Northleach • THE SOUTH COTSWOLDS

local ceramicists, artisans and artists to inspire and transform your interior designs. Open M, Tu, Th & F 10-3, Sa 10-1.
decou.co.uk

Lechlade & Bushleaze Trout Fisheries. Stocked with Brown and Rainbow trout (& the odd Pike) for day and half-day, and evening fishing exploits. Tackle shop, loos, tuition and boat hire on hand. (M8) 01367 253266
lechladetrout.co.uk

SLEEP...

The Lakes By Yoo, Claydon Pike. High end luxurious resort hosts cabins and apartments to rent by the day with views of Marley Lake. Access to The Lakes Spa, Wellness Centre and **The Lakes Bar & Kitchen**. 01367 254269 (K9)
thelakesbyyoo.com

Weston Farm, Buscot Wick. 500-acre organic farm with C17 farmhouse. All tastefully decorated and furnished, inviting comfort and relaxation, both in the house and garden. (M10) 01367 252222

SPECIAL PLACES TO VISIT...

Cotswold Water Park. This covers an area of 42 square miles of countryside and is split into three sections: the Western section, the Keynes Country Park and the Eastern Section (near Fairford). waterpark.org. There are 180 lakes, 74 fishing lakes, 10 lakes with SSSI status, 40 different lake owners and 150km of pathways, bridleways and cycleways. 20,000 people live in the park's 14 main settlements. The extraction of the gravel and sand deposits from the 'catchment area' of the Upper Thames left large holes that were in 1967 designated to become a water park. From its humbled beginnings at the South Cerney Sailing Club, the park now attracts more than half-a- million visitors a year. Children love the sandy beach and sculptures at Keynes, whilst the more active are beckoned to the wakeboarding and slalom skis at **WM Ski** on Spine Road wmski.com A visit to the new **Visitor Centre Open 11-3 at W/Es and daily school hols** on Spine Road is recommended before you explore the park where you can eat and drink at the **Gateway Café** daily from 9-5. Just opposite, the retailer, **Cotswold Outdoor**, for all your walking and camping supplies. Further down the road overlooking Spring Lake, the **Lakeside Brasserie** for coffees, beers, pizzas, burgers and childrens meals. (D10) waterpark.org

Lodge Park (NT). A 'little' property with a big (boozy) history. A grandstand (folly) built by John 'Crump' Dutton in 1634 so he could watch deer coursing in comfort, and share his passion for gambling, drinking and entertaining his friends. Open selected weekends - see NT website. (H3) 01451 844130
nationaltrust.org.uk

Sherborne Park Estate (NT). Waymarked walks through woods and parkland with fine views. (J2) nationaltrust.org.uk

Windrush Valley. A slow, trickling stream in summer with a tendency to flood in winter. The river snakes its way through quiet golden villages, creating the idyllic Cotswold scene. (K2)

The Lakes By Yoo ss

| 1709 | The building of Blenheim Palace begins | 1714 | Cirencester Park's landscape is designed by Alexander Pope | 107 |

THE SOUTH COTSWOLDS

Church of St Margaret's, Bagendon

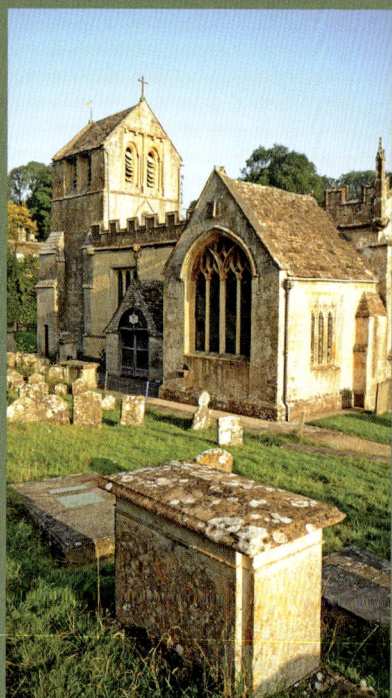

Church of All Saints, North Cerney

Church of St James, Coln St Dennis

Autumn at Lodge Park

Sherborne Brook at Dawn

PASTORAL SCENES

Slad Valley

Macoroni Downs, Eastleach

Stowell Park Estate, Chedworth

Summer's Dawn, Sherborne Brook

Footpath into Lower Slaughter

Sheepscombe Vale

THE EAST COTSWOLDS

Brewing, scenic villages, blanket making, Blenheim, Birthplace of Sir Winston Churchill.

The East Cotswolds extends from the flat Thames basin in the south up into the more typically hilly undulating countryside around Chipping Norton and the beautiful Windrush Valley dissects the region.

This area has traditionally been a coaching route on the A40 London to Gloucester route. It is awash with hostelries and now has a broad selection of pubs with an excellent reputation for eating and drinking. One of the areas best independent breweries, Hook Norton, is based here too.

Minster Lovell Hall

THE EAST COTSWOLDS

Burford was home to one of the area's most famous historic incidents involving the Burford Levellers who are famed with having started civil rights in this country. During the English Civil War, three Parliamentarian soldiers who felt Cromwell was getting too big for his boots stood up against him and were put to death in Burford churchyard for their troubles. This event is celebrated annually with much gusto and beer.

Many of the villages in the East Cotswolds are feeder villages for Oxford. Great Tew is arguably one of the most beautiful villages in the Cotswolds. Witney is a former blanket making town and was, along with the hilltop village, Chipping Norton, a wool trading market town. And, of course, there is Blenheim, famously the birthplace of Winston Churchill.

A B C D E F

124

BURFORD, WITNEY

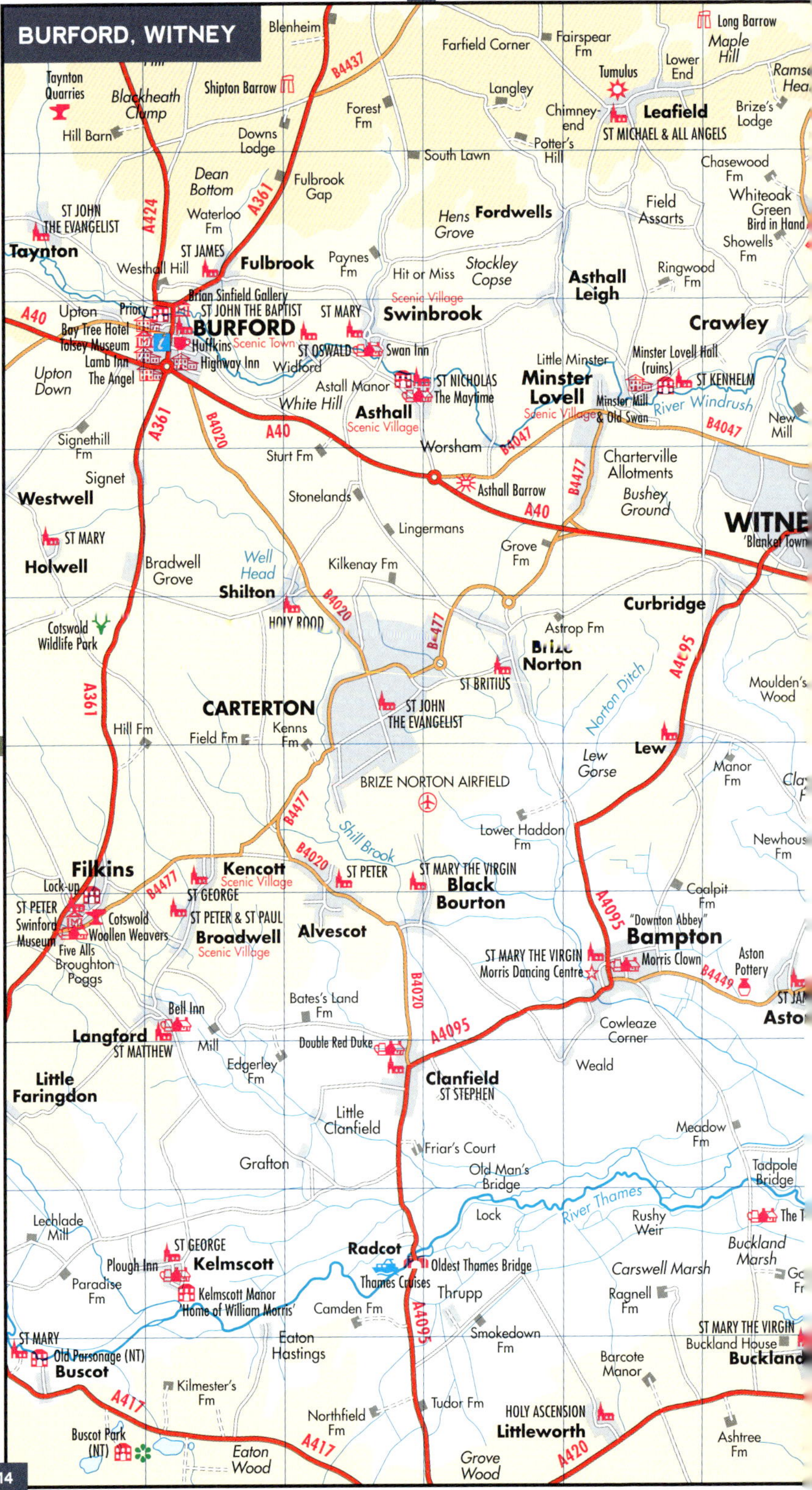

1 2 3 4 5 6 7 8 9 10

89

A B C D E F

125

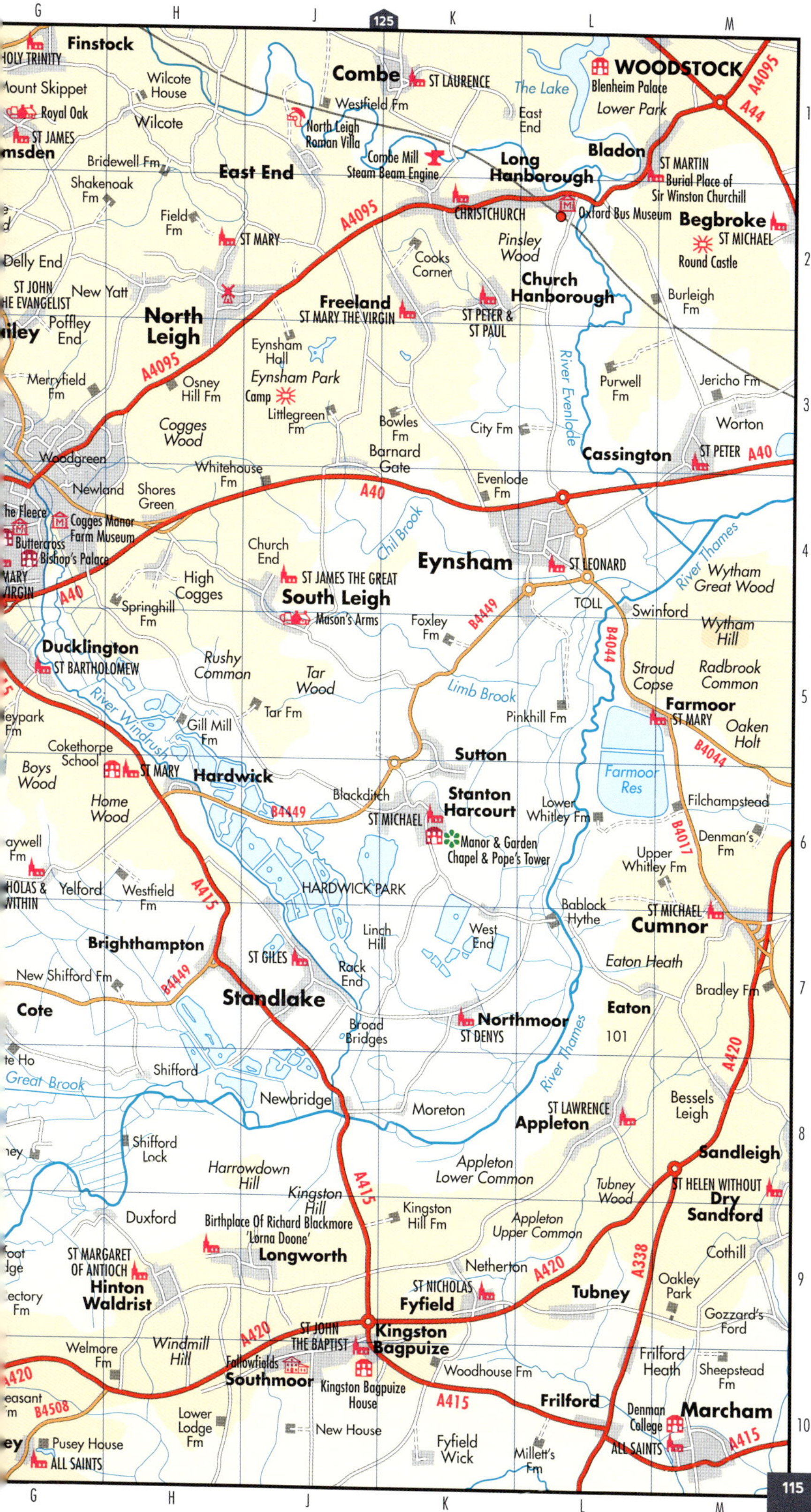
G
H
J
K
L
M
1
2
3
4
5
6
7
8
9
10
Finstock
HOLY TRINITY
Mount Skippet
Wilcote House
Royal Oak
Wilcote
ST JAMES
msden
Bridewell Fm
Shakenoak Fm
East End
Field Fm
ST MARY
Delly End
ST JOHN THE EVANGELIST
New Yatt
Poffley End
North Leigh
Merryfield Fm
Osney Hill Fm
Cogges Wood
Woodgreen
Newland
Shores Green
Whitehouse Fm
The Fleece
Cogges Manor Farm Museum
Buttercross
Bishop's Palace
MARY VIRGIN
A40
A4095
High Cogges
Springhill Fm
Church End
ST JAMES THE GREAT
South Leigh
Mason's Arms
Ducklington
ST BARTHOLOMEW
Rushy Common
Tar Wood
Tar Fm
River Windrush
Gill Mill Fm
Cokethorpe School
ST MARY
Boys Wood
Home Wood
Hardwick
B4449
Blackditch
Combe
ST LAURENCE
Westfield Fm
North Leigh Roman Villa
Combe Mill Steam Beam Engine
CHRISTCHURCH
Cooks Corner
Freeland
ST MARY THE VIRGIN
ST PETER & ST PAUL
Eynsham Hall
Eynsham Park Camp
Littlegreen Fm
Bowles Fm
Barnard Gate
City Fm
Evenlode Fm
Chil Brook
Eynsham
ST LEONARD
TOLL
Foxley Fm
Limb Brook
Pinkhill Fm
Sutton
Stanton Harcourt
ST MICHAEL
Manor & Garden Chapel & Pope's Tower
HARDWICK PARK
Linch Hill
West End
Rack End
ST GILES
Standlake
Broad Bridges
Northmoor
ST DENYS
The Lake
Blenheim Palace
Lower Park
East End
WOODSTOCK
A44
Bladon
Long Hanborough
ST MARTIN
Burial Place of Sir Winston Churchill
Oxford Bus Museum
Begbroke
ST MICHAEL
Round Castle
Pinsley Wood
Church Hanborough
Burleigh Fm
River Evenlode
Purwell Fm
Jericho Fm
Worton
Cassington
ST PETER
River Thames
Wytham Great Wood
Swinford
Wytham Hill
B4044
Stroud Copse
Radbrook Common
Farmoor
ST MARY
Oaken Holt
Farmoor Res
Lower Whitley Fm
Filchampstead
B4017
Denman's Fm
Upper Whitley Fm
Bablock Hythe
ST MICHAEL
Cumnor
Eaton Heath
Bradley Fm
Eaton
101
A420
Haywell Fm
NICHOLAS & WITHIN
Yelford
Westfield Fm
A415
Brighthampton
New Shifford Fm
Cote
te Ho
Shifford
Great Brook
Newbridge
Moreton
Appleton
ST LAWRENCE
Bessels Leigh
Sandleigh
Shifford Lock
Harrowdown Hill
Kingston Hill
Appleton Lower Common
Tubney Wood
ST HELEN WITHOUT
Dry Sandford
Duxford
Birthplace Of Richard Blackmore 'Lorna Doone'
Kingston Hill Fm
Appleton Upper Common
Longworth
ST MARGARET OF ANTIOCH
Hinton Waldrist
Rectory Fm
Netherton
A338
Cothill
Oakley Park
ST NICHOLAS
Fyfield
Tubney
Gozzard's Ford
Welmore Fm
Windmill Hill
ST JOHN THE BAPTIST
Kingston Bagpuize
Fallowfields
Southmoor
Kingston Bagpuize House
Woodhouse Fm
Frilford Heath
Sheepstead Fm
Frilford
A415
Denman College
Marcham
Pheasant Fm
B4508
Lower Lodge Fm
New House
Fyfield Wick
Millett's Fm
ALL SAINTS
Pusey House
ALL SAINTS

THE EAST COTSWOLDS • Burford, Witney

Burford's High Street

Burford Town House

| 116 | 1715 | Mineral springs are discovered in Cheltenham | 1721 | Construction of Witney's Blanket Hall |

Burford, Witney • **THE EAST COTSWOLDS**

BURFORD

The first major Cotswold town you come to if travelling from the East, and what an introduction. The wide High Street, with its classical gables atop some gracious houses, slopes down to the dreamy, River Windrush. It was once an important coach and wool centre bursting with activity, hostelries and dens of rumbustious entertainment. A history of civil rights and religious tolerance prevailed here with the Burford Levellers. On 17 May 1649, three soldiers were executed in Burford Churchyard on the orders of Oliver Cromwell. These three had sort to undermine the authority of Cromwell whom they considered to be a dictator rather than a liberator. This event is celebrated every year with song, dance and speeches. Today, there are the splendid inns and pretty cottages hidden down the side streets.

The churchyard is a quiet spot with some beautifully decorated table tombs. The town has a wide selection of hotels, inns and tearooms and a couple of delis to make up lunchtime sandwiches. 'Feast of the Dragon' and Street Fair in June. (B3)

SPECIAL PLACES OF INTEREST...

Cotswold Wildlife Park. A full score of animals, birds and reptiles from all corners of the globe, beautifully laid out in 120-acres of gardens and parkland. Adventure playground. Tropical House. Children's farmyard. Facilities for the disabled. Picnic area. Café. Open daily 10-6 (winter til 4). 01993 823006 (A5) cotswoldwildlifepark.co.uk

Parish Church of St John the Baptist. One of the great Cotswold churches built in the C15 with proceeds earned by the local wool merchants. Hence, the term 'Wool' church. It has a spacious interior more akin to a small cathedral. The porch and spire c.1450 are outstanding, as are the sculptured table tombs in the churchyard. Inside, don't miss the intricate medieval stained glass and the monuments (painted figures). Open daily 9-5, except during services. (B3)

Burford Priory. This was the former home of Benedictine nuns who have since moved to Broad Marston. It is hidden behind high walls and is Jacobean in style and has a history dating from the C13 when it was a Hospital of St John in 1226. More recently sold as a private residence to a Mr Freud. (B3)

Tolsey Museum. Burford's social and industrial history; charters, dolls house, objects of many rural trades. Open daily April to October, W/Es Nov-Dec 2-5. (B3) 01993 823196 burfordtolsey.org

Brian Sinfield Gallery, 127 The Hill. Highly respected gallery featuring changing exhibitions of modern and contemporary paintings, sculpture and ceramics. Open Tu-Sa, 9.30-5. (B3) 01993 824464 briansinfield.com

THE EAST COTSWOLDS • Burford, Witney

LIGHT BITES...

Quite a choice. Herewith, my favourites, starting at the bottom of the hill with: **Mrs Bumbles of Burford, 31 Lower High Street.** A Lancashire lass who knows, and loves her food. A deli to prepare for a walker's picnic. Try her olives, sumptuous cheeses, scotch eggs and pastas..... Open 8.30-5.30. Moving up the High Street, **The Priory (B&B), 35 High Street.** Open every day for breakfast, lunch, cream teas and early suppers. Child friendly. Open 9.30-5, W/Es 9-5. 01993 823249 prioryrestaurantburford.co.uk Up the street is **Bakery On The Hill** where I breakfasted twice at an early hour. Friendly and recommended.

An alternative for afternoon teas is **Huffkins** a home from home for many wanderers. A little further up the street the **Lynwood & Co Café** noted for their exceptional coffees and savouries. Cross the road for **The Cotswold Cheese Co., High Street.** Sample a cut of cheese or charcuterie accompanied by a glass of wine. 01993 823882 cotswoldcheese.com

Parish Church of St John the Baptist, Burford

1746 William Kent designs Badminton House   1747 Minster Lovell Hall demolished

Burford, Witney • **THE EAST COTSWOLDS**

EAT... DRINK... SLEEP...

Bay Tree Hotel, Sheep Street. This is Burford's most luxurious and smartest hostelry, for that is what they are on this old coaching route, hostelries. It is a traditional and charming inn with oak panelled rooms, stone fireplaces and tapestries. We hear favourable notices of the Chef and his creations. There is a secluded walled garden for pre-prandials and intimate conversation. (B3)
01993 822791
cotswold-inns-hotels.co.uk/the-bay-tree-hotel

Burford House, 99 High St. Full of character and charm, and you'll never sleep alone in a 4-poster again; there's a teddy bear on every bed! Coffees, Lunch & Dinner. No dogs. (B3)
01993 823151
stayinburford.com

Greyhounds B&B, 19 Sheep Street. Stylish, exceptional, luxurious, relaxing, immaculate, knockout - adjectives that one does not use lightly. Michael Taubenheim has created a refuge of delight and wonder in a historic build. Formerly home to the Countryman Magazine, before that built for a wool merchant in the C15.
01993 822780/07711 342608
greyhoundsburford.com

THE EAST COTSWOLDS • Burford, Witney

Highway Inn, 117 High Street. A choice of 11 cosy bedrooms furnished in a mix of antique and modern styles. The Highway Inn has plenty of character and prides itself on offering an informal and individual experience akin to visiting friends in the country. Simple food made using local and seasonal produce. (B3) 01993 823661
thehighwayinn.co.uk

Lamb Inn, Sheep St. Your typical olde English hostelry: flagstone floors, low ceilings, nooks and crannies, galore, fine ales and now with luxurious bedrooms and intimate lounges. Restaurant. (B3) 01993 823155
cotswold-inns-hotels.co.uk/the-lamb

Manfred Schotten Antiques & B&B, High Street. Manfred and his wife Gabi are legends in the world of antiques, sports antiques and memorabilia, as well as classic and vintage motor cycles, living here the past 40-years. Their top floor houses a luxurious double bedroom with bathroom. Staying here is an experience that will live with you forever. 01993 822302
sportantiques.co.uk

The Angel, 14 Witney St. Relaxed, stylish brasserie in C16 coaching inn provides mediterranean dishes and enormous breakfasts specifically cooked for the adventurous traveller. Is this the best cuisine in town? (B3) 01993 822714
theangelatburford.co.uk

SPECIAL PLACES OF INTEREST... MINSTER LOVELL

Arguably, one of the most beautiful villages in the Windrush Valley. There is a fine C15 bridge leading to a street of pretty cottages and the C15 Church which rests beside the ancient Hall. The Manor House has been associated with the rhyme 'Mistletoe Bough.' (E3)

Minster Lovell Hall (EH). A picturesque C15 ruin beside the River Windrush. Reputed to be the haunted seat of the Lovell family. Open daily. Don't miss the Church, next door. (E3)

EAT...DRINK...SLEEP...

Minster Mill. The latest addition to the Andrew Brownsword stable of exclusive hotels lies beside and amidst lush water meadows and the dreamy River Windrush. The bedrooms are of the 'Skandi' style, the cuisine is for Fine Dining and the Garden Spa will seduce your hedonistic appetites. (E3) 01993 774441
minstermill.co.uk

Old Swan. A luxurious Inn With Rooms describes this old country pub and Spa. Little sister to the Mill next door. (E3) 01993 862512 oldswan.co.uk

WITNEY

The largest shopping centre in West Oxfordshire, and a dormitory town to Oxford that has seen much rapid expansion in the past 25 years. A town of hustle and bustle with a good share of attractive limestone buildings. Note, the C17 Butter Cross with gabled roof, clock turret and sundial, the Town Hall with room overhanging a piazza

Cotswold Woollen Weavers, Nr. Lechlade. The story of wool and woollen cloth has woven its way into every fabric of Cotswold life, as has the stone that has built the barns, churches, manor houses and villages. The stone is brilliantly displayed by the masons' sculptures and workmanship. The cloth, and the garments made up in their many guises (scarves, handbags, throws, jackets, skirts, coats, upholstery, as well as rolls of cloth) mirror the delights of this unique establishment. Coffee shop. Picnic area. Open W-Sa 10-6. (A7) 01367 860660
cotswoldwoollenweavers.co.uk

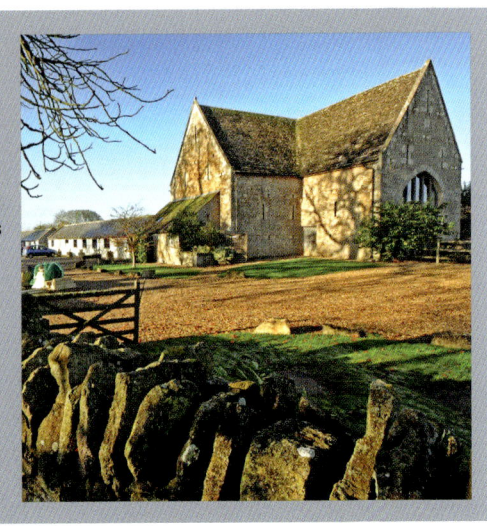

Burford, Witney • THE EAST COTSWOLDS

LIGHT BITES...

In need of intellectual sustenance and nourishment? Head for the **Blanket Hall** for coffee and their Pieshop where you can sit als fresco beside the river. Almost next door is **The Plough Inn**, a popular hostelry with garden beside the same river. Witney has a fair compliment of ancient hostelries and the **Angel Inn** overlooking Church Green is steeped in history, often populated by ancient Witneyites. Ethnic restaurants are plentiful and diverse in their culinary arts: The **Witney Azis** is highly recommended for Asian cuisine.

The Fleece, 11 Church Green. A fine Georgian building originally the home of Clinch's Brewery and reputedly a favourite watering-hole of one Dylan Thomas who lived in South Leigh. Overlooks the beautiful Church Green with al fresco seating. B&B. (G4) 01993 892270 fleecewitney.co.uk

Bird in Hand Inn, Hailey, near Witney. A Grade II listed inn that has been renovated yet retains its charm and original features. Traditional British and European cuisine with a modern twist. Restaurant open for breakfast, lunch and dinner. B&B. (G2) 01993 868321 birdinhandinn.co.uk

and across Church Green the unusually handsome spire to the Parish Church, visible from far and wide. There have been signs of Iron Age and Roman settlements but the first records of any activity date from 969 AD. The Bishop of Westminster built a palace in 1044 which was eventually excavated in 1984. In 1277 the town's business centred on the fulling and cloth mills. In the Middle Ages gloves, blankets and brewing were the staple industries. Earlys of Witney, the blanket makers were in business for 300 years until quite recently. All of this has been ably recorded by the **Blanket Hall** and **Cogges Manor Farm Museum. (F4)**

SPECIAL PLACES OF INTEREST...

Blanket Hall, 100 High St. When it was built in 1721 every blanket woven in Witney came to Witney Blanket Hall to be tested for quality, and upstairs the weavers sat in court to regulate their affairs. Now, blanket making has gone, but the Witney Blanket Hall still proudly stands with its beautiful Great Room, and its famous one-handed clock. A pocket-sized tribute to a proud past. Now, it has once more come to life, as a place where visitors can explore the intricate mysteries of the blanket trade. There's the 1920s blanket warehouse, the soundscape on the grand oak staircase, the re-planted C18 garden by the river... and not forgetting the Blanket Hall Pieshop! Open W-Sa 10-5. (G4) 01993 706408
blankethall.co.uk

Bishops Palace. The site of the Bishop's Palace situated near to the Church on Church Green, is one of 24 luxurious residencies in the Diocese and dates from the C12. The archaeological remains of the great hall and other features are exposed under a modern roof and were discovered in the early 1980s. (G4)

Cogges Manor Farm Museum, Church Lane. Historic buildings, exhibitions, traditional breeds of animals, daily demos and special weekends. Garden, orchard and riverside walk. Location for Downton Abbey. Kitchen Café. Open daily 9.30-5, cafe 9-4.30. (G4) 01993 772602 cogges.org.uk

Witney Museum, High Street. Lies within a traditional Cotswold stone building once the home of Malachi Bartlett, the proprietor of a well known local building firm. Illustrates the history of Witney and surrounding area, featuring local industries: Witney Blankets, glove making and brewing, together with photographs and artefacts relating to Witney. Open Apr to Oct, W-Sa 10-4. Children free. (G4) 01993 775915 witneymuseum.org.uk

SPECIAL PLACES OF INTEREST...

Aston Pottery. Working pottery, demonstrations, shop and tearoom. Open daily. (F7) 01993 852031. astonpottery.co.uk

Buscot Park (NT). C18 house with park and superb water garden designed by Harold Peto. Collection of art: Italian, Dutch, Flemish, Spanish and English Schools. Chinese porcelain. Tea room. Open late Mar to Sept W Th & F (including Good F, East W/Es) 2-6, and alternate W/Es in each month 2-6. Grounds M & Tu 2-6. (A10) 01367 240786 buscot-park.com

Kelmscott Manor. The Elizabethan home of William Morris, the C19 poet, craftsman and socialist. Houses his furnishings which can be identified as examples from

THE EAST COTSWOLDS • Burford, Witney

the Arts & Crafts Movement. Paintings by his fellow pre-Raphaelite, Dante Gabriel Rossetti. Tearoom & Gift shop. Open Apr to Oct Th-Sa 10.30-5. Group bookings on Th by arrangement. (B9) 01367 252486 sal.org.uk

Kingston Bagpuize House. A beautiful early C18 manor house in parkland setting. The garden contains shrubs, bulbs and herbaceous borders. Teas. Small gift shop. Open all BHs and various Su, Feb to Sept 2-5. (J10) 01865 820259 kbhevents.uk

North Leigh Roman Villa (EH). This ruin was excavated in 1813 and 60 rooms were revealed surrounding the courtyard with a beautiful mosaic pavement. A charming spot beside the River Evenlode. Open daily in summer. (J1)

Oxford Bus Museum, BR Station Goods Yard. 35 vehicles including the Morris Motors Museum. Open Su, W & BHs 10.30-4.30. (L2) 01993 883617 oxfordbusmuseum.org

Stanton Harcourt Manor House & Gardens. A unique collection of medieval buildings. The house contains fine pictures, silver, furniture and porcelain. Moat and stew ponds. Pope's Tower. Limited opening, call for details. (K6) 01865 881928

Swinford Museum. Agricultural, craft and domestic bygones. Open May to Sept first & third Su 2-5, and by appointment. (A7)

CHURCHES OF INTEREST...

Swinbrook. Fettiplace monuments. Mitford family memorials. (C3)

Kelmscott. Wall painting. William Morris tomb by Philip Webb. (B9)

EAT...DRINK...SLEEEP WITHIN AN INN WITH ROOMS...

Bell Inn, Langford. A country pub that knows what its all about. Simple things done well: sincere hospitality, tasty nosh, blazing fire and stone-flagged floors. 8 Luxurious bedrooms. 01367 860249 (B7) thebelllangford.com

Double Red Duke, Clanfield. It's different; a little crazy and hip. Certainly, friendly and quirky. Indeed, a rare beast for the Duke's a jolly fellow. 01367 810222 (C8) countrycreatures.com

Five Alls, Filkins. A comfortable C18 coaching inn offers log fires, agreeable nosh and luxurious bedrooms, and maybe, the odd celeb in mufty enjoying a Cotswold repast. 01367 860875 thefiveallsfilkins.co.uk

Maytime Inn, Asthall. Set in an authentic Cotswold stone building situated in a quiet country village. On a winter's day you can duck through the low door into the homely bar and imagine the pub as it was centuries ago. B&B. (C3) 01993 822068 themaytime.com

Plough, Kelmscott. It's a pretty Grade 11 listed building of character, good food and 8 luxurious bedrooms. Cottage garden for alfresco dining, and hidden Hideaway Bar in the old stable block. 01367 253543 theploughinnkelmscott.com

Swan Inn, Swinbrook. Formerly owned by the late, Dowager Duchess of Devonshire (the former Deborah Mitford, the last of the infamous Mitford sisters). A beautiful dining pub, in a delightful location, with a fair balance between traditional and modern cuisine. Luxurious B&B. (C3) 01993 823339 theswanswinbrook.co.uk

EAT...DRINK...SLEEP... WITHIN A COUNTRY INN...

Royal Oak, Ramsden. A listed Coaching Inn dating from the C17 that was used as a watering hole for the London to Hereford stagecoach. Traditional rustic bar and restaurant with an excellent reputation for food. Lovely bedrooms. (G1) 01993 868213 royaloakramsden.com

The Trout, Tadpole Bridge. Remote location beside the Thames footpath manages to be busy at lunchtime. Well worth a visit. Children & dogs welcome. B&B. (F9) 01367 870382 troutinn.co.uk

Kelmscott Manor

Three Fettiplace Rogues, Swinbrook Church

123

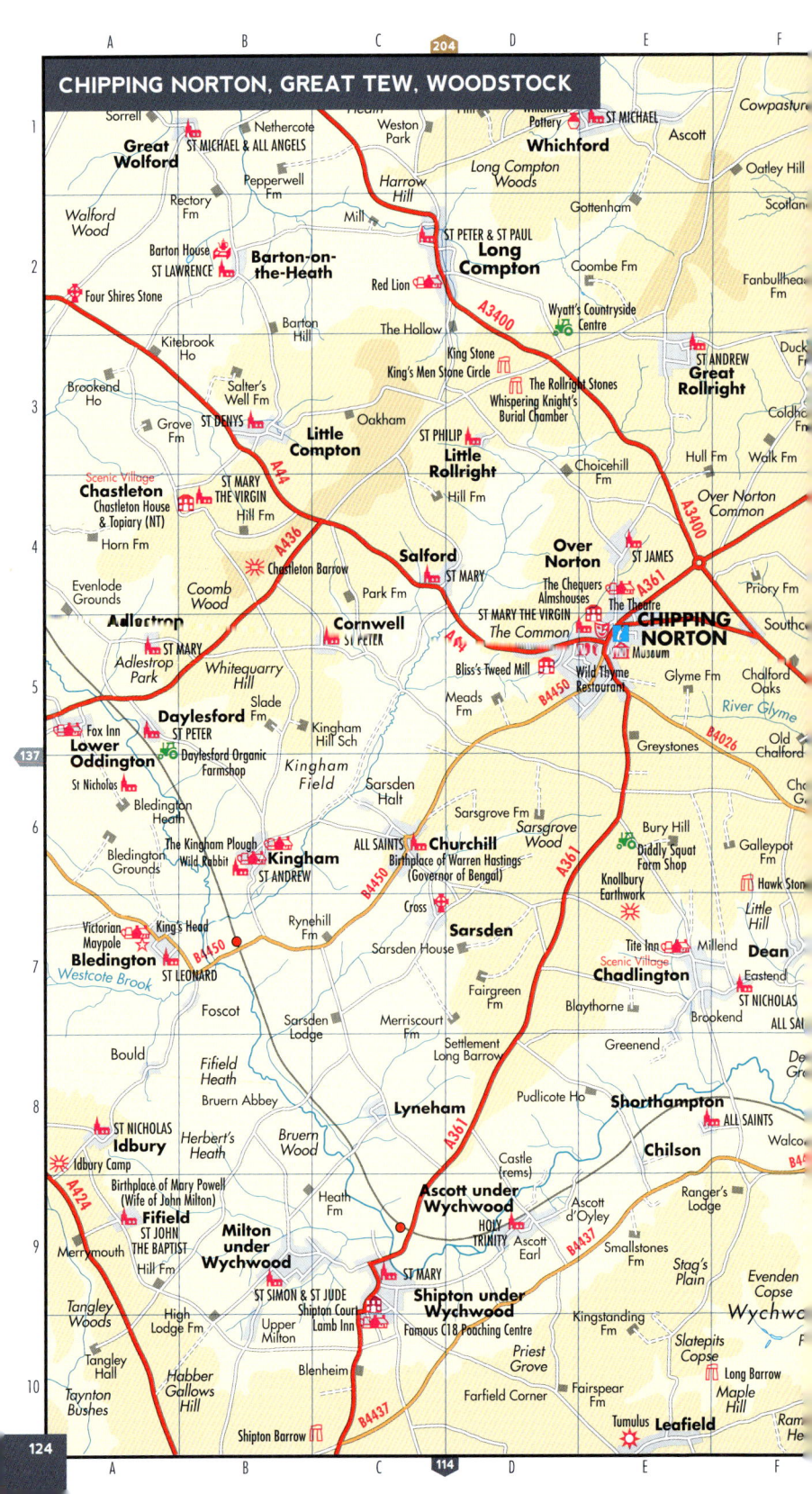

CHIPPING NORTON, GREAT TEW, WOODSTOCK

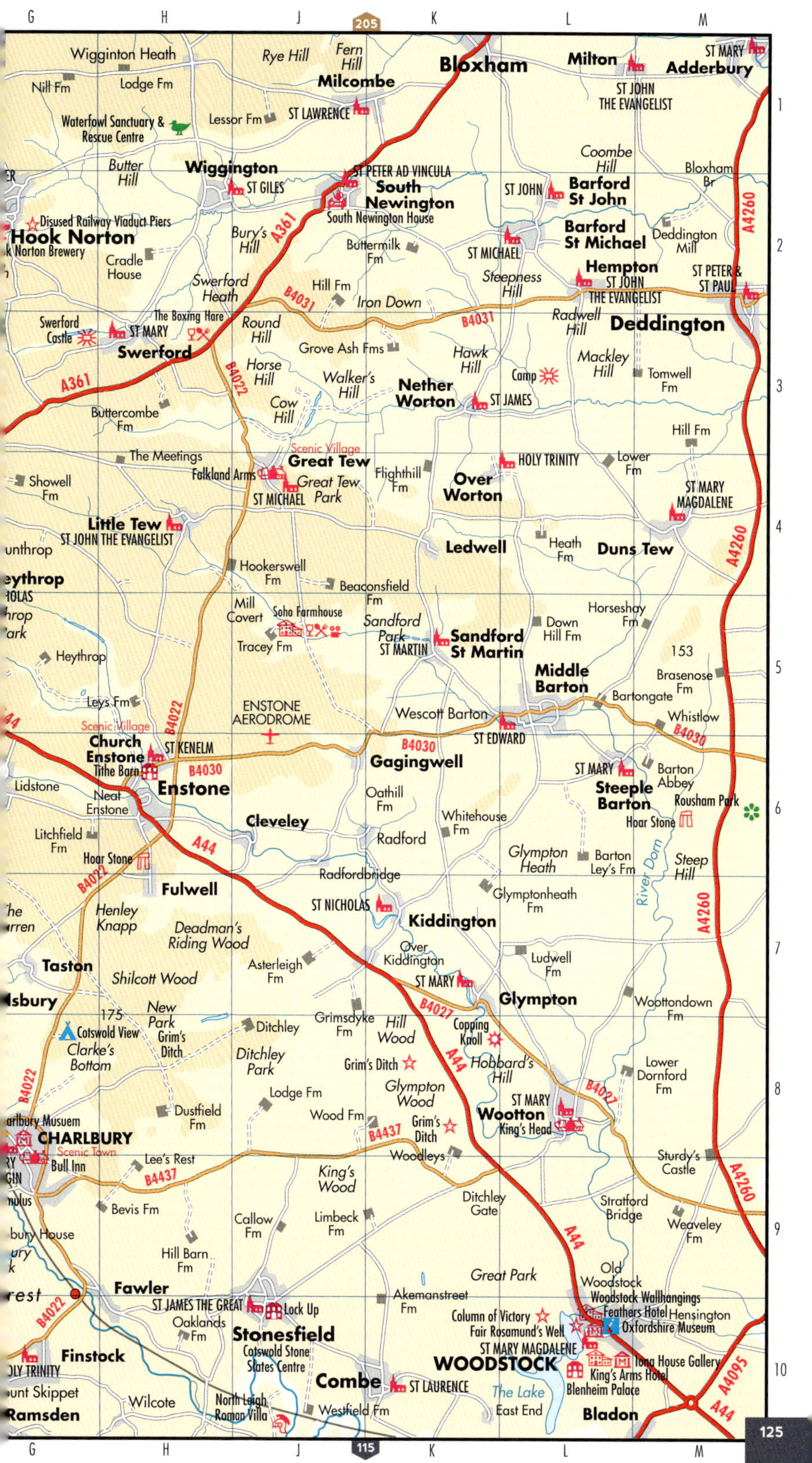
G
H
J
205
K
L
M
Wigginton Heath
Rye Hill
Fern Hill
Milcombe
Bloxham
Milton
ST MARY
Adderbury
Nill Fm
Lodge Fm
ST JOHN THE EVANGELIST
Waterfowl Sanctuary & Rescue Centre
Lessor Fm
ST LAWRENCE
Coombe Hill
Butter Hill
Wiggington
ST GILES
ST PETER AD VINCULA
South Newington
South Newington House
ST JOHN
Barford St John
Bloxham Br
Disused Railway Viaduct Piers
Hook Norton
Hook Norton Brewery
Bury's Hill
A361
Buttermilk Fm
ST MICHAEL
Barford St Michael
Deddington Mill
A4260
Cradle House
Swerford Heath
Hill Fm
Steepness Hill
Hempton
ST JOHN THE EVANGELIST
ST PETER & ST PAUL
B4031
Iron Down
Radwell Hill
Deddington
Swerford Castle
ST MARY
The Boxing Hare
Round Hill
Grove Ash Fms
Hawk Hill
Swerford
B4022
Horse Hill
Walker's Hill
Camp
Mackley Hill
Tomwell Fm
A361
Nether Worton
ST JAMES
Cow Hill
Buttercombe Fm
Hill Fm
Scenic Village
The Meetings
Great Tew
Flighthill Fm
HOLY TRINITY
Lower Fm
Showell Fm
Falkland Arms
Great Tew Park
ST MICHAEL
Over Worton
ST MARY MAGDALENE
Little Tew
ST JOHN THE EVANGELIST
Ledwell
Heath Fm
Duns Tew
Enslow/Heythrop
Hookerswell Fm
Beaconsfield Fm
Mill Covert
Soho Farmhouse
Sandford Park
Horseshay Fm
Down Hill Fm
Tracey Fm
ST MARTIN
Sandford St Martin
Heythrop
153
Middle Barton
Brasenose Fm
Leys Fm
ENSTONE AERODROME
Wescott Barton
Bartongate
Whistlow
Scenic Village
B4022
ST EDWARD
B4030
Church Enstone
ST KENELM
Tithe Barn
B4030
Gagingwell
ST MARY
Barton Abbey
Lidstone
Enstone
Oathill Fm
Steeple Barton
Rousham Park
Neat Enstone
Cleveley
Whitehouse Fm
Hoar Stone
Litchfield Fm
Radford
A44
Glympton Heath
Barton Ley's Fm
Steep Hill
River Dorn
Hoar Stone
B4022
Radfordbridge
Fulwell
ST NICHOLAS
Glymptonheath Fm
Kiddington
A4260
Henley Knapp
Deadman's Riding Wood
Over Kiddington
Ludwell Fm
Taston
Asterleigh Fm
ST MARY
Shilcott Wood
Glympton
Woottondown Fm
175
New Park
Grimsdyke Fm
B4027
Cotswold View
Grim's Ditch
Ditchley
Hill Wood
Copping Knoll
Clarke's Bottom
Ditchley Park
Grim's Ditch
A44
Hobbard's Hill
Lower Dornford Fm
B4022
Lodge Fm
Glympton Wood
ST MARY
B4027
Charlbury Museum
Dustfield Fm
Wood Fm
Grim's Ditch
Wootton
King's Head
CHARLBURY
Scenic Town
B4437
Bull Inn
Lee's Rest
Woodleys
Sturdy's Castle
B4437
King's Wood
A4260
Bevis Fm
Ditchley Gate
Callow Fm
Limbeck Fm
Stratford Bridge
Weaveley Fm
A44
Hill Barn Fm
Great Park
Old Woodstock
Fawler
Akemanstreet Fm
Woodstock Wallhangings
ST JAMES THE GREAT
Lock Up
Column of Victory
Feathers Hotel
Hensington House
B4022
Oaklands Fm
Fair Rosamund's Well
Oxfordshire Museum
Stonesfield
ST MARY MAGDALENE
Finstock
Cotswold Stone Slates Centre
WOODSTOCK
Tong House Gallery
HOLY TRINITY
Combe
ST LAURENCE
King's Arms Hotel
A4095
Mount Skippet
Wilcote
North Leigh Roman Villa
The Lake
Blenheim Palace
Ramsden
Westfield Fm
East End
Bladon
A44
G
H
J
115
K
L
M
1
2
3
4
5
6
7
8
9
10

THE EAST COTSWOLDS • Chipping Norton, Great Tew, Woodstock

Bliss Tweed Mill, Chipping Norton

CHIPPING NORTON

A well situated hill-top town affording spectacular views over the surrounding countryside. Mentioned in the Domesday Book. The new Market Place was built in 1205 and is today surrounded by elegant houses with Georgian facades. But it was the Wool industry established in the C13 that brought wealth to this corner of Oxfordshire and, like so many before them and after, the wealthy merchants invested their coppers in the C15 'Wool' church in order to guarantee a place in heaven. Its attraction is that it is very much a small market town responding to the demands of the local populace and is little affected by Cotswold tourism. It is home to some celebrities: Jeremy Clarkson, and, until his death, Ronnie Barker, who ran an antique emporium. The Chipping Norton Set, is a close group of powerful politicians and media elite, amongst them is included, The former Prime Minister, David Cameron, and his friends, Rebekah and Charlie Brooks, Matthew Freud and Elisabeth Murdoch (daughter of media mogul, Rupert Murdoch). Fine bookshop in **Jaffe & Neale** and around the corner on Spring Street the **Chequers Inn**, a cosy pub to assuage your thirst and halt your hunger. Mop Fair in September. (E5)

SPECIAL PLACES OF INTEREST...

Almshouses. A picturesque row of C17 houses still in use today. The occupants were to be 'Honest women of godly life and conversation.' (E5)

Bliss Tweed Mill. Built by William Bliss in 1872 to house his textile factory. He was instrumental in encouraging the railways to reach Chipping Norton. The mill closed as a factory in 1980 and was converted into domestic apartments. It is still quite a sight from the road and was apparently one of Sir John Betjeman's favourite buildings. (D5)

Chipping Norton Museum, 4 High St. Agricultural equipment, a 30s kitchen and local Co-op. Open Easter to October M-Sa & BH Ms 2-4. (E5) 01608 641712

Diddly Squat Farm Shop, Chadlington. Jeremy Clarkson may irritate you, bore you with his petrol-head vigour but there is no stopping him being loved and admired within the farming community. His down-to-earth, soul-searching and humble TV series about life on his farm has won him many plaudits and fans. Shop open Th-Su 9.30-4.30, Big View Cafe 10-3 (E4)

diddlysquatfarmshop.com

Hook Norton Brewery. Visitor Centre displays brewing artefacts from 1849 to today. Two-hour tours M-Su. Shop open M-Sa 8-6, Su 9-4. Cafe M-Sa 8-4.30, Su 9-3. (G2) 01608 730384 hooky.co.uk

Rollright Stones. The King's Men is a Bronze Age stone circle 100 feet in diameter, 2,000-1,800 BC and is easily accessible from the road. Just 400 yards east of this circle are The Whispering Knights, remains of a Bronze Age burial

---

1788 — George II visits Cheltenham thus stamping approval of the spa's waters and healing powers

1789 — Northleach Prison built by Sir Onesiphorous Paul, a pioneer of prison reform

Chipping Norton, Great Tew, Woodstock • **THE EAST COTSWOLDS**

Three Views of Great Tew

| 1789 | The Thames & Severn canal is opened connecting Bristol with London via the Thames at Lechlade | 1790 | Newark Park remodelled by James Wyatt | 127 |

THE EAST COTSWOLDS • Chipping Norton, Great Tew, Woodstock

chamber. And, isolated in a field, the King's Stone. (D3)

The Theatre, Goddards Lane. Flourishing little theatre puts on dance, music, plays, films, workshops, and is host to touring companies. (E5) 01608 642349
chippingnortontheatre.com

SLEEP...

Cotswold View Campsite, Enstone Road, Charlbury. Spacious pitches set in rolling, wooded farmland. Well-signed trails where you can see a variety of farm animals. Children's playground. Tennis court, skittle alley and well stocked shop, and off license. Open late Mar to Oct. (G8) 01608 810314
cotswoldview.co.uk

CHARLBURY

A small town overlooking the Evenlode Valley, towards the Wychwood Forest. Group of stone-roof houses with 30-yard stretch of wisteria. Fine walking and cycling country; the Oxfordshire Way passes through the town, and the Glyme Valley is also a popular walker's destination. Easy rail access to London and Oxford. Charlbury Deli and Café. (G8)

GREAT TEW

A sensationally beautiful village lined with ironstone cottages covered in thatch and stone tiles. Many fell into disrepair but have now been restored to their former glory. Much of the village was designed by the Scottish architect, John Claudius London. The Falkland Arms is named after Lord Falkland who lived here, and who died fighting for Charles 1 at the Battle of Newbury. (J4)

Cornbury Music Festival (The Original), Great Tew Park. Now establishing itself as a more personal alternative to Glastonbury. Three days in early July with a full lineup of stars. Camping/Glamping on site. (J4)

EAT... DRINK...SLEEP...

The Falkland Arms B&B. A traditional pub with flagstone floors, oak beams, inglenook fireplace, mugs and bric-a-brac hanging from the ceiling and ale in many potions to whet your senses. Average pub-grub. (J4) 01608 683653
falklandarms.co.uk

Soho Farmhouse. An exclusive club originally founded for the creative industries but now accepts those with a healthy bank balance. All set in 100-acres of Oxfordshire countryside with 40 cabins, a Main Barn, Mill Room for eating, a Boathouse, indoor and outdoor pools and the Cowshed spa, plus a lot more for your hedonistic pleasures. It is also eco and PC. (J5) 01608 691000
sohohouse.com

Quince & Clover, The Old Post Office. Herewith, a stylish café serving breakfast, brunch and lunch, and their home-made ice creams. Open daily except Tu from 8.30 to 3pm. (J4) 01608 683225
quinceandclover.co.uk

WOODSTOCK

A pretty town of stone built houses, interesting shops and smart hotels, and a practical centre for exploring the eastern Cotswolds and West Oxfordshire. Famous for glove-making in the C16, and for Blenheim Palace, the birthplace of Sir Winston Churchill (1874-1965) who is buried nearby in Bladon churchyard. There are a number of antique shops, art galleries and a fascinating museum plus a melee of delis, inns, restaurants, tearooms and coffee shops. (L10)

SPECIAL PLACES OF INTEREST...

Blenheim Palace. This is the home of the Dukes of Marlborough and was built as Queen Anne's gift to John Churchill, 1st Duke of Marlborough, for his defeat of Louis XIV in 1704 - 'a monument to commemorate a military victory, and to glorify the Queen.' It is considered to be Vanbrugh's C18 baroque masterpiece, although much of the detail was by Nicholas Hawksmoor. There are fine

Daylesford ss

Chipping Norton, Great Tew, Woodstock • **THE EAST COTSWOLDS**

Blenheim Palace, Woodstock ss

paintings, Churchill Exhibition, tapestries, a 10,000 volume library and parkland designed by 'Capability' Brown. Plus, other attractions: the Butterfly House, Marlborough Maze, Adventure Play Area and Herb Garden. Restaurant. Palace & Gardens open daily 10.30-5.30 (last admission 4.45pm). Park open daily, all year, for rambling and dog walking, 9.30-6. (L10) 01993 810530 blenheimpalace.com

Combe Mill. A restored C19 beam engine and a breast shot waterwheel. Blacksmith's forge in operation. Open Days are advertised locally.
combemill.co.uk

Grim's Ditch. Disconnected series of ditches and banks built by Iron Age tribes (Belgic) to defend their grazing enclosures. Best sections in Blenheim and Ditchley Parks. Grim is one of the names of Woden - the masked one, the god of victory, death and magic power, the high god of the Anglo-Saxons, before their conversion to Christianity in the C7. (K8)

Iona House Gallery. Paintings, etchings, prints, sculpture, ceramics, glass, textiles, silver and wood. Open M-Sa 10-5.15, Su 11-5. (L10) 01993 811464
ionahousegallery.org

Oxfordshire Museum, Park Street. An exhibition of Oxfordshire, and its people, from earliest times to the present day. Changing exhibitions. Coffee shop. Open daily Tu-Sa 10-5, Su 2-5. (L10) 01865 897519
oxfordshire.gov.uk

Woodstock Wallhangings, Town Hall. Story of Woodstock from Norman times, told in thirteen embroidered scenes. See Museum for opening times. (L10) 01993 811216

LIGHT BITES...

My visits to Woodstock always start here at **Hampers** on Oxford Street. This great deli and café provides a wide range of sandwiches, paninis and cakes - you can sit down, relax and enjoy the craic. Open daily. (L10) Across the road (careful) **The Woodstock Coffee Shop**, lauded as producing the best cofffee in Oxfordshire. The double-espresso + two sugars is delicious, believe me! Moving into the village is **Brothertons**. For pasta, pizzas and burgers, home-made soups, daily specials. A family business serving unpretentious and good-value fare. Opens M-Su 12-2.30 for lunch & dinner 6 till late. 01993 811114 brothertonsbrasserie.co.uk

For a pint of ale and pub-grub, a good choice of two: The **Woodstock Arms, Market Street.** This is considered by many locals as the best pub in Woodstock. Their food is considered great value and available most of the day. (L10) 01993 811251 thewoodstockarms.com. The other choice would be **The Back Lane Tavern, 11 Park Lane.** A hostelry since 1735. Cosy and comfy. One could settle down here for an age. Tempting. Kitchen serves tapas-style food. Open daily, times vary. (L10) 01993 810826 backlanetavern.co.uk

| 1794 | Sharpness founded with the digging of the Gloucester & Sharpness Canal | 1796 | Edward Jenner invents the small pox vaccine | 129 |

THE EAST COTSWOLDS • Chipping Norton, Great Tew, Woodstock

Zuleika Gallery, 6 Park Street. C20 Modern British and British Contemporary art. Specialising in the Primary and Secondary markets; Nigel Hall RA, Nicola Green, Rachel Gracey RE... Open W-Sa 10-5, Su-Tu by appoint. 07719 060962 (L10) zuleikagallery.com

Rachel Gracey, R.E., Zuleika Gallery, Woodstock ss

EAT...DRINK...SLEEP...

Feathers Hotel, Market Street. This romantic C17 top-notch hotel has a labyrinth of rooms on all levels; the bedrooms are plush, intimate and hidden up narrow stairwells. The restaurant has been producing superb food for years. Add the Gin Bar, log fires and contemporary furnishings, all makes for a winning combination. (L10) 01993 812291 feathers.co.uk

Kings Arms Hotel & Restaurant, 19 Market Street. This has the feel of a trendy wine bar: leather chairs and pine tables and a smart cocktail bar. Upstairs, the bedrooms are trendy with low-slung, sexy beds you can crawl into. (L10) 01993 813636 kingshotelwoodstock.co.uk

| 130 | 1800 | Broadway Tower built | 1800-1825 | 200 cloth mills built in the Stroud area |

Chipping Norton, Great Tew, Woodstock • **THE EAST COTSWOLDS**

Chastleton House

Marlborough Arms B&B, Oxford Street. This stunning 15th century coaching inn will endear you with its luxurious bedrooms. Breakfast only. Ample parking. (L10) 01993 811227 themarlborougharms.co.uk

EAT...DRINK...SLEEEP IN DINING VENUES TO SAVOUR...

The Boxing Hare, Swerford. Let the bout commence. Those listed below have some serious competition. This new venture has blue-blooded experience of running top-notch restaurants having gathered various Rosettes and Stars. Naturally, a place of style and gourmet delectables. Child and dog friendly. Open for Lunch and Dinner from 12-9. Closed M, Tu & Su eves. (H3) 01608 683212 theboxinghare.co.uk

The Chequers Inn, Churchill. All very civilised and jolly with scrubbed tables, scrummy food and nectar-like ales, the odd Cocktail and general bonhommie. It's what life's about, not so? (C6) 01608 659393 lionearth.co.uk

The Kings Head, Bledington. A former C16 cider house (now hostelry) that has a dream-like setting on a village green beside a meandering brook. Produce comes from University Farm in Bledington. The bedrooms are top-notch. Do visit the Church - magical. (A7) 01608 658365 thekingsheadinn.net

The Plough at Kingham. A long-term favourite of foodie aficionados in West Oxfordshire. You have the laid-back pub area serving local and draught ales and exceptional bar food. The dining room serves English Classic fare and you have the 6-luxurious bedrooms. (B6) 01608 658327 thekinghamplough.co.uk

The Red Lion, Long Compton. This is Richard's favourite, my local spymaster who hs been turfed out of many a hostelry. He finds this inn hard to fault for food, service, hospitality and atmosphere. I liked its simplicity. 4 bedrooms. 01608 684221 (C2) redlion-longcompton.co.uk

The Wild Rabbit, Kingham. A Daylesford creation (or warren, ha-ha) designed for the upwardly mobile Londoner, and or, media-type. It is all glass and food in prep whilst the clientele are busily monitoring their laptops and

1801 Jane Austen arrives in Bath   1805 Sezincote remodelled in Indian style   131

THE EAST COTSWOLDS • Chipping Norton, Great Tew, Woodstock

iPads, or enjoying the log fires, comfy seating and classy bedrooms. (B6) 01608 658389
thewildrabbit.co.uk

SPECIAL PLACES OF INTEREST...

Charlbury Museum. An exquisite little museum with Oxfordshire hay wagon, old photographs and domestic bric-a-brac from a bygone age. Open Apr-Sept Sa 10.30-12.30, Su & BH Ms 2.30-4.30. (G8) 01608 810656
charlburymuseum.org.uk

Chastleton House & Topiary (NT). Jacobean Manor associated with the Gunpowder Plot retains its faded glory with a superb collection of tapestries, original furniture and ornamental topiary. Don't miss the church next door. Open Mar to October W-Su 1-5 (B4) 01608 674981

Daylesford Organic. This is the doyen of farmshops (locals call it The Mothership). On display are the fine foods direct from their 2,350 acres of organic fields and pastures. Kitchen and bakery. Café. Accommodation in Cottages and Bamford Haybarn Spa. Cookery School on: 01608 731620. Behind Bamford Spa is the new exclusive venture, The Club by Bamford. Open daily M-Sa 8-8, Su 9-6. (A5) 01608 731700
daylesford.com

Enstone Tithe Barn, Rectory Farm. Dates from 1382 and is built with some magnificent timbers. Used for local functions: craft fairs, harvest festivals. Open days. (H6)

Rousham Park, House & Garden. Castellated house built c.1635 by Sir John Dormer. Remodelled by William Kent c.1773 to a Gothic style. Royal Garrison in Civil War. Beautiful garden with temples, dovecote and walled garden. No children under 15. No dogs. Garden open all year, 10-4.30. House open May to September for groups by prior arrangement. (M6)
01869 347110
rousham.org

Waterfowl Sanctuary & Rescue Centre. A centre for rare breeds, with an emphasis on giving children a "hands-on" experience with the farm animals. Baby barn. Open Tu-Su & BHs 10.30-dusk. (H1) 01608 730252

Wyatts Plant Centre. Farm shop with ice cream parlour in organic conversion, plus a garden nursery, animal and play area, farmshop and tearoom. Open M-Sa 9-5, Su 10-4. (D2) 01608 684835
wyattsgardencentre.co.uk

Rousham Park Gardens ss

GREAT PUB-GRUB

Scallops, Seven Tuns, Chedworth ss

The Swan at Southrop ss

The Wild Rabbit, Kingham ss

THE CENTRAL WOLDS

Galloping country, stonewalls, sheep pastures, hill top towns and villages, honey-pot villages, three Gloucestershire towns, three choirs festival, racing stables.

If the Central Wolds are the centre of the Cotswolds, then Stow-in-the-Wold, sitting atop its hill, is the absolute heart of the region. This is due in part to the original route taken by the all important Fosse Way, a route which passes through Stow.

To the left of the Central Wolds lie three significant and interesting towns: Tewksbury, Cheltenham and Gloucester. The landscape is very flat here. As you move east, the terrain becomes more undulating and hilly. The Windrush river runs through the Wolds from east to west.

Cheltenham is a Georgian Spa town with interesting architecture and a range of decent places to stay and eat. Tewksbury and Gloucester are older, medieval towns with magnificent churches. Gloucester Cathedral is thought by some to be the birthplace of fan vaulting and Perpendicular architecture.

As well as the towns, there are also many pretty feeder villages to Cheltenham in the area including the Slaughters, the Swells, the Rissingtons and the twin villages of Stanton and Stanway.

This area is host to a number of festivals and cultural events including the Cheltenham Festivals, the Guiting Festival, and the Three Choirs Music Festival.

Stanway

THE CENTRAL WOLDS

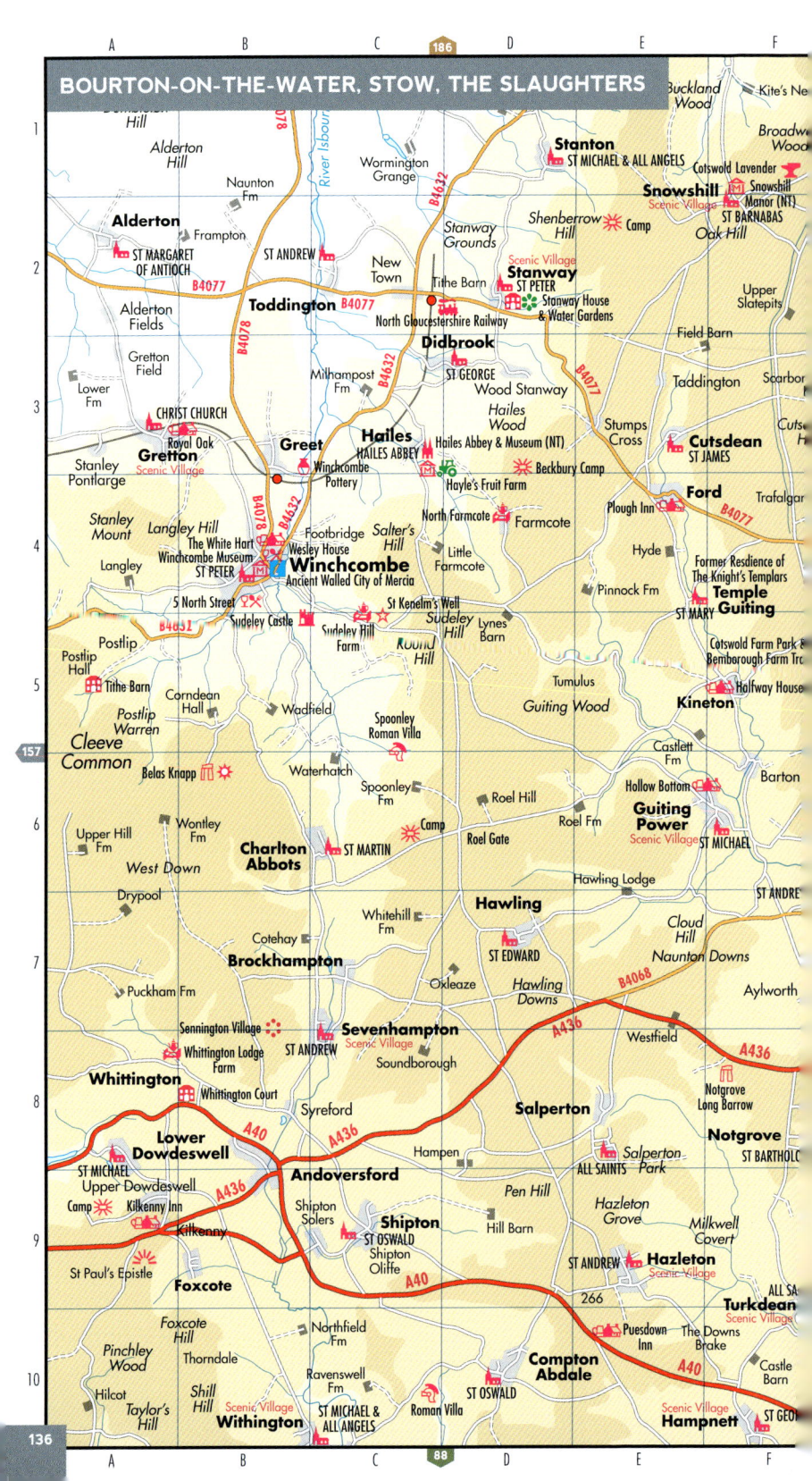

BOURTON-ON-THE-WATER, STOW, THE SLAUGHTERS

G H J 187 K L M

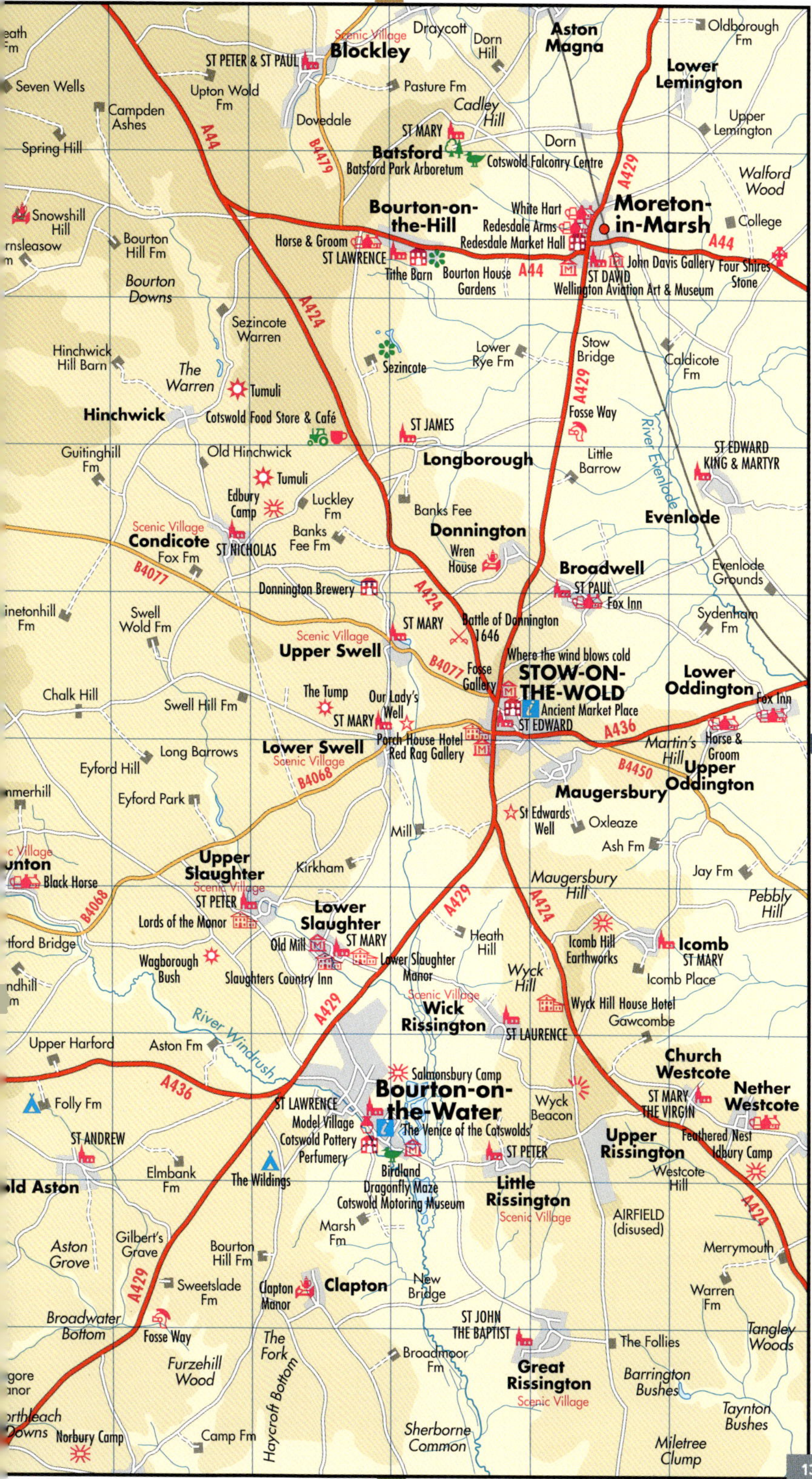

G H J 89 K L M

THE CENTRAL WOLDS • Bourton-On-The-Water, Stow, The Slaughters

Two Views of Bourton-On-The-Water

BOURTON-ON-THE-WATER

One of the most popular destinations in the Cotswolds but best visited out of season or at daybreak. It can be charming on a quiet, frostbitten morning when only the postman is out and about, so be advised to avoid a busy bank holiday when the hordes arrive in coaches and their charabancs. With ice cream in hand the visitors sit beside the river wetting their bare feet in the Windrush, and there's not a stitch of green grass visible through all the paraphernalia. The tourist brochures describe it as 'The Venice of the Cotswolds,' no doubt, because the River Windrush is spanned with low graceful bridges. You must, however, look beyond the crowds and the tackey gift shops and wander the little streets for there are some beautiful houses to admire. Bourton may not thrill the jaded teenager or hard-bitten traveller, but it will delight small children - mine loved to run across the little bridges, paddle in the river and feed the ducks, and you have, of course, Birdland, the Model Village, the Motoring Museum, all devised for family fun and rainy days. The village is built above Salmonsbury Camp, a Roman settlement, and also above a former underground reservoir. It is not an uncommon sight to see a sprightly pensioner move into the village, and within eighteen months, be seen wobbling along the lane, bent double by the damp. Bourton has its fair share of pubs that cater for the tourist. Tearooms are plentiful. Water Game - August BH M. (J8)

| 1805 | The Fettiplace's (former highwaymen) Swinbrook mansion is demolished | 1806 | Jane Austen stays at the Old Rectory (now Adlestrop House) in Adlestrop |

Bourton-On-The-Water, Stow, The Slaughters • THE CENTRAL WOLDS

SPECIAL PLACES OF INTEREST…

Birdland Park & Gardens. Home to over 500 birds on banks of the River Windrush; Penguins, tropical and sub-tropical birds. Feed the penguins, and adopt a bird. Open daily from 10. (J8) 01451 820480 birdland.co.uk

Cotswold Farm Park. A unique survival centre for rare historic breeds of British farm animals including the Cotswold Lions (the Golden Fleece), lies elevated, high on the Central Wolds, three miles from Bourton. Pets and tots corner. Farm trail. Lambing, shearing and seasonal exhibitions. Camping. Café. Open daily 9.30-5. (F5) 01451 850307 cotswoldfarmpark.co.uk

Cotswold Motoring Museum. Motorcycles and vintage racing cars in an C18 water mill. Collection of old advertising signs. Open daily mid-Feb to mid-Dec 10-6. (J8) 01451 821255 cotswoldmotoringmuseum.co.uk

Cotswold Perfumery. Locally produced fragrances. Exhibition of perfumery. Factory tours. Open M-Sa 9.30-5, Su & BHs 10.30-5. (J8) 01451 820698 cotswold-perfumery.co.uk

Cotswold Pottery. Traditional rustic pots, hand-thrown using local materials. Bronze sculptures too. Open daily from 11. (J8) 01451 820173 cotswoldpottery.com

Dragonfly Maze, Rissington Road. Search for the Dragonfly within a traditional Yew Hedge Maze with a Rebus Puzzle and look upon the sculptures crafted by Kit Williams. Gift shop. Open daily from 10 Apr-Oct. (J8) thedragonflymaze.com

Model Village, Old New Inn. Bourton in miniature, at the scale of 1/9th of the original. Lovingly tended gardens. Open daily from 10. (J8) 01451 820467 theoldnewinn.co.uk

Oxfordshire Way. A long distance footpath from Bourton-on-the-Water to Henley-on-Thames, linking the Cotswolds with the Chilterns. Follows the ancient tracks of the county through meadows and woods, along quiet river valleys, and over windy escarpments through many a delightful village. Waymarked. (K8)

Salmonsbury Camp. The Romans' second legion of 5,000 soldiers was encamped here and built Lansdown Bridge to ford the Windrush on the Fosse Way. (K8)

The Lakes. These are flooded gravel pits from the 1960s and 70s. Now used for a carp farm and angling lake. There is a great abundance of wildlife: plants, insects and birds. (K8)

Windrush Valley. A slow, trickling stream in summer, with a tendency to flood in winter. The river snakes its way through quiet golden villages to create the idyllic Cotswold scene. (K10)

Brough Superior SS80, Cotswold Motoring Museum ss

1807   The Prince Regent visits Sezincote and demands the new Brighton Pavilion design be copied, per se   1810   Kennet & Avon Canal opened   139

IN MEMORIAM TO THE FALLEN - POPPIES IN A COTSWOLD GARDEN

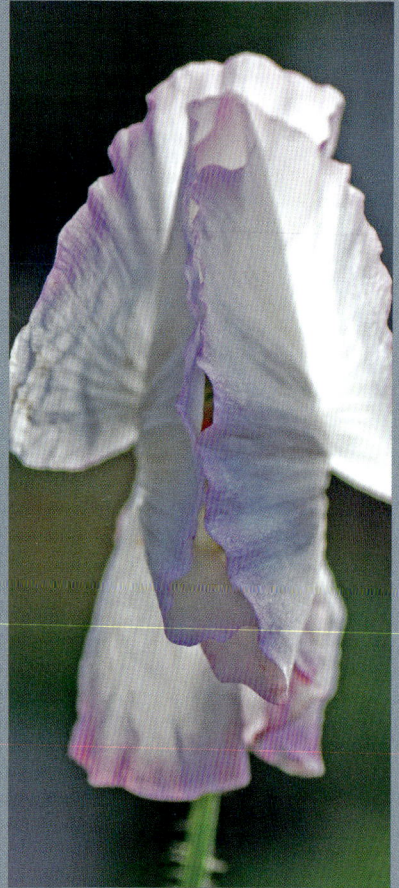

Courtesy of the late Andrew Dawkes, The Glebe, Bourton-On-The-Water

Magnolias in Bloom, Batsford Arboretum

THE CENTRAL WOLDS • Bourton-On-The-Water, Stow, The Slaughters

LIGHT BITES...

I always head to **Bakery On The Water** located just past the bridge, opposite the Cotswold Motoring Museum. An established business for 90-years run by the 4th generation, and now 10-years in Bourton. An artisan bakery, serving a simple breakfast (no fry ups), homemade cakes and bread - all made on the premises. 01451 822748
bakeryonthewater.co.uk

Down river next to the Post Office is **La Reine** where the food is made on the premises: breakfast, coffee and cakes, sandwiches, soup of the day. Opposite, the **Coffee Hub** run by enthusiasts who will serve you an espresso, or two.

EAT...DRINK...SLEEP...

Clapton Manor B&B, Clapton-on-the-Hill. Stunning Grade II listed Tudor house with a beautiful garden created by your host - a garden designer and historian serving fabulous organic breakfasts. (J9) 01451 810202
claptonmanor.co.uk

The Old New Inn B&B, Bourton. Originally a Queen Anne coaching inn that now provides traditional comfort within 9-luxurious bedrooms. Home to the Model Village. (J8) 01451 820467
theoldnewinn.co.uk

The Plough Inn B&B, Cold Aston. A fine country pub offering the full gamut: home-cooked fresh food, real ales, craft beers, great wines, flagstone floors, original beams and a roaring fire. Plus, 3 luxurious double-bedrooms with bathroom. (G8) 01451 822603
coldastonplough.com

The Wildings Campsite, Lankett Lane. A quiet, cool place offering solitude within a family farm: pods, bell tents, yurts - just bring your own bedding/sleeping bags. A Cook House is available with cooking facilities and more comforts. (J9) 01451 518869
thewildingscampsite.co.uk

MORETON-IN-MARSH

Perhaps the first Cotswold town you'll visit if coming from the north along the ancient Fosse Way. And, what an impressive site it is, too. The wide, main street built by the Abbot of Westminster in 1220 for the sheep and arable sales is today a lively scene on market day, every Tuesday since King Charles I granted the town a Charter in 1637. But, its origins go back to the Romans who built a military camp around 43-50 AD whilst planning the construction of the Fosse Way. It remains the largest town in the North East Wolds and is dominated by the Market Hall built in 1887 by Lord Redesdale, father of the infamous Mitford sisters. Look out for the Curfew Tower, an unusual phenomenon on the corner of Oxford Street, dated 1633, which rung until 1860. A fine centre given to a number of inns, art galleries and independent retailers. Associated with the English Civil War, for the Royalist Cavalry were based here. Just out of town on the Chipping Norton road is the Fire Services' College and HQ of the Institute of Fire Engineers. Moreton (agricultural & horse) show - 1st Saturday in September. (L2)

SPECIAL PLACES OF INTEREST...

Batsford Arboretum & Garden Centre. These 56 acres of rare, and beautiful trees, all part of one of the largest private collections of trees in Britain. Visitor centre, café, garden and gift shop. Dogs welcome. Open daily, all year from 9.30 (10 on Su & BHs). (K2) 01386 701441
batsarb.co.uk

Bourton House Garden. 3-acres of intense planting; topiary, knot garden, potager and a profusion of herbaceous borders and exotic plants. The wonderful C16 tithe barn is host to a gallery of contemporary arts and crafts. Lunches, teas, café & shop open May-Sept from 10.30. Garden open Apr-Oct, Tu-F from 10. (K2) 01386 700754
bourtonhouse.com

Cotswold Falconry Centre, Batsford Park. The centre is dedicated to the conservation of eagles, hawks, falcons and owls, with many breeding pairs. Flying displays throughout the day. New parliament of owls. Open daily Feb to Nov, 10.30-3. (K2) 01386 701043
cotswold-falconry.co.uk

John Davies Gallery, The Old Dairy Plant. A much-respected Cotswold gallery established in 1977. Six fully catalogued annual exhibitions. Fine period, post impressionist and contemporary paintings. Open W-F 10.30-4.30, Sa 11-3. (L2) 01608 652255
johndaviesgallery.com

Sezincote House & Garden. House designed in the Indian style (and inspiration for the Brighton Pavilion) is beautifully set in an oriental water garden.

Bourton-On-The-Water, Stow, The Slaughters • **THE CENTRAL WOLDS**

The Slaughters

Bourton House Garden

Sezincote ss

THE CENTRAL WOLDS • Bourton-On-The-Water, Stow, The Slaughters

LIGHT BITES...

A wide choice: Start the day at the **Café, in the Old Market Way** for great homemade food - breakfasts, lunch and Artisan Gelato.

Across the High Street towards Stow, **Mrs T Potts, 5 High St.,** specialise in gluten-free dishes. They bake all their cakes and serve an all-day breakfast from 9am. If a fascination for coffee is your delight,

Grouch Coffee at 3 New Road may alight your senses. Home baking is Kelly's speciality.

In need of a treat? Lunch, Dinner...one turns to **Henne** on the High Street. They tick all the right boxes if British, local, seasonal, sustainable, ethical, personable is your want. Recommended.
01608 544 603
restauranthenne.com

House open May to Sept W Th F & BH Ms 11-5. Garden open Jan to Nov W Th F & BH Ms from 11. (J3) 01386 700444
sezincote.co.uk

Wellington Aviation Museum & Gallery. A funky, very personal collection of the late Gerry Tyack's (amateur racing driver) RAF memorabilia, with a corner dedicated to motorsport, plus a choice of 250 aviation prints for sale. Open Su 10-4. (L2)
01608 812387
wellingtonaviation.org

EAT...DRINK...SLEEP...

Horse & Groom, Bourton-on-the-Hill. A modern, and airy ambience permeates this Grade II listed Georgian inn which is peacefully set in a large garden on the hilltop. Bar, en-suite bedrooms and a blackboard menu changes daily.
01386 700413 butcombe.com

Manor House Hotel, Moreton in Marsh. A C16 coaching that developed into a hotel in the C19 with the coming of the railways. Today it is comfortable, colourful and furnished with some flair. Stunning Gothic windows, a sheltered garden, a conservatory for dining make up the hotel's worth. (L2)
01608 650501
cotswold-inns-hotels.co.uk

Redesdale Arms, Moreton in Marsh. An old coaching inn that mixes the traditional with contemporary designs. (L2)
01608 650308
redesdalearms.com

Wren House, Donnington. Wren House accommodation comprises three en-suite bedrooms in the C15 house, recently renovated to a high standard, and the C17 Grade II listed Cotswold stone cottage - an old granary - which has been converted into a surprisingly spacious one bedroom self-catering cottage. (K4)
01451 831787 wrenhouse.net

SPECIAL PLACES OF INTEREST... THE SLAUGHTERS

Lower Slaughter is one of the most popular villages in the Cotswolds. Little bridges cross the eye stream which runs beside rows of golden cottages. The much painted C19 red-brick Corn Mill stands on the western edge of the village. Upper Slaughter is a couple of miles upstream and has an old Manor House once lived in by the Slaughter family, an old post office with a beautiful kitchen garden and, along a lane past the church, a ford crosses the stream hidden beneath lush greenery. (J7)

Old Mill, Lower Slaughter. This iconic and charming, much photographed, C19 flour mill was lovingly restored into a small museum and was the life-blood of the village. New ownership and new developments we await with interest. (J7)

EAT...DRINK...SLEEP...

Lords of the Manor, Upper Slaughter. Classy, well established country house hotel with C17 origins set in 8-acres of parkland. Child and dog friendly. The former home of the Reverend F E B Witts, Rector of this parish who wrote his famous chronicle of the C18, 'The Diary of a Cotswold Parson.' Afternoon Teas. (H7) 01451 820243
lordsofthemanor.com

Slaughters Country Inn, Lower Slaughter. This C17 hotel, once an Eton cramming school, stands in 4-acres of beautiful grounds alongside the river eye. A hostelry, with a pleasing mix of contemporary and historic features, and a reputation for fine food. Afternoon Teas. Fish and Pie Nights. (J7) 01451 822143
theslaughtersinn.co.uk

Slaughters Manor Hotel. If you seek a hotel with style, and old-fashioned virtues, this perfectly proportioned C17 Cotswold manor house may well be to your liking. There are large, spacious rooms furnished with antiques and classic art. No children U-12. No dogs. (J7) 01451 820456
slaughtersmanor.co.uk

Bourton-On-The-Water, Stow, The Slaughters • **THE CENTRAL WOLDS**

NAUNTON

A pretty village surrounded by rolling sheep pastures, and overlooked by some steep gallops. A noted centre for National Hunt racing stables. The handsome church has some interesting gargoyles, and a stone pulpit. (G6)
Naunton Church. Idyllic country setting on edge of village below rolling pastures. Gargoyles. (F6)

SNOWSHILL

(Pronounced Snosill). This charming and unspoilt hilltop village is a short distance by car from Broadway. There's a striking church, a pub and a row of much photographed cottages opposite Snowshill Manor. (F1)

Cotswold Lavender. Lavender fields to roam in where you can sniff the perfumed plants and buy their Essential Oils. Tearoom/Plants/Shop. Open daily June to Aug 10-5. (F1) 01386 854821
cotswoldlavender.co.uk

Snowshill Manor & Garden (NT). A Cotswold manor house containing Charles Paget Wade's extraordinary collection of craftsmanship and design, amounting to some 22,000 items; from toys to musical instruments, Samurai armour, to clocks, and bicycles. Open daily mid-Mar to 30 Oct 11-5.30, House from 11. (F1) 01386 852410
nationaltrust.org.uk

STANTON

Charming village with houses of warm honey-coloured stone. Restored by Sir Philip Scott, 1903-37. Centre for equine excellence in the Vine, a popular horse riding centre. **The Mount Inn** is a welcome refuge if one's tackling the Cotswold Way, or a fine spot to sink a pint, take in the view, and sample some tasty cuisine. (D1) themountinn.co.uk

Stanton Church of St Michael. Impressive Perpendicular tower. Much is C12-15 with wall paintings, Jacobean pulpit, but its fame was associated with the many visits of John Wesley, the Methodist preacher.(D1)

STANWAY

This village is dominated by the outstanding Manor House. In its grounds stands one of the country's finest tithe barns designed with the Golden Proportion in mind, and across the road, a thatched cricket pavilion set on staddle stones. The beautiful Gatehouse is C17 and was probably built by Timothy Strong of Little Barrington. It bears the arms of the Tracy family. The little church of St Peter has C14 origins and some amusing gargoyles. (D2)

Stanway House & Water Garden. This exquisite Jacobean Manor House and Gatehouse is built from the local stone known as Guiting Yellow which lights up when the sun touches it. All is set within an enchanting and ancient parkland designed by a numerologist, the home of the Earl of Wemyss and March. The restored C18 cascade (fountain) and canal was designed by the highly respected Charles Bridgman. Open as locally advertised. (D2) Groups/Private Tours: 01386 584469
stanwayfountain.co.uk

Slaughters Manor Hotel

THE CENTRAL WOLDS • Bourton-On-The-Water, Stow, The Slaughters

STOW-ON-THE-WOLD

With a name like this it is bound to attract visitors, and it has, and does so to this day, for with its exposed position at the intersection of eight roads, (one being the Fosse Way) Stow has been party to some momentous events in history. The Romans used Stow as an encampment and route centre. The Viking merchants traded down the Fosse Way, but it was the Saxon hill farmers who laid the foundations for the "fleece" which created wealth for the wool merchants who used the great Market Place for sheep sales of 20,000, or more. The Kings Arms is named after Charles Stuart who stayed here in 1645 before the Battle of Naseby. In March 1646, the Battle of Stow was the last skirmish, or battle of the English Civil War. Stow has a number of historic hostelries, and is thus, an agreeable place in which to succumb to fine ales and wine, and the comfort of a four-poster bed. Today, the town is a busy and pleasing place to be. It still has free parking and you may wander freely about, and admire and visit the art galleries, antique shops, bookshops and delis. 'Where the wind blows cold' so the song goes. (K5)
stowonthewold.info

SPECIAL PLACES OF INTEREST...

Donnington Brewery. Established in 1865 by Thomas Arkell who used the spring water to concoct his delicious potions. The brewery remains independent and supplies 15 tied houses and a number of free trade outlets. (J4)
01451 830603
donnington-brewery.com

Fosse Gallery, The Square. Well-established gallery displaying paintings; contemporary and modern, most artists are RA, RAI, ROI members. Open M-Sa 10.30-5. (K5) 01451 831319
fossegallery.com

Market Cross. The lantern head represents four meanings: 'A Rood (crucifix/cross),' St Edward, The Wool Trade and The Civil War. (K5)

Parish Church of St Edward the Confessor. Set behind the Market Place in the centre of town. The building is a mix of the C11 and C15. Originally of Saxon origins, it has an impressive tower of 88 feet

Cotswold Lavender, Snowshill

| 1829 | The first trees are planted at Westonbirt by the 21-year old Robert Holford | 1830 | Edwin Budding of Stroud patents the first lawnmower |

Bourton-On-The-Water, Stow, The Slaughters • **THE CENTRAL WOLDS**

Back Door, Church of Edward the Confessor, Stow

that was built in 1447. Modern stained glass is of interest. Seek out the back door within a tree. (K5)

Red Rag Gallery, Church Street. Original paintings from living artists. Sculpture. Scottish art. Open daily. (K5) 01451 832563
redraggallery.co.uk

Stow Horse Fair. This is held twice a year, in the spring and autumn. Its origins have been lost in time, but today it is very much a Romany get-together. They come from far and wide, to trade in ponies, tack and odds and sods. It's quite a sight, but one visit will probably suffice and satisfy your curiosity. On arriving in Stow, one can't help but notice that the police (and RSPCA) presence is considerable, and that most of the shops, tearooms and inns are closed. No doubt the matrons of the town have also locked up their daughters! As you make your way towards the site, gaggles of young girls showing more flesh than common sense (often in freezing conditions), strut their apparel. A rustic type of "Passeggiata." All apparently (according to a 10-year old Romany) to attract members of the opposite sex. I can't imagine that they were successful because the only males I saw were well into their 40s, possibly older, and only intent on doing a deal, often clasping wodges of £50 notes. The elderly female Romanies were fun to talk to, and chivvy with and were there to meet up with old friends, and to experience the camaraderie of times past. What did impress me was their collection of new motors: black Golf Gtis for the women, and black Land Rovers for the men folk. I was later informed, by what I took to be a reliable source, that they do not pay VAT, corporation or income tax, or are lumbered with hefty mortgages. Well that beats the system I thought. Perhaps they have something to teach us? (K5)

Peter Martin Gallery, 2 Digbeth Court. An artistic, and creative impression of life in Venice and Paris, through the medium of black-and-white images. Open daily 10-5. 07479 610511
petermartingallery.com

1835 — William Henry Fox Talbot invents the negative process at Lacock Abbey

1840 — The process of Enclosure (building of stone walls) is almost complete

STOW HORSE FAIR

Bourton-On-The-Water, Stow, The Slaughters • **THE CENTRAL WOLDS**

LIGHT BITES..

Starting from the **Borzoi Bookshop** in Digbeth Court just off the Market Square. Opposite is **The New England Coffee House** for all your coffees, hot chocs, cakes, with a smile. Along the street to a haven of New York brilliance: **D'Ambrosi Fine Foods**. Gourmet Takeaways; seafood, roasted meats, salads of delectable tastes, an understatement. If enthusiasm be the food of life, this New Yorker has it, bygad. 01451 833888
dambrosi.co.uk

Le Patissier Anglais on The Square will be a delectable experience for those with a passion for pastries, home-made mousses, savoy quiches, and coffee. No bread. The Proprietor is a Chocolatier who trained with Albert Roux. So, if you seek a personal service, and to chat with a Maestro...Open M-Sa from 9. 01451 870571

If you seek a fresh, custom-made sandwich you have two choices, either **Cotswold Baguettes** on Church Walk. 01451 831362
cotswoldbaguettes.co.uk

At the other end of the Square, opposite the Stocks, **The Little Stocks Coffee Shop** run by a Hungarian pastry chef where you can be served soups, savouries and delish cakes. 01451 830666. Now for some Donnington Cotswold ale. Across the Square to **The Queens Head Inn.** Log fire, ancient settles and pub-grub. Note the splendid Sign of Her Majesty. 01451 830563

EAT...DRINK...SLEEP...

Kings Arms, The Square. Fine pub in Market Square set on two levels. Lively and comfortable, matched by well prepared ingredients. Greene King and Hook Norton beers. Children & dogs welcome. B&B. (K5) 01451 830364
thekingsarmsstow.co.uk

The Old Butchers, Park Street. This is a family-run business that has kept Cotswold folk who adore seafood, in the pink, and happy for many years. Open Tu-Sa for lunch and dinner. (K5) 01451 831700
theoldbutchers.squarespace.com

The Porch House, Digbeth Street. Claims to be the oldest Inn in England, dating from 947 AD. It has a had a complete make-over, and a new name. It is thus, now a luxurious hostelry; cosy and comfy, backed up by fine dining. 13-bedrooms. Adjacent, The Pub and Conservatory for informality. (K5) 01451 870048
porch-house.co.uk

EAT... DRINK...SLEEP... OUTSIDE STOW...

Horse & Groom, Upper Oddington. This inn dates back to 1580, and has retained some original features since its early days as a simple hostelry. Set in a beautiful conservation village, this freehouse provides sustenance and comfort. B&B. 01451 830584
horseandgroomcotswolds.co.uk

WINCHCOMBE

This small Cotswold town lies cradled in the Isbourne Valley. It was an ancient Saxon burh (small holding) and famous medieval centre visited from far and wide for the market, horse fair and monastery which was destroyed in the C16. You can still walk the narrow streets beside the C16 and C18 cottages, but do look up and admire the many fine gables above the shop fronts. There's a local saying: "Were you born in Winchcombe?" which is directed at those of us who leave doors open. It can be a wee bit drafty. (B4)

SPECIAL PLACES OF INTEREST...

Belas Knap Long Barrow. In Old English translates 'beacon mound.' A burial chamber, 4,000 years old. Opened in 1863 to reveal 38 skeletons. In superb condition and good viewpoint beside the Cotswold Way. Steep footpath from road. (B6)

Folk & Police Museum. Town Hall. History of the town, police and weapons. TIC. Open East/Apr-Oct M-Sa 10-4.30. (B4) 01242 609151

Hailes Abbey (EH/NT). Built in 1246 by Richard, Earl of Cornwall, brother of Henry III, having vowed he would set up a religious house if he survived a storm at sea. Museum. The abbey became a popular place of pilgrimage in the Middle Ages until Henry VIII closed it down. It remains an attractive ruin with many surviving artefacts on display in the museum. Open daily Apr-Oct 10-dusk. (C3) 01242 602398
nationaltrust.org.uk

Hayles Fruit Farm. Wide range of locally produced fruit, cider and home-cured hams. Tea room. Two nature trails. Camping. Open daily 9-5. (D3) 01242 602123
haylesfruitfarm.co.uk

Parish Church of St Peter. One of the great 'Wool' churches. It is of a C15 Perpendicular design but is

THE CENTRAL WOLDS • Bourton-On-The-Water, Stow, The Slaughters

LIGHT BITES...

There are a number of choices for tea, coffee, pastries, a pre-walk breakfast, and or, brunch and light lunch. Park outside the Church, or in the Square. Taking the **RH** pavement, you first come to **The Old Bakery,** open for breakfast W-Sa from 9.30. Dogs welcome.

Moving on to **The White Hart,** and **Wesley House** (described below). Cross the street to the Town Clock/Museum and enter North Street to **North Street Bakery** for pasties, pies and filled rolls.

A few steps to the food hall, **William's of Winchcombe, 12 North St.**, a deli and coffee shop serving quiches, cheeses, pates, pastries and cold meats. Open daily. food-fanatics.co.uk

Just past the turning into North Street continue to **Honey Bea's Café**, open Tu-Sa 10-4 for a personable service and wholesome food.

---

strangely plain, yet dignified. Not as elaborate as some of the other 'Wool' churches. For example, it has no chancel arch. The gargoyles are the one notable feature, and a circumnavigation of the exterior is advised. The weathercock is the county's finest. (B4)

Postlip Hall & Tithe Barn. A former Jacobean Manor House set in fifteen acres. Postlip Hall has been for the past 40 years a co-housing idyll. Eight families live in separate dwellings, working the organic kitchen garden and grounds, and pursuing their own creative pleasures; be it writing, painting, sculpting or inventing. The original tithe barn is also in continual use except when it is hired out as a venue for weddings, parties and beer festivals. (A5)

Salt Way. This prehistoric track runs east of Winchcombe from Hailes, south towards Hawling along Sudeley Hill. It was used in medieval times to carry salt from Droitwich and coastal salt towns, salt being the essential meat preservative. (D6)

Sudeley Castle. A Tudor house and the original home of the Seymour family. Katherine Parr, widow of Henry VIII lived here and lies buried in the chapel. There is a fine collection of needlework, furniture and tapestries, plus paintings by Van Dyck, Rubens and Turner. All surrounded by award-winning gardens and open parkland. Café. The Castle is open daily Apr to 5 Nov 10-5. (B5) 01242 604244
sudeleycastle.co.uk

Winchcombe Pottery. One of the country's most respected potteries, known throughout the ceramic world. A large variety of hand-made domestic ware on sale in the shop. Open daily M-F 8-5, Sa 10-4. (B3) 01242 602462
winchcombepottery.co.uk

EAT... DRINK...SLEEP...

5 North Street. Has gained a healthy respect from fellow restaurateurs in the Cotswolds. You have a small, and well-run restaurant with low-beamed ceiling in a quaint C17 building providing a relaxed and friendly atmosphere. (B4) 01242 604566
5northstreetrestaurant.co.uk

Lion Inn, 33 North Street. A comfortable hostelry serving good-value food within a sympathetically decorated building. You can eat/drink in the bar (and nestle up to the log fire), or dining room; tapas for lunch, Dinner is more dynamic, and sleep in their luxurious bedrooms. 01242 603300 (B4)
butcombe.com

Wesley House, High Street. Deserved reputation for excellent food. Locals travel miles to this gastronomic fest. Five bedrooms. (B4) 01242 602366
wesleyhouse.co.uk

White Hart, High Street. Variously viewed as an inn or a hotel, the White Hart offers last-minute deals. This C16 inn is a popular 'local' with eight en-suite bedrooms and a bar/restaurant (B4) 01242 602359
whitehartwinchcombe.co.uk

EAT...DRINK... SLEEP...OUTSIDE WINCHCOMBE...

North Farmcote. A working family farm producing sheep and cereals situated high on the Cotswold escarpment. Built around 1840 as a dower house for Lord Sudeley's mother, the house is surrounded by a large garden where guests can have afternoon tea. Visit their specialist herb garden (open May to Sept). (C4) 01242 602304
northfarmcote.co.uk

Sudeley Hill Farm. Comfortable C15 listed farmhouse with panoramic views onto a working sheep/arable farm of 800 acres. Three en-suite bedrooms. (C4) 01242 602344

Bourton-On-The-Water, Stow, The Slaughters • **THE CENTRAL WOLDS**

The Fox, Oddington

SPECIAL PLACE OF INTEREST...

Whittington Court. An impressive, statuesque Cotswold stone house beside a pretty church. Next door, home of the Whittington Press, Letterpress specialist. Open Easter fortnight, then mid to end Aug, 2-5. (B8) 01242 820556
whittingtoncourt.co.uk

WHERE TO STAY...

Whittington Lodge Farm, Whittington. Your hostess takes your comfort and enjoyment very seriously and the bedrooms are perfect down to the smallest details. The farm has a special emphasis on conservation and wildlife and you can take farm wildlife tours and walks. (B8) 01242 820603
whittingtonlodgefarm.com

EAT...DRINK...IN LOCAL INNS...

Black Horse, Naunton. A Donnington Brewery tied-house, so naturally, there is an excellent selection of beers on offer. A little off the beaten track, so ideal for those wishing to avoid the crowds. B&B (G6) 01451 850565

Fox Inn, Broadwell. Picturesque inn with a large beer garden situated opposite the village green, thus making it an ideal pit stop for families. Real ales and tasty pub-grub from the kitchens. Jus Purrfik, Ma Larkin! (L5) 01451 832134
thefoxbroadwell.com

The Halfway at Kineton. Two hospitality crazy/foodie nuts Nathan and Liam, along with their families have turned this lovely ancient C17 Inn into a cosy, comfy pub. Three knockout bedrooms. (F5) 074259 70507
thehalfwayatkineton.com

The Fox, Oddington. A Daylesford Re-Creation to empower C11 origins; flagstone floors, open fireplaces and wooden beams. To whit wholesome pub grub, comfort and plush bedrooms. On leaving, if you have a moment, walk to the Church of St Nicholas for solitude and spiritual enlightenment. (M5) 01451 767000
thefoxoddington.com

The Plough at Ford. The first pub my 90-year old Grandmother entered, and surprisingly, she was markedly impressed at how civil and well behaved everyone was. She was drawn to the advertised, asparagus. Its all flagstone floors, beams and old-worlde charm. (E4) 01386 584215
theploughinnford.co.uk

Sudeley Castle

1854 — Founding of Cheltenham Ladies College
1854 — Woodchester Mansion is designed by Pugin

151

THE CENTRAL WOLDS • Bourton-On-The-Water, Stow, The Slaughters

Guiting Power

GUITING POWER

A hidden, somnolent estate village that surprisingly manages to support two pubs, a village shop serving coffee and cakes, a deli, a nursery school and an active village hall. The blue-grey cottages belong to the Cochrane Estate (or Guiting Manor Amenity Trust) that has thankfully saved this village from greedy developers and second homers. The Church of St Michael & All Angels lies on the edge of the village and has some Norman features, a beautiful Tympanum and some weather-beaten tombstones. It was an early Anglo-Saxon settlement called Gyting Broc. A classical and jazz music festival is held in late July for the past 39 years and attracts many artists of international renown. guitingfestival.org

EAT… DRINK… SLEEP…

The Cotswold Guy, Church Lane. This is a new boutique farm shop with a passion for fresh, locally sourced produce. Takeaway Meals and a bespoke food distribution service, dinner parties etc. Open M-Su 9-4, 01451 851955
thecotswoldguy.co.uk

Farmers Arms, Winchcombe Road. A proper locals country pub whose untarnished exterior does not do justice to the welcome, or basic food served. My children used to love coming here. Donnington Ales. Don't expect nouvelle cuisine or al dente veg.
01451 850358
farmersarmsguiting.co.uk

Guiting Guest House, Post Office Lane. C16 Cotswold stone former farmhouse which has been tastefully modernised. Candlelit and tasty evening meals by arrangement. Garden. Children and dogs welcome. 01451 850470
guitingguesthouse.com

Hollow Bottom. Out on the road to Winchcombe. Herewith, a friendly pub popular with the racing fraternity. Now owned by Youngs Brewery. 01451 539890
hollowbottom.com

The Lion Inn, Winchcombe ss

| 152 | 1856 | St Lawrence Church, Bradford-on-Avon is discovered behind cottages | 1859 | Katherine Parr's tomb is rediscovered and restored |

WINCHCOMBE GARGOYLES

The word gargoyle is a derivation from the French word gargouille meaning throat or pipe. The carved gargoyles were invented to channel water off, or away, from the roofs of buildings in Egypt and Ancient Greece. Their popularity became almost endemic in Europe during the Middle Ages. Fine examples are to be seen on Notre Dame in Paris, and on Rouen's Cathedral in northern France. In Britain, the Cotswold churches, especially Winchcombe's have some fine, amusing examples, as illustrated.

The reason for these strange and often ugly designs is open to conjecture. Some believe they are caricatures of the clergy, or that they are there to ward off evil spirits. Perhaps, to protect the church's building from the devil. Others believe they are transformed into ghosts and ghoulies at night! They were certainly a popular architectural ornament during dark days of the superstitious, Middle Ages.

COTSWOLD CHURCHES

Church of St Mary's, Bibury

Church of St Matthew, Coates

Church of St Kenelm, Sapperton

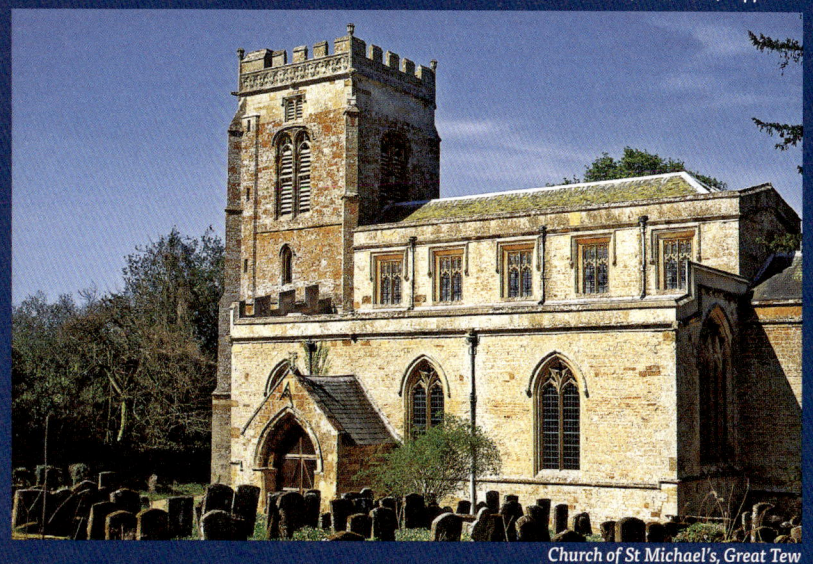

Church of St Michael's, Great Tew

CHELTENHAM, GLOUCESTER, TEWKESBURY

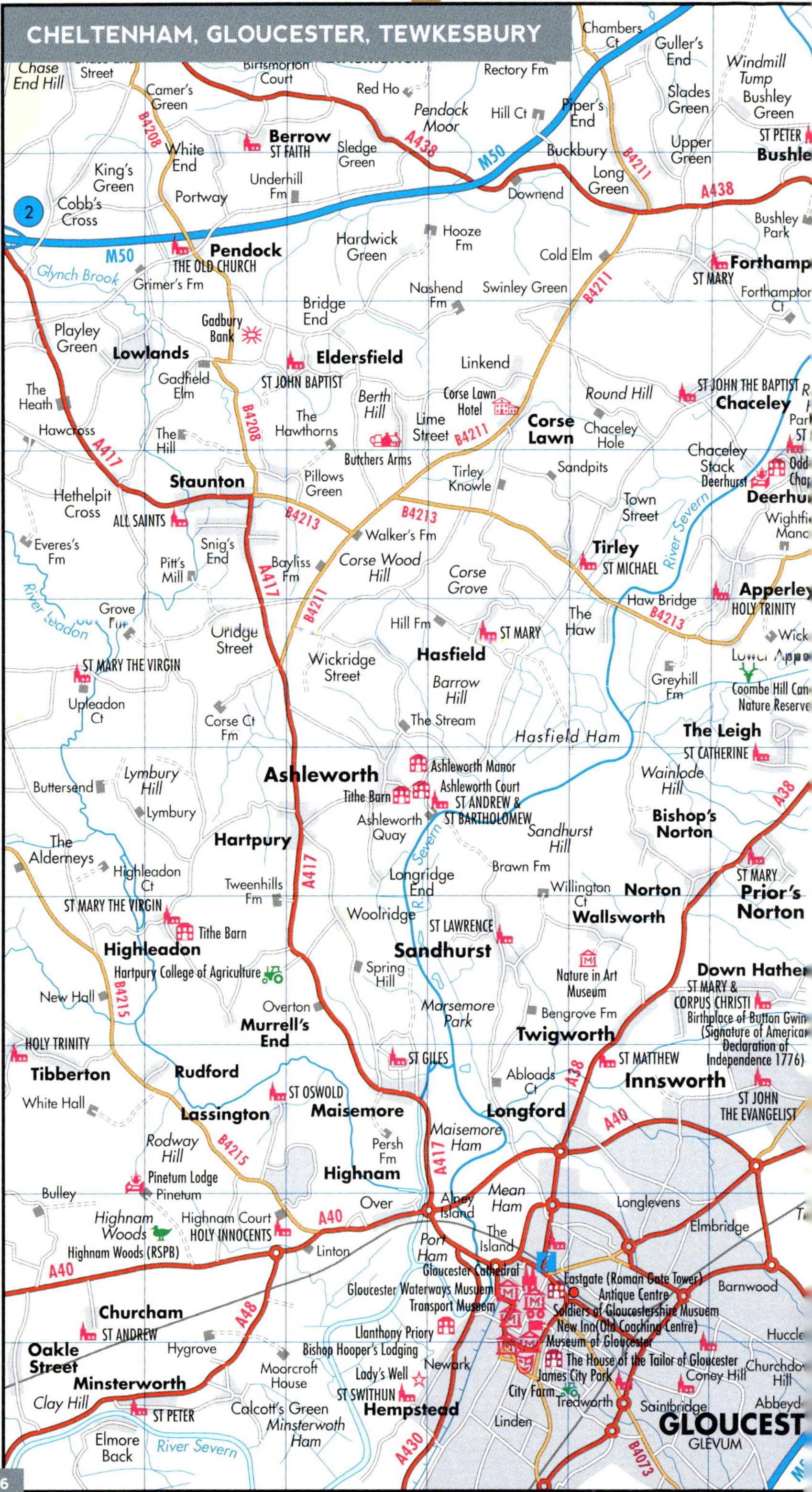

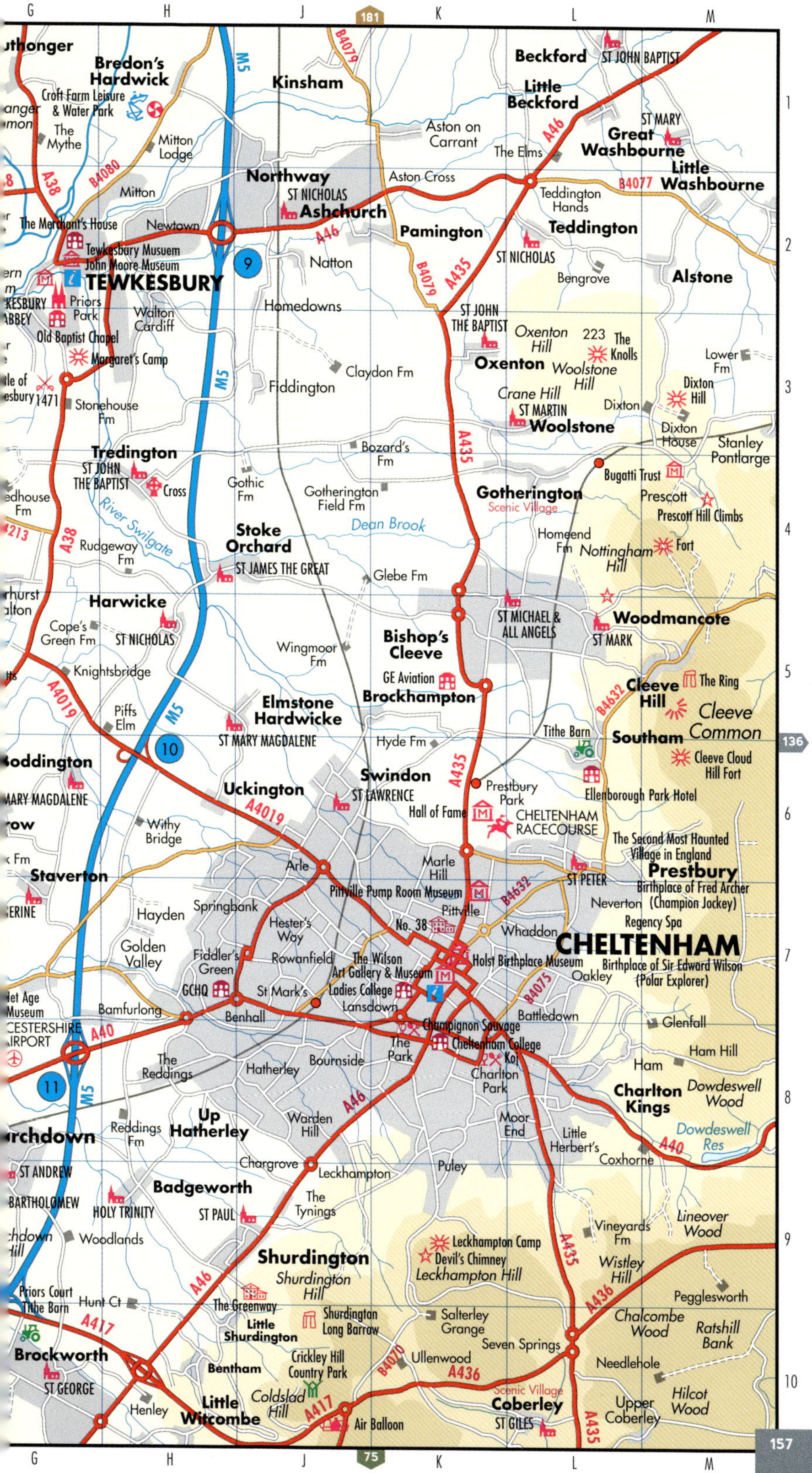
G
H
J
181
K
L
M
Bredon's Hardwick
Croft Farm Leisure & Water Park
The Mythe
Mitton Lodge
Mitton
Kinsham
Beckford
ST JOHN BAPTIST
Little Beckford
Aston on Carrant
The Elms
ST MARY
Great Washbourne
Little Washbourne
Northway
ST NICHOLAS
Ashchurch
Aston Cross
Teddington Hands
B4077
Teddington
The Merchant's House
Newtown
Tewkesbury Musuem
John Moore Museum
TEWKESBURY
Natton
Pamington
ST NICHOLAS
Bengrove
Alstone
Priors Park
Walton Cardiff
Old Baptist Chapel
Margaret's Camp
Homedowns
ST JOHN THE BAPTIST
Oxenton Hill
223
The Knolls
Lower Fm
Claydon Fm
Oxenton
Woolstone Hill
Fiddington
Crane Hill
Dixton Hill
1471
Stonehouse Fm
ST MARTIN
Woolstone
Dixton
Dixton House
Stanley Pontlarge
Tredington
ST JOHN THE BAPTIST
Cross
Bozard's Fm
Gothic Fm
Gotherington Field Fm
Gotherington
Scenic Village
Bugatti Trust
Prescott
Prescott Hill Climbs
River Swilgate
Rudgeway Fm
Dean Brook
Stoke Orchard
ST JAMES THE GREAT
Homeend Fm
Nottingham Hill
Fort
Glebe Fm
Harwicke
Cope's Green Fm
ST NICHOLAS
ST MICHAEL & ALL ANGELS
Woodmancote
ST MARK
Wingmoor Fm
Bishop's Cleeve
Knightsbridge
GE Aviation
Brockhampton
Cleeve Hill
The Ring
Elmstone Hardwicke
Cleeve Common
Piffs Elm
ST MARY MAGDALENE
Hyde Fm
Tithe Barn
Southam
Cleeve Cloud Hill Fort
Boddington
MARY MAGDALENE
Swindon
ST LAWRENCE
Prestbury Park
Ellenborough Park Hotel
Uckington
Hall of Fame
CHELTENHAM RACECOURSE
Withy Bridge
The Second Most Haunted Village in England
Staverton
Arle
Marle Hill
ST PETER
Prestbury
Birthplace of Fred Archer (Champion Jockey)
Pittville Pump Room Museum
Neverton
Pittville
Regency Spa
Springbank
Hayden
Hester's Way
No. 38
Whaddon
CHELTENHAM
Golden Valley
Fiddler's Green
Rowanfield
The Wilson Art Gallery & Museum
Holst Birthplace Museum
Oakley
Birthplace of Sir Edward Wilson (Polar Explorer)
GCHQ
St Mark's
Ladies College
Jet Age Museum
Bamfurlong
Lansdown
Benhall
Battledown
Glenfall
Champignon Sauvage
Cheltenham College
The Park
The Reddings
Hatherley
Bournside
Koj
Charlton Park
Ham Hill
Ham
Charlton Kings
Dowdeswell Wood
Up Hatherley
Warden Hill
Moor End
Little Herbert's
Dowdeswell Res
Reddings Fm
Coxhorne
Chargrove
Puley
Leckhampton
ST ANDREW
Badgeworth
The Tynings
BARTHOLOMEW
HOLY TRINITY
ST PAUL
Vineyards Fm
Lineover Wood
Woodlands
Leckhampton Camp
Devil's Chimney
Leckhampton Hill
Wistley Hill
Shurdington
Shurdington Hill
Priors Court
Tithe Barn
Hunt Ct
The Greenway
Little Shurdington
Shurdington Long Barrow
Salterley Grange
Chalcombe Wood
Ratshill Bank
Pegglesworth
Seven Springs
Brockworth
ST GEORGE
Bentham
Crickley Hill Country Park
Ullenwood
Needlehole
Scenic Village
Hilcot Wood
Henley
Little Witcombe
Coldslad Hill
Air Balloon
Coberley
ST GILES
Upper Coberley
M5
9
10
11
A38
A46
A435
A4019
A40
A417
A436
B4079
B4080
B4632
B4075
B4070
136
1
2
3
4
5
6
7
8
9
10
75

CHELTENHAM

Pittville Park

Cars, Imperial Square

Lansdown Parade

Cheltenham, Gloucester, Tewkesbury • **THE CENTRAL WOLDS**

CHELTENHAM

A smaller version of Bath, often described as 'the most complete Regency town in England.' Elegant Regency buildings overlook the crescents, squares, tree-lined avenues and spacious parks. Cheltenham remains, in historic terms, a young town of a mere 300-years. It grew as a spa after George III had approved the waters in 1788. Thereafter, distinguished visitors such as George Handel and Samuel Johnson came to be revitalised. The Promenade is one of the most attractive shopping streets in England which becomes progressively more independent and up-market as you trudge with heavy bags and depleted purse west towards Montpelier. Style and fashion epitomise this smart town. Youth and hedonism, a-plenty. Cheltenham has seen a phenomenal explosion of new nightclubs, bars and restaurants patronised by the ever-increasing student population and, come the evening, by an influx of visitors from Birmingham, Bristol and Gloucester and, not least from the surrounding villages and small towns. It is no longer the home of Colonel Blimps and tweedy ladies of means. Cheltenham is proud of its calendar of festivals: Antique, Folk, Jazz, Literature, Music, Science...but it is during the Cheltenham Festival of National Hunt Racing which takes place in March that the town takes on a carnival atmosphere. The Irish arrive in thousands and this brings out the Cheltonians hospitality. Hotel rooms are like gold dust so many of Cheltenham's citizens open their homes and do a brisk and highly profitable B&B trade for three or four nights. A centre of administration, commerce, education, high-tech industries and secret surveillance. The Countryside Commission and UCAS have their headquarters here. So do a number of large organisations: the Chelsea Building Society, Dowty Rotol and Endsleigh Insurance. The University of Gloucestershire has expanded its faculties to countenance the weight of the highly regarded private schools. What stands out for those of us who arrive from the Gloucester side, is the large circular building known as GCHQ, locally known as the Puzzle Palace. This was established after WWII as a secret surveillance centre for the Foreign Office. It is a most congenial town that could well be described as the centre for the Cotswolds. Its motto Salubritas et Eruditio 'Health and Education.' If you can achieve either of these, then your luck is in. (L7)

Cheltenham College

SPECIAL PLACES OF INTEREST...

The Wilson - Cheltenham Art Gallery & Museum, Clarence Street. World-renowned Arts & Crafts Movement collection inspired by William Morris. Rare Chinese and English ceramics. The Paper Store, an open archive of local heroes, including the great Edward Wilson, Antarctic Explorer. Social history of Cheltenham. C17 Dutch and C17-20 British paintings. **Wilson Café. TIC**. Open Tu-Sa 10-6, Su 10-4. (K7) 01242 528764
cheltenhammuseum.org.uk

Pittville Pump Room

THE CENTRAL WOLDS • Cheltenham, Gloucester, Tewkesbury

Bugatti Trust ss

Bugatti Trust, Prescott Hill. A small exhibition illustrates the work of Ettore Bugatti the genius of industrial design and invention. Study Centre with drawings, photos and some cars. Open M-F 10-4, and during Hill Climb days. (M4)
01242 677201
bugatti-trust.co.uk

Cheltenham College. An independent Public School of architectural renown, distinguished by the superb Chapel and Refectory. The ground for the oldest cricket festival in the world (first staged in 1872) which takes place every summer. (K8) To visit contact 01242 265600
cheltenhamcollege.org

The Paragon Gallery, 4 Rotunda terrace, Montpelier Street. A refreshing, new gallery with a diverse range of stylish, bold, bright and contemporary artworks. The service is friendly and unstuffy, and dog-loving. (K7)
01242 233391
paragongallery.co.uk

Cheltenham Ladies College, Bayshill Road. If you see young ladies dressed in green apparel walking at pace through the streets of Cheltenham (in twos and threes) you can be sure they are educated at this, the most elitist of academies. Its buildings are undistinguished, modern and rarely favourably commented upon. However, the aesthetics of the buildings have no effect on the school's academic achievements, for it usually comes in the Top 3 of all A-Level results. (K7)
01242 520691
cheltladiescollege.org

Cheltenham Racecourse Hall of Fame. The story of steeple chasing and its immortals, in sight and sound, from Cheltenham's first Gold Cup in 1818 to Desert Orchid's heart-stopping win in 1989. Open Race Days. Free. (L6)
01242 513014
thejockeyclub.co.uk/cheltenham

Gustav Holst Birthplace Museum, Clarence Road, Pittville. Memorabilia of composer's life. Period furnished rooms. Open all year Tu-Sa 10-4. (K7) 01242 524846
holstvictorianhouse.org.uk

Pittville Pump Room, East Approach Drive. A masterpiece of C19 Greek Revivalism, adorned with colonnaded facades, portico, pillared and balconied hall. Open daily, except during private functions. (K7)
01242 528724
pittvillepumproom.org.uk

Seven Springs. One of the sources of the River Thames. There is a stone plaque here with a Latin inscription which reads, roughly translated: 'Here thou, O Father Thames, hast thy sevenfold beginning.' (L10)

NATURAL PLACES OF INTEREST...

Cleeve Hill. At 1,083 feet this is the highest point in the Cotswolds and thus a superb viewpoint across to the Malvern Hills, Welsh Mountains, and northwards across the Cotswold landscape. A popular dog walking area and, in winter snow, ideal for tobaggan runs. In 1901 a tramway was built from Cheltenham to Cleeve Cloud but sadly closed in 1930. Cleeve Cloud is the site of an Iron Age hill fort and just below the scarp is The Ring, a site of religious/pagan rituals, 100 feet in diameter. Castle Rock is popular with novice rock climbers. (M5)

Cleeve Common. A vast expanse of common land where you are free to roam, with dog and friends. It is more like a piece of wild moorland with its extensive horizons, and you may be forgiven for believing you are in the midst of a National Park. There are wild flowers, the Gallops (for exercising race horses) and tracks that lead off in all directions. Park in the golf course, or in the lay-byes, on the B4632. (M5)

Coombe Hill Canal Nature Reserve. Two-mile stretch of canal closed in 1876. Habitat of birds, dragonflies, aquatic and bankside plants. Open all year. (F5)

Crickley Hill Country Park. Nature trails, geological and archaeological trails are signposted, as is the Cotswold Way. Traces of Stone Age and Iron Age settlements. Fine views. Cafe. Open daily. (J10)

1863 — Belas Knapp long barrow is excavated   1864 — Thomas Keble, vicar of Bisley church devises the Ascension Day Well Blessing Ceremony

Cheltenham, Gloucester, Tewkesbury • THE CENTRAL WOLDS

LIGHT BITES...

Cheltenham provides an amazing choice of bars, coffee shops, hotels, pubs and restaurants. I have selected three areas of the town: Montpelier, The Promenade/Regents Street area and Suffolk Parade. Where to start? Montpelier - which is the smart area of town. First up, **The Montpelier Wine Bar,** an old favourite (and the first in town), which has received a facelift. It has character, and a pedigree.

Continue down the street to the **Chaplais** for European delights and combative conversation, cross the road and you come to **John Gordons, 11 Montpelier Arcade.** You will be impressed by the bottles on display. 200+ malt whiskeys, 50 gins, 30 rums, an off-license and bar, plus coffee, cakes and tapas with seating outside, too. 01242 245985 johngordons.co.uk

Leave and turn R, cross the street to **Lazy Graze** in The Courtyard. I often stop here for a hot-choc and breakfast. Lovely people.

Leave Montpelier and with the **Queens Hotel** on your R descend to the Imperial (Square) Gardens area. **No. 131** is worth a look in. It's all about the lifestyle of being chic and watched, narcissism. Ask to see **Yoku (Japanese restaurant) or Gin & Juice** for cocktails. This boutique restaurant is always booked up way in advance. Breakfast is from 8-11am, lunch 12-3, supper 5-7.30, sunday lunch 12-4. There's an outside bar and seating with views over the gardens. 01241 822939 no131.com.

Across the road you may see folk in repose on the grass with glass in hand supplied by the **Imperial Garden Bar** established in 1903. Open daily from Easter at 10.30am until the close of the Literary Festival in October. A popular, al fresco dining experience, where you can meet up with family and friends. Tapas menu. It has a secret garden for intimate assignations. Now, if all this is a bit much, and you just seek to gather your energy and thoughts before tackling the shopping delights of **The Promenade** where you can buy a fresh coffee from the man with the Coffee Station.

Behind the Promenade, is Regent Street where there is a multiple of coffee shops. If you start from the High Street end you hit **Caffe La Scala,** then **Fat Tonis Pizzeria**, **The Cheeseworks** for a full selection of cheeses, fresh bread, oils.....**KIBOU**, a Japanese hot kitchen and bar serving sushi and ramen, and comfort...

We are now entering the domain of some serious coffee houses/eateries. Its your choice: **WoodKraft the Artisan Eatery**, then **The Coffee Dispensary** then onto **The Find** - some choice. You can not miss them. To reach Suffolk Parade you must retrace your steps. Walk to the top of Montpelier Gardens to the roundabout and turn L down Montpelier Terrace, and take the first R into Suffolk Parade. This area has a full panoply of independent shops, cafés and bars, lighting, antiques and a florist. A town within itself.

The Retreat at 10 Suffolk Parade is an old favourite that has had a loyal following since it opened 30+ years back. Food is served at lunchtime Tu-Sa 12-12 where you can have ham, egg and chips, to new potatoes and a casserole to a steak sandwich and rocket salad. A pleasing ambience with red walls and bare floors gives way to a buzz, come the evening. 01242 235436 theretreatwinebar.co.uk

Devil's Chimney. A 50 foot high limestone rock which according to local superstition 'rises from hell.' Its origins resulted from quarrying the surrounding stone. (K9)

Highnam Woods Nature Reserve. 300 acres of broadleafed woodland, with bluebells in spring. Nightingales call (if you are listening). Open daily. (A9) 01594 562852 rspb.org.uk

Leckhampton Hill. A popular dog walking area for Cheltenians that provides superb views towards the Malvern Hills, and Wales. The golden stone of 'Regency' Cheltenham was quarried here. Iron Age and Roman camps. (K9)

EAT...

Coconut Tree, 59 St Paul's Rd. Something different: Sri Lankan street food, vegan dishes, cocktails to fire you up in this laid-back dive. Open daily from 12-late. Takeaways 12-9. 01242 465758 (K7) thecoconut-tree.com

THE CENTRAL WOLDS • Cheltenham, Gloucester, Tewkesbury

Curry Corner, 133 Fairview Road. If you enjoy Indian cuisine stop here for some nourishment and hospitality. The Krori family have been delighting their customers for nigh on 40+ years. Takeaways. Open Tu-Su 5-10. 01242 528449
thecurrycorner.com

Daffodil, 18-20 Suffolk Parade. Converted from a 1920's art deco cinema to a restaurant and mezzanine circle bar and original features, posters advertising films with the original projectors. No longer a restaurant but available for Events and Private Hire. (K7) 07355 055201
thedaffodil.com

Ginger & Garlic, 334 High St. A South Korean restaurant that conjures up all manner of Asian delights. Indeed, a mix of Japanese, Chinese and Korean. Quite an adventure. 01242 519888 (K7) ginger-garlic.co.uk

Morans Eating House, 123-129 Bath Road. Family owned restaurant, and wine bar that has been popular and busy since its inception 30-years ago. Squeeze amongst the regulars for a glass of wine or good value, homespun fare, from brunch to a bedtime snack. (K8) 01242 581211
moranseatinghouse.co.uk

Prithvi, Bath Road. The quality of the Indian cusine, the service and ambience would be the envy of other restaurants such is the praise that shines down on "Mother Earth" 01242 226129 (K7)
prithvirestaurant.com

Purslane, Rodney Road. Gareth Fulford is the Chef/ Patron of this family-run restaurant specialising in seafood caught in British waters and Cotswold produce who has been cooking for Cheltenham folk the past ten years. Keep going Gareth! Open Th-Sa 12-4.30, 6-12.30. (K7) 01242 321639
purslane-restaurant.co.uk

EAT...DRINK...SLEEP...

Cleeve Hill Hotel. Ideally situated to tackle the Cotswold Way, and or, two or three walks over an energetic weekend. You will enjoy stunning views from their light and airy rooms. And, sleep the dreams of rambling over hills and dales. (M5) 01242 672052
cleevehillhotel.co.uk

Ellenborough Park Hotel, Southam. If you seek space, style, spa treatments and affable staff with local knowledge, all within jumping distance of Cheltenham's Racecourse it is all here within a 90-acre estate. At its heart a Cotswold manor house dating back to the 1500s surrounded by sweeping lawns and new buildings quarried from a local quarry to provide authenticity and the wow factor. The bedrooms are luxurious and contemporary, the food is of a very high quality. Dogs welcome. 01242 545454
ellenboroughpark.com

No. 131 The Promenade. You really can't find a better location in this Regency town. Smack opposite Imperial Gardens and a short walk onto the finest shopping street in England. The 36 rooms are all independently decorated, and designed with locally sourced materials. Lavish and a wee bit over the top but good fun. And, not forgetting the stupendously popular Gin & Juice Bar and Yoku Japanese Restaurant in the basement. 01242 822939
no131.com

No. 38 Evesham Road. An intimate, Georgian town house overlooking Pittville Park and a short walk to the Racecourse and town centre. This a perfect venue for a house party catering to 13-rooms. Can be yours for a small song. Now part of Youngs Brewery. 01242 394014
no38thepark.com

Hotel du Vin & Bistro, Parabola Road. A little bit of France within a Regency townhouse. The bedrooms are moody, dark and contemporary. The Bistro is inspired by French home-style cooking. The Spa will rejuvenate the senses you thought were missing. 01242 370584
hotelduvin.com

The Greenway Hotel & Spa, Shurdington. Elizabethan manor house provides elegance, peace and self-indulgent comfort with easy access to the M5 motorway. (J9) 01242 862352
thegreenwayhotelandspa.com

The Greenway ss

1866   Vulliamy designs the neo-Baroque Westonbirt (school)   1866   The Tyndale Monument is built

Cheltenham, Gloucester, Tewkesbury • **THE CENTRAL WOLDS**

Purslane ss

No. 131 The Promenade ss

THE CENTRAL WOLDS • Cheltenham, Gloucester, Tewkesbury

Warehouses, Gloucester Docks

GLOUCESTER

The county town of Gloucestershire and its administrative centre is set to the west of the Cotswold Hills, south of the Malvern Hills, and to the east of the Forest of Dean. Originally a port connected to the tidal Bristol Channel and strategic point developed by the Romans into the fort Glevum. This ancient city is today dominated by the magnificent Cathedral. The other great attractions are Gloucester Docks and Gloucester Quays where the spectacular C19 warehouses have been restored for commercial and leisure uses. It is not unknown to spy tall ships, and ships in the dry dock for renovations. The City has undergone a great deal of new development on the south side just off the Bristol road. The history of Gloucester is immense and this is well covered in the many museums listed below. (E10)

SPECIAL PLACES OF INTEREST...

Eastgate. Roman and Medieval Gate. Towers and medieval stone-lined horse pool (moat). Open as locally advertised. (D9)

Glevum, Gloucester. Occupied since Neolithic times. Became of strategic importance to Early Man and the Roman legions. Fort at Kingsholm beside the River Severn. Lost out to Corinium (Cirencester) in importance in the C3 AD. (D9)

Gloucester Cathedral. The Cathedral Church of St Peter and the Holy and Undivided Trinity. Without exception the most magnificent building in Gloucestershire and one of the finest of all English cathedrals. The building's foundation stone was laid down by Abbot Serlo in 1089 on the site of a religious

Jet Age Museum, Gloucester Airport ss

| 164 | 1871 | William Morris moves into Kelmscott Manor | 1874 | Gustav Holst is born in Cheltenham |

Cheltenham, Gloucester, Tewkesbury • **THE CENTRAL WOLDS**

house founded by Osric, an Anglo-Saxon prince living here in about 678-9 AD. The Nave was completed in 1130. Its architecture is Romanesque, with some early Perpendicular. The reconstruction of the Quire followed the burial in 1327 of Edward II. The East Window behind the altar had at its installation the largest display of medieval stained glass in the world and dates from 1350. The same year, fan vaulting was invented here at Gloucester and its intricate design covers the roof of the cloisters. Some would argue that Gloucester also saw the birth of Perpendicular architecture. In the south transept survives the oldest of all Perpendicular windows. Allow a couple of hours to wander around this spiritual hot house. There are tours of the crypt and tower. You will also be shown the location used for part of Hogwarts in the Harry Potter films. Evensong is a most magical experience not to be missed, as is the Christmas Carol service. Cream Teas 10-4.30, Su 11-4. Open daily 10-5, Su 12-5. (D9) 01452 528095 gloucestercathedral.org.uk

Gloucester & Sharpness Canal. Opened in 1827 and built above the River Severn. It's 16 miles long and was originally used by ocean-going ships in transit to Gloucester. (D9)

Gloucester Waterways Museum, Llanthony Warehouse. A major national exhibition about the history of the inland waterways. Historic boats and leisure cruises on hand. Café. Open daily 11-4, July-Aug 10.30-5. (D9) 01452 318212
gloucesterwaterwaysmuseum.org.uk

Holy Innocents Church, Highnam. A masterpiece of Victorian design and Thomas Parry's monument to his beloved, Isabella. Henry Woodyer (disciple of Pugin), Hardman and Parry completed this in 1851 with no expense spared. Wallpaintings dominate the Nave, the floor with Minton tiles, the exterior with crockets and pinnacles. Open weekends. (B9)

Jet Age Museum, Meteor Business Park, Gloucester Airport. Collection of Gloucester built aircraft with artefacts representing the county's contribution to aviation. Frank Whittle Exhibition. Open W/Es & BHs 10-4. (G7) jetagemuseum.org

Nature in Art Museum

Museum of Gloucester, Brunswick Road. Roman relics, dinosaurs, art exhibitions, treasures of days gone by, a whole panoply of this great county's history. Open Tu-Sa 10-5, Su 11-4. (D9) 01452 396131 museumofgloucester.co.uk

Nature In Art Museum, Wallsworth Hall. The world's first museum dedicated exclusively to Art inspired by Nature. Life-size sculptures in the garden. Artists at work (Feb-Nov). Coffee shop. Play area. Open all year Tu-Su & BHs 10-5. (E7) 01452 731422 natureinart.org.uk

Soldiers of Gloucestershire Museum, The Docks. 300 years' service portrayed by sound effects and life-size models, weapons and uniforms. Open W-Su & Easter 10-4. (D9) 01452 522682 soldiersofglos.com

WHERE TO STAY...

Pinetum Lodge, Churcham. This historic Victorian hunting lodge sits well off the beaten track, situated in 13 acres of woodland garden (otherwise known as a Pinetum) planted by Thomas Gambier Parry in 1844. The owners encourage you to shrug off the city on your arrival, and to surround yourself with nature. (A8) 07798 563536 thepinetum.co.uk

---

LIGHT BITES...MED BITES...ASIAN DELIGHTS...

Head for the Docks where you will find a plethora of cafés close to the entrance to Gloucester Quays shopping arcades. If you seek a more substantial repast, mediterranean delights are to be had at the **Trattoria Settebello** 01452 937655 settebello.co.uk and next door **Greek On The Docks** 01452 524574 greekonthedocks.co.uk

The Italian is a wee bit pricier. Both have Al Fresco dining and overlook the Marina. However, if you seek a rare Asian meal or Takeaway to **Joy Kitchen** must you journey to at: 157 Southgate Street, Gloucester. 01452 923120 joykitchen-gl.co.uk My New York friends from D'Ambrosi of Stow and Chelsea wax lyrical and joyfully of their cuisine.

GLOUCESTER CATHEDRAL

Fan Vaulting, The Cloisters

GLOUCESTER CATHEDRAL

THE CENTRAL WOLDS • Cheltenham, Gloucester, Tewkesbury

TEWKESBURY

One of England's finest medieval towns set at the confluence of the rivers Avon and Severn. Just look up at the gables of the many ancient buildings and admire (or venture into) one of the 30 narrow alleyways that make up this historic place so magnificently brought to life in John Moore's Brensham Trilogy. In the Middle Ages Tewkesbury was a flourishing centre of commerce: flour milling, mustard, brewing, malting, shipping. Today, it has its flourmills and is a centre for boating and tourism. It is still a busy market town of half-timbered buildings, overhanging upper storeys and carved doorways. Following the recent floods the town has a new energy and purpose. Note the new Tourist Information Centre and Out of the Hat Museum which symbolises the ambitions of the Town's elders. (G2)

SPECIAL PLACES OF INTEREST...

Old Baptist Chapel. Reputed to be the first Baptist Chapel in southern England. Restored in 1976. Open daily. (G3)

John Moore Countryside Museum, 41 Church Street. Dedicated to children and all aspects of nature conservation displayed in a C15 timber framed house. Open Apr to Oct Tu & Sa & BHs, 10-1 & 2-5. (G2) 01684 297174
johnmooremuseum.org

Tewkesbury Abbey. Founded in 1087 by the nobleman Robert Fitzhamon. However, the present building was started in 1102 to house Benedictine monks. The Norman abbey was consecrated in 1121. The Nave and roof finished in the C14 in the Decorated style. Much is Early English and Perpendicular, although it is larger than many cathedrals and has according to Pevsner 'the finest Romanesque Tower in England.' The Abbey opens its doors to three major music festivals: Musica Deo Sacra, the Three Choirs Festival and the Cheltenham Music Festival. You can park opposite and take a tour. Info on: 01684 850959 Shop and tearoom. Open daily 8.30-4.30 (G2)
tewkesburyabbey.org.uk

Merchant's House, 45 Church Street. Restored medieval merchant's house. Open Apr to Oct Tu & Sa & BHs 10-1 & 2-5 (G2) 01684 297174

Tewkesbury Museum, Barton Street. Local folk history and heritage centre in stunning black and white timbered building. Open summer Sa-M 11-4, Tu & W 12-3, Th 1-4. (G2) 01684 292901
tewkesburymuseum.org

SPECIAL PLACES OF INTEREST BESIDE THE RIVER SEVERN...

Ashleworth Court. C15 limestone manor with a notable stone newel staircase. Closed to the public. All is overlooked by the tithe barn, next door which can be visited. (D6)

Ashleworth Manor. C15 timber framed and E-shaped. Open by written appointment for parties of eight or more. (C6) 01452 700350

Ashleworth Tithe Barn (NT). This C15 barn has an impressive stone-tile roof and two projecting porch bays. The roof timbers are held together by Queenposts. Open daily all year dawn-dusk. (C6) 01452 814213
nationaltrust.org.uk

Deerhurst (St Mary). C9 Saxon with superb font. (F4)

Deerhurst (Odda's Chapel). One of the few surviving Saxon chapels left in England. Earl Odda dedicated this rare chapel to the Holy Trinity on the 12th April 1056, in memory of his brother. Open daily. (F4)

EAT...DRINK...

The Butchers Arms, Lime Street, Eldersfield. Are you on a quest to discover the perfect pub-grub? A haven of fresh vegetables, beef from a locally reared herd of Hereford cattle. Ale from the Wye Valley. A set menu W-Su & F/Sa luncheon. The Block Family will have you purring with delight. 01452 840381 (C3)
thebutchersarms.net

LIGHT BITES...

I would recommend **Miss Muffets Delicatessen**, next door to **Out of the Hat Museum.** They know their coffee, hot chocolates, and can make up super sandwiches from their chutneys, cheeses and salads. 01684 273593

Left out of here to **The Hide**, 89 Church St., for a light lunch of homemade soup, steak pie, vegan. veggie options, too, or just a pot of tea. Child/dog friendly. Opens from 10 M, W-Su. 01684 290601
thehidecafe.co.uk

Cheltenham, Gloucester, Tewkesbury • **THE CENTRAL WOLDS**

Tewkesbury Abbey following floods and snowfall

MEDIEVAL TEWKESBURY

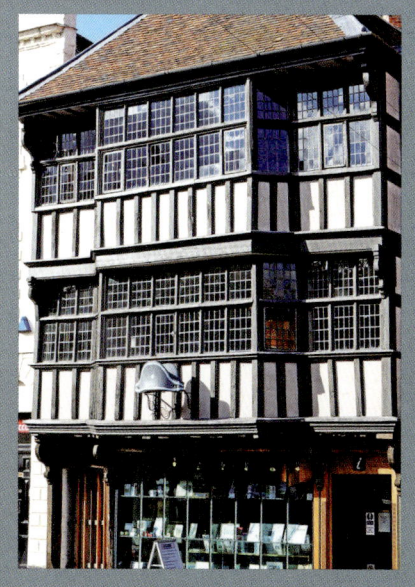

MEDIEVAL TEWKESBURY

172

173

ESTATE AND TITHE BARNS

Bredon Tithe Barn

Tithe Barn, Swalcliffe

Bredon

The tithe barns were built by the Church to store one-tenth of the peasant's (farmer's) produce, known as a tithe. This tax went to support the clergy and church. The estate barns belonged to the Manor or the Court House (see Frocester). Today, these majestic buildings are either used as museums (see Swalcliffe and Cogges Manor) or have been left to gather dust and decay. Unless they have been substantially developed for modern use (see Tetbury Tythe Barn - sic), the barns practical use is not fit for purpose. Bredon Barn is a majestic building, but the aged design allows pigeons to merrily defecate over all below them, so its potential use as a venue for barn dances, parties and weddings has been overlooked.

Both types of barns are a wonderful testament to our agricultural heritage and the Cotswolds has some of the finest examples in Britain and Northern Europe.

Stanway

SAXTON'S MAP 1576

CHRISTOPHERVS SAXTON DESCRIPSIT
AVGVSTINVS RYTHER ANGLVS
SCVLPSIT AN DNI 1577

THE NORTHERN COTSWOLDS

Theatre, festivals, Elgar and Shakespeare, Bredon Hill, poets laments, Cotswold jewels, Blossom Trail...

The Northern Cotswolds incorporates Stratford-on-Avon, the birthplace of England's greatest poet, William Shakespeare, and site of many Shakespearian locations of interest. The area was also the birthplace of England's finest composer – Edward Elgar, who hailed from Lower Broadheath, on the outskirts of Worcester. Perhaps there was, and still is, something in the water!

This area also contains a pair of villages of note which are the jewels in the Cotswold crown: Chipping Campden and Broadway. Chipping Campden is an outstanding example of medieval architecture whilst behind the high walls and hedges of Broadway stand the very epitome of Cotswold domestic architecture

THE NORTHERN COTSWOLDS

Just off the North Cotswold escarpment, the Evesham Vale, a verdant and productive fruit and vegetable farming area with many farm produce stores beside the road. And, in late May you can follow the annual Blossom Trail, a bonanza of colour and new growth.

Bredon Hill is in the centre of the region and is a very beautiful spot. So beautiful, that poets and writers have been moved to describe it in verse and prose. A E Houseman and John Moore wrote poems and novels about this area. The Gloucestershire composer Ralph Vaughan Williams' 'Lark Ascending' could have been inspired from a field atop this hill, for from the peak are stunning views across to the Cotswolds, the Malverns and the distant, Welsh hills.

Broadway Tower

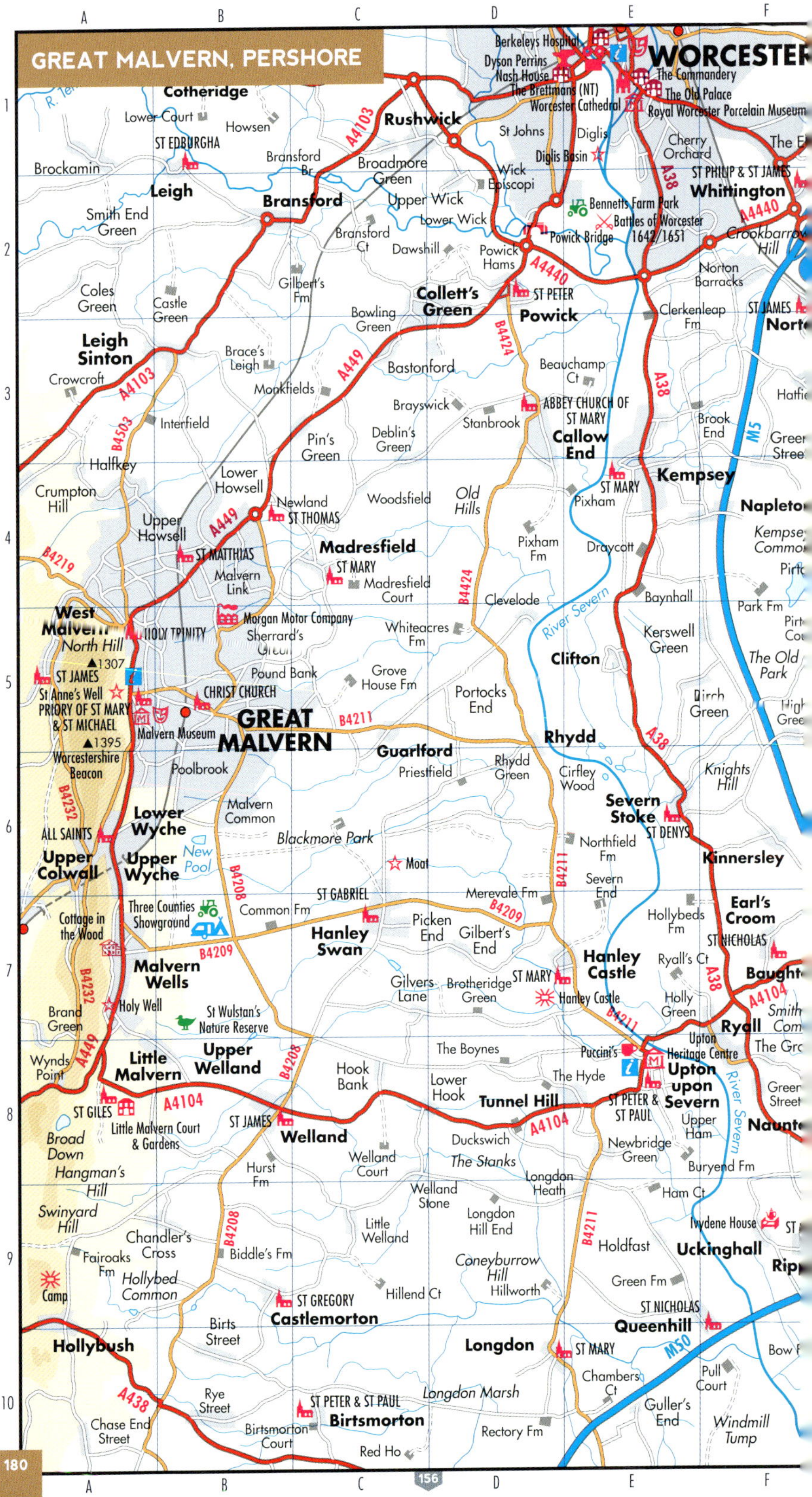
WORCESTER
Berkeleys Hospital
Dyson Perrins
Nash House
The Commandery
The Old Palace
The Brettmans (NT)
Worcester Cathedral
Royal Worcester Porcelain Museum
Cotheridge
R. Teme
Lower Court
Howsen
Rushwick
St Johns
Diglis
Cherry Orchard
ST EDBURGHA
Bransford Br
Broadmore Green
Diglis Basin
Wick Episcopi
Brockamin
ST PHILIP & ST JAMES
Leigh
Bransford
Upper Wick
Whittington
Smith End Green
Lower Wick
Bennetts Farm Park
Battles of Worcester 1642/1651
Bransford Ct
Powick Bridge
Crookbarrow Hill
Dawshill
Powick Hams
Gilbert's Fm
Norton Barracks
Coles Green
Castle Green
Collett's Green
ST PETER
Powick
Clerkenleap Fm
ST JAMES
Norton
Bowling Green
Leigh Sinton
Brace's Leigh
Bastonford
Beauchamp Ct
Crowcroft
Monkfields
Hatfield
Brayswick
ABBEY CHURCH OF ST MARY
Stanbrook
Brook End
Callow End
Interfield
Deblin's Green
Pin's Green
Green Street
Halfkey
Kempsey
Lower Howsell
ST MARY
Crumpton Hill
Newland
Woodsfield
Old Hills
Pixham
Napleton
ST THOMAS
Upper Howsell
Kempsey Common
Pixham Fm
Draycott
Madresfield
ST MATTHIAS
ST MARY
Madresfield Court
Malvern Link
Clevelode
Baynhall
Park Fm
West Malvern
Morgan Motor Company
Whiteacres Fm
River Severn
HOLY TRINITY
Sherrard's Green
Kerswell Green
North Hill
1307
Pound Bank
Grove House Fm
Clifton
The Old Park
ST JAMES
St Anne's Well
CHRIST CHURCH
Portocks End
Birch Green
PRIORY OF ST MARY & ST MICHAEL
GREAT MALVERN
B4211
1395
Malvern Museum
Rhydd
Worcestershire Beacon
Guarlford
Priestfield
Rhydd Green
Cirfley Wood
Knights Hill
Poolbrook
Severn Stoke
Malvern Common
ST DENYS
ALL SAINTS
Lower Wyche
Blackmore Park
Northfield Fm
Upper Colwall
Upper Wyche
New Pool
Moat
Kinnersley
Severn End
ST GABRIEL
Merevale Fm
Three Counties Showground
Common Fm
Hollybeds Fm
Earl's Croome
Cottage in the Wood
Picken End
Gilbert's End
Hanley Swan
ST NICHOLAS
Malvern Wells
Hanley Castle
Ryall's Ct
Gilvers Lane
Brotheridge Green
ST MARY
Holy Well
Holly Green
Brand Green
St Wulstan's Nature Reserve
Ryall
Smith Common
Wynds Point
Little Malvern
Upper Welland
The Boynes
Upton Heritage Centre
Puccini's
The Grove
Hook Bank
Upton upon Severn
Lower Hook
The Hyde
Green Street
ST GILES
Tunnel Hill
ST PETER & ST PAUL
Little Malvern Court & Gardens
ST JAMES
Welland
Upper Ham
Naunton
Broad Down
Duckswich
Newbridge Green
Welland Court
The Stanks
Hurst Fm
Buryend Fm
Hangman's Hill
Longdon Heath
Ham Ct
Welland Stone
Swinyard Hill
Longdon Hill End
Ivydene House
Little Welland
Chandler's Cross
Holdfast
Uckinghall
Fairoaks Fm
Biddle's Fm
Coneyburrow Hill
Hollybed Common
Green Fm
Hillworth
Camp
Hillend Ct
ST GREGORY
ST NICHOLAS
Castlemorton
Queenhill
Birts Street
Hollybush
Longdon
ST MARY
Bow Farm
Chambers Ct
Pull Court
Rye Street
Longdon Marsh
Guller's End
Windmill Tump
ST PETER & ST PAUL
Chase End Street
Birtsmorton
Birtsmorton Court
Rectory Fm
Red Ho
A4103
A449
A4440
A38
A4104
A438
B4424
B4503
B4219
B4232
B4208
B4209
B4211
M5
M50
156
A
B
C
D
E
F
1
2
3
4
5
6
7
8
9
10

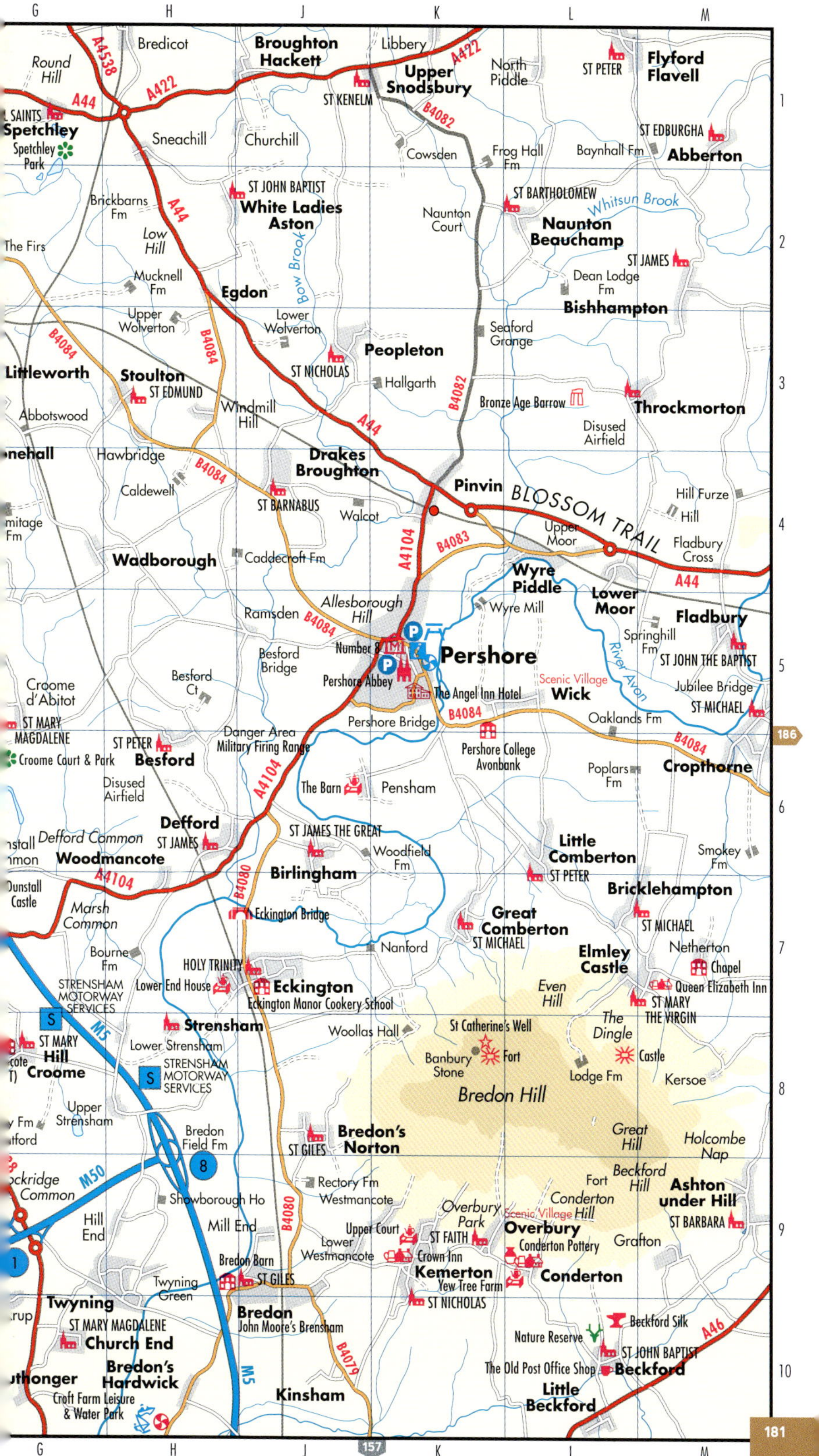
G
H
J
K
L
M
1
2
3
4
5
6
7
8
9
10
Round Hill
Bredicot
Broughton Hackett
Libbery
Upper Snodsbury
North Piddle
ST PETER
Flyford Flavell
A4538
A44
A422
ST KENELM
B4082
SAINTS
Spetchley
Spetchley Park
Sneachill
Churchill
Cowsden
Frog Hall Fm
Baynhall Fm
ST EDBURGHA
Abberton
ST JOHN BAPTIST
White Ladies Aston
Brickbarns Fm
Naunton Court
ST BARTHOLOMEW
Whitsun Brook
Naunton Beauchamp
Low Hill
The Firs
Bow Brook
ST JAMES
Mucknell Fm
Egdon
Dean Lodge Fm
Bishhampton
Upper Wolverton
Lower Wolverton
Seaford Grange
B4084
Peopleton
Littleworth
Stoulton
ST EDMUND
ST NICHOLAS
Hallgarth
Bronze Age Barrow
Throckmorton
Abbotswood
Windmill Hill
Disused Airfield
nehall
Hawbridge
Drakes Broughton
Caldewell
Pinvin
BLOSSOM TRAIL
ST BARNABUS
Walcot
Hill Furze
Hill
mitage Fm
Upper Moor
Fladbury Cross
A4104
B4083
Wadborough
Caddecroft Fm
Wyre Piddle
Lower Moor
Wyre Mill
Allesborough Hill
Ramsden
Fladbury
Springhill Fm
River Avon
Number 8
Pershore
ST JOHN THE BAPTIST
Besford Bridge
Besford Ct
Pershore Abbey
Scenic Village
Wick
Jubilee Bridge
Croome d'Abitot
The Angel Inn Hotel
ST MICHAEL
ST MARY MAGDALENE
Pershore Bridge
Oaklands Fm
Danger Area Military Firing Range
Pershore College Avonbank
ST PETER
Besford
Croome Court & Park
Poplars Fm
Cropthorne
Disused Airfield
The Barn
Pensham
Defford
Defford Common
ST JAMES THE GREAT
stall
mon
ST JAMES
Woodfield Fm
Little Comberton
Smokey Fm
Woodmancote
Birlingham
ST PETER
Bricklehampton
Dunstall Castle
B4080
Marsh Common
Eckington Bridge
Great Comberton
ST MICHAEL
Bourne Fm
Nanford
Elmley Castle
Netherton
Chapel
HOLY TRINITY
STRENSHAM MOTORWAY SERVICES
Lower End House
Eckington
Even Hill
Queen Elizabeth Inn
Eckington Manor Cookery School
ST MARY THE VIRGIN
The Dingle
S
M5
Strensham
Woollas Hall
St Catherine's Well
ST MARY
Hill Croome
Lower Strensham
Banbury Stone
Fort
Castle
cote
STRENSHAM MOTORWAY SERVICES
Lodge Fm
Kersoe
Bredon Hill
Upper Strensham
Fm
tford
Bredon Field Fm
Great Hill
Holcombe Nap
Bredon's Norton
ST GILES
8
M50
ckridge Common
Rectory Fm
Westmancote
Fort
Beckford Hill
Ashton under Hill
Showborough Ho
Overbury Park
Scenic Village
Conderton Hill
Hill End
Mill End
Upper Court
ST FAITH
Overbury
ST BARBARA
Lower Westmancote
Conderton Pottery
Grafton
1
Bredon Barn
Crown Inn
Twyning Green
ST GILES
Kemerton
Yew Tree Farm
Conderton
Twyning
Bredon
John Moore's Brensham
ST NICHOLAS
rup
ST MARY MAGDALENE
Beckford Silk
Church End
B4079
Nature Reserve
ST JOHN BAPTIST
A46
Bredon's Hardwick
The Old Post Office Shop
Beckford
uthonger
M5
Little Beckford
Croft Farm Leisure & Water Park
Kinsham
186
157

THE NORTHERN COTSWOLDS • Great Malvern, Pershore

GREAT MALVERN

Pull the word Malvern out of a hat and what does its name conjure up? Edward Elgar, education, festivals, open-top sports cars, spring water, stained glass, walking holidays...quite a diverse spectrum of interests. There has been a settlement here since Iron Age man built forts at the British Camp on Herefordshire Beacon and on the southern tip at Midsummer Hill. Work began on the Priory in the C11 and continued well into the C16. But, it was not until a Dr Wall promoted 'Taking The Waters' that Malvern developed as a spa town in 1756. The town's true popularity took shape when the Baths and Pump Room opened in the 1820s. It even attracted the desperate Charles Darwin to bring his beloved ten-year old daughter Annie here for a cure. She had developed scarlet fever and possibly tuberculosis. She died and was buried in the Priory's churchyard. Her death had a profound and lasting effect on Darwin's attitude and philosophy.

It remains a popular walking centre and once up on the hill there are fine views across to Wales, the Severn Vale and the Cotswolds. The healthy rigour of the town encouraged the Victorians to open schools for both sexes. Even George Bernard Shaw visited and help co-found the Theatre. The busy calendar of events is made up of various arts festivals: Elgar, Fringe, Music, Three Counties. The show goes on. Be prepared for some steep climbs - take comfy footwear. There are a number of coffee shops and delis on the main street below the Elgar statue. C15 Priory Church with famous medieval stained glass and tiles. (B5)

SPECIAL PLACES OF INTEREST...

Croome Court & Park (NT). A mid-C18 Neo-Palladian mansion surrounded by 'Capability' Brown's first significant landscape project for the 6th Earl of Coventry. The Park has a man-made lake and river, as well as Gatehouses, Grotto and Church. A major restoration plan of dredging and replanting the Lake Garden took place. The Court's interior was partially designed by Brown and Robert Adam with plasterwork by G Vassalli. The Walled Garden has been restored under separate ownership. The secretive WW11 RAF Defford is now the Visitor Centre. Open daily all year 11-5. (G6) 01905 371006 nationaltrust.org.uk

Little Malvern Court & Gardens. Former Benedictine monastery. Home of the Russell and Berington families since the Dissolution. Priors Hall with needlework, family and European furniture and paintings. 10 acre garden; spring bulbs, rose garden and views. Open late April to late July W & Th only 2-5. (A8) 01684 892988 littlemalverncourt.co.uk

LIGHT BITES...

Seek out the entrance to **The Priory,** and on the corner before you is **Abbey Road Café** where you can have breakfast, a light lunch and afternoon teas. Opens M-Sa 7.30-6.30, Su 8-5.

Up the steps and over the road is the **Mulberry Tree,** 50 Bellevue Terrace. A friendly and pleasant restaurant and bar, and civilised pit stop before you tackle the Malvern Hills. Opens for Brunch, lunch and dinner. 01684 561837 (A7) mulberrytree.co

Malvern Hills. A superb viewpoint. 6 paths and more criss-cross these hills. The highest point is Worcestershire Beacon at 1,394 feet. (A5)

Malvern Hill's Ancient Settlements. A natural location for Early Man; Herefordshire Beacon is the site of the Iron Age, British Camp. At the southern end is the monument and fort, Midsummer Hill. Superb views. (A5)

Morgan Motor Company. Morgan is the iconic British sports car and in its 112-year history was family owned with a community of 5,000 owners.

Morgan Car

---

182 | 1890 Cotswold Lion Sheep considered by Harmon to be the hardiest of English breeds | 1892 The Cotswold Sheep Society is formed

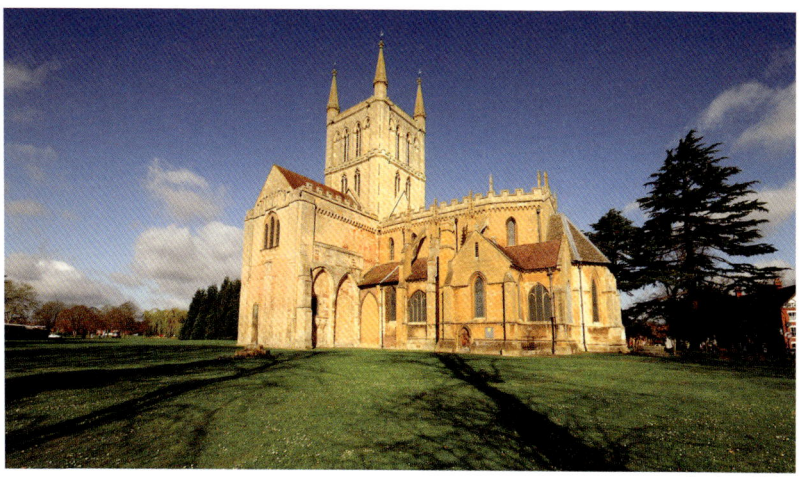

Great Malvern, Pershore • **THE NORTHERN COTSWOLDS**

Pershore Abbey

It was recently taken over by an Italian venture capital group to develop the brand. You can take a factory tour M-Sa, pre-book on 01684 573104 (B4) morgan-motor.com

Spetchley Park. The Berkeley family home for 400 years who have lovingly planted acres of rare and unusual trees and shrubs from all over the World. Open Mar to Oct W-Su & BH Ms 10.30-5, Oct W/Es 10.30-4. Special Weeks to view the exceptional collection. (G1) 01905 345106 spetchleyparkestate.co.uk

EAT... DRINK... SLEEP...

The Cottage in The Wood, Holywell Rd. Superb hillside location with panoramic views across the Severn Vale towards the Cotswold Hills. Walks from hotel onto the Malvern Hills. A boutique-style hotel that is elegant, chilled and comfortable. Child/dog friendly. (A7) 01684 588260 cottageinthewood.co.uk

PERSHORE

A very attractive market town known for its plums and elegant Georgian buildings.

The Abbey was founded c.689, and established in the late C10 by the Benedictine monks who later built the six-arched bridge across the River Avon. Plentiful supply of independent shops, cafés and delis. (K5)

SPECIAL PLACES OF INTEREST...

Number 8, High Street. This is Pershore's community centre for the arts: Cinema, Theatre and Gallery. It holds live events, creative courses for adults and children. Coffee shop. Open daily. (K5) Box office: 01386 555488 number8.org

Pershore Abbey. Established in the late C10 by Benedictines. C14 tower and the superb vaulting of the Prestbytery, remain. Beautiful Early English Choir, but sadly much was destroyed by Henry VIII. Visitor Centre open summer weekends. Look out for the intricate wooden sculpture in the grounds. Open daily 8-5.30. (K5) 01386 552071 pershoreabbey.org.uk

Eckington Manor Cookery School, Manor Road, Eckington. This is a cookery school with state of the art facilities and a team of passionate tutors who use fresh, locally sourced seasonal ingredients, and much more. The accommodation is run separately from the school and restaurant. One of the oldest houses in Worcestershire; a period house full of character, renovated with the emphasis on quality and style. Hence, the luxurious bedrooms. Perfectly located for walking on the nearby Bredon or Malvern Hills. (J7) 01386 751600 eckingtonmanorcookeryschool.co.uk

LIGHT BITES...

For those who wish to improve their lifestyle a visit to **SIP Coffeehouse & Patisserie at 24 High St.** may well fit the bill. Open M-Sa 10-4. Smart cakes, smart gear and cocktails served in their garden come summer sundown.

If you seek breakfast, porridge, a takeaway toastie and coffee, down the street to **Baristas** opposite the car park.

THE NORTHERN COTSWOLDS • Great Malvern, Pershore

Beckford Silk. Hand printers of silk, with silk store, digital print room, hand print rooms, dye kitchen and tenter room. Open M-F 9-4 (Coffee shop for light meals Tu-Sa, 10-4). (L10) 01386 881507 beckfordsilk.co.uk

EAT... DRINK...SLEEP...

Benvenuti, Belle House, Bridge Street. There are a number of good reasons to visit. The exterior and interior architecture, the Italian restaurant's mouth-watering fare and a restaurant run with great enthusiasm and good manners. Set luncheon menu. Open daily from 12. (K5) 01386 426772
benveniutbellehouse.co.uk

The Angel Inn Hotel, High Street. Refurbished inn marries period detail with contemporary décor in a stylish format. Special weekend breaks with coffee, lunch and dinner for two. (K5) 01386 552046
theangelpershore.co.uk

OUTSIDE PERSHORE...

The Barn B&B, Pensham. A large and spacious barn ideally suited for a large family or group. No dogs or children U-12. (J6) 01386 555270
pensham-barn.co.uk

UPTON-UPON-SEVERN

An attractive town beside the River Severn that has been an important river crossing and route centre for centuries. There's profusion of medieval buildings and hostelries. The 2007 floods left a devastating mark on the town, so much so, that many inns were closed for 12 months. It is cettainly worth a visit, for apart from the profusion of inns, the shops are independents which makes the High Street of interest to window-shoppers. A visit to the International Map Shop may endear you to further adventures. (E8)

Upton Heritage (& Information) Centre. History of the town, and the River Severn's activities. Civil War connections. Open daily. (E8) 01684 592679

SPECIAL PLACES OF INTEREST...BREDON HILL & VILLAGES

A circumnavigation of Bredon Hill is a fine introduction to the beautiful villages of Kemerton, Overbury, Conderton, Ashton-under-Hill and Elmley Castle. A lovely mixture of Cotswold stone, and black-and-white timbered buildings with many fine Inns, and peaceful churchyards. Various footpaths lead up to the summit from Elmley and Kemerton. Superb views from this isolated limestone hill at 961 ft. (K8)

Bredon Barn (NT). A beautifully constructed large medieval threshing barn extending to 132 feet. Expertly restored after fire. Temporarily closed. (H9) 01452 814213
nationaltrust.org.uk

Bredon Hill Fort. Iron Age fort with two ramparts. Scene of great battle at time of Christ, possibly against the Belgic invaders. The hacked remains of 50 men were found near entrance. Superb views over to Wales, Vale of Evesham, the rivers Severn and Avon, and to the Cotswolds. (K8)

| 1898 | The Whiteway Colony is established | 1898 | Arthur Gibbs of Ablington Manor publishes A Cotswold Village |

Great Malvern, Pershore • **THE NORTHERN COTSWOLDS**

LIGHT BITES...

I first head to **The Shack** where a warm welcome and coffee aromas set the scene. Opens for breakfast, toasties and their homemade soups will tempt you. Playroom and Chill Out Garden. (E8)

In need of ale, **The Kings Head** is an option. It overlooks the river. Good pub-grub. It could be the start of a pub crawl? Some locals recommend **The White Lion**. An amazing Signatory over the doorway but a bit out of date for my taste.

Conderton Pottery. Distinctive stoneware pots by specialist saltglazed country potter, Toff Milway. Open M-Sa 9-5. (L9) 01386 725387 toffmilway.co.uk

Croft Farm Leisure & Water Park. Bredons Hardwick. Lake and river fishing, camping and glamping pods, water sports tuition and supervised health centre (Gym & Tonic). Café. Open daily 9-5 (H10) 01684 772321 croftfarmwaterpark.com

Eckington Bridge. Built between the C16 and C17s. A car park beside the river with a map board detailing a circular walk. (H7)

EAT... DRINK... SLEEP...

Meadows Home Farm B&B, Bredons Norton. Family run working farm in a quiet setting. One ensuite double bedroom and one ensuite room with a double and a single bed. Garden and patio area, TV lounge, ample parking. Farm shop and cottage to rent. 01684 772322 meadowshomefarm.co.uk

The Queen Elizabeth Inn, Elmley Castle. 16th Century (community run) Inn serving breakfast, lunch and dinner; pub-grub and local ales. (M7) 01386 710251 elmleycastle.com Within is the **The Polka Dot Tearoom**, serving cup cakes, teas and coffees.

The Star Inn, Ashton-under-Hill. Perfect rest stop for walkers. Children and dogs welcome. Large garden. Delicious home-cooked food to eat in or takeaway. 01386 881325 thestar-ashtonunderhill.co.uk

The Old Post Office, Beckford. A worthy pit stop for their grilled open sandwiches, pizzas and rolls. Out back a plethora of antiques, reclamation, local arts and crafts, an emporia of garden furnishings. Open daily 9-4. (L10) beckfordcoffeeshop.co.uk

Upper Court, Kemerton. Self-catering within a very grand house. Minimum stay for 2 nights. 0333 3355246 uppercourt.co.uk

Yew Tree Inn, Conderton. One of the most popular local pubs around Bredon Hill. Conveniently situated for pre- or post-walk, refreshments. Basic pub grub. (L9) 01386 725364 yewtreepub.com

Overbury Court, Overbury

1899 — J M Barrie (of Peter Pan fame) visits Stanway House and designs the cricket pavilion

1902 — Sir Edward Lutyens builds Abbotswood

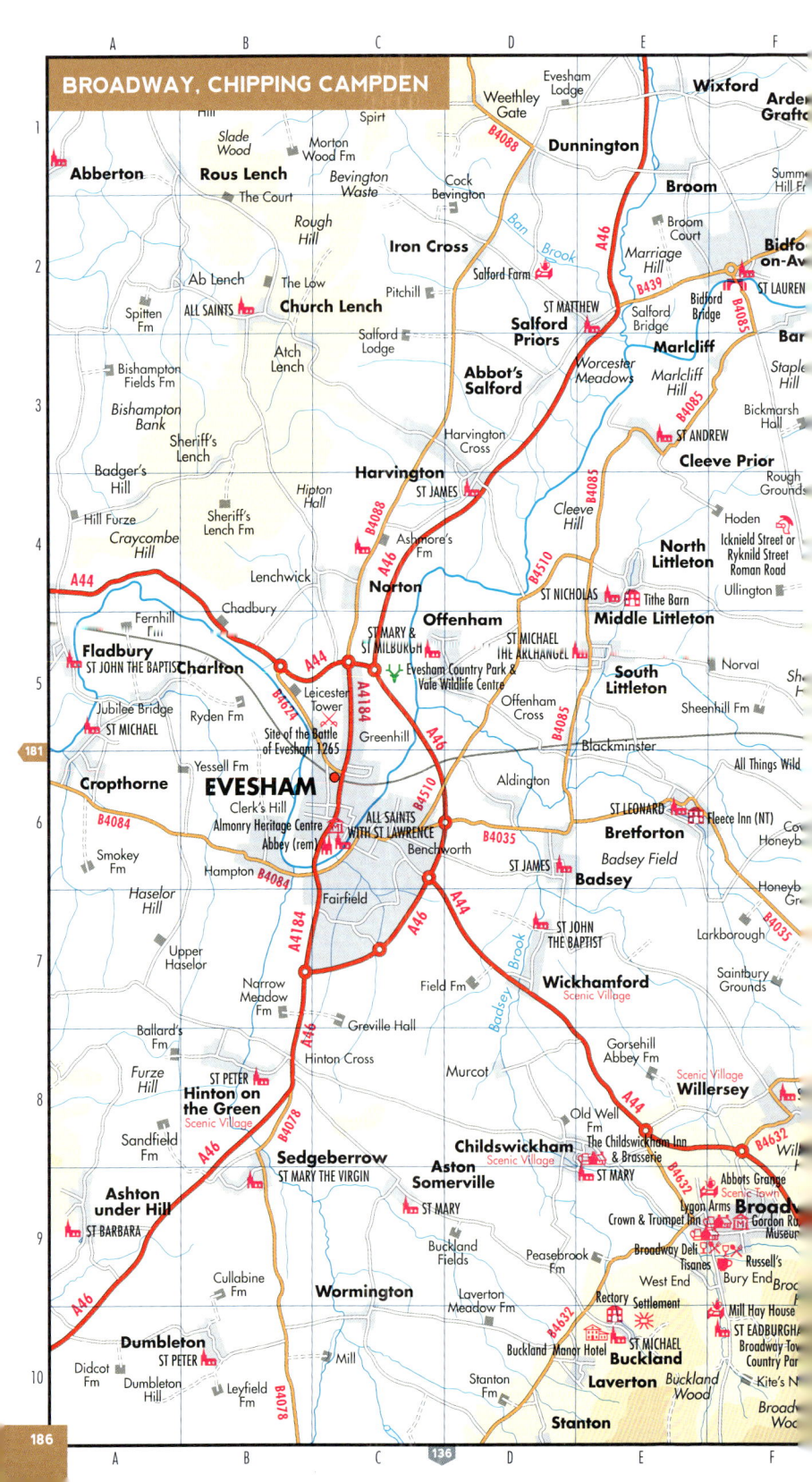

BROADWAY, CHIPPING CAMPDEN

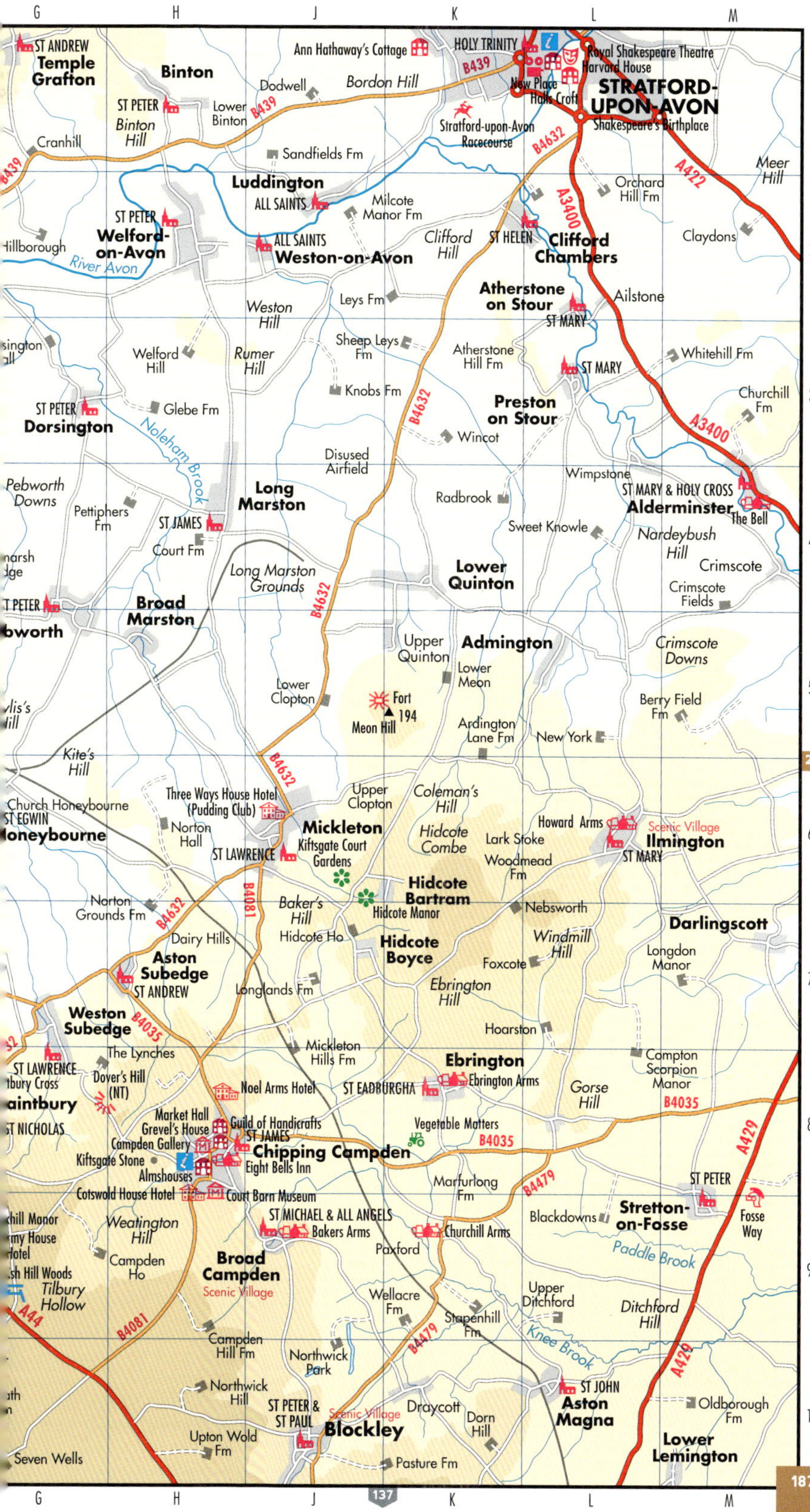
G
H
J
K
L
M
1
2
3
4
5
6
7
8
9
10
ST ANDREW
Temple Grafton
Binton
ST PETER
Binton Hill
Lower Binton
B439
Dodwell
Bordon Hill
Ann Hathaway's Cottage
HOLY TRINITY
Royal Shakespeare Theatre
Harvard House
New Place
Halls Croft
STRATFORD-UPON-AVON
Shakespeare's Birthplace
Stratford-upon-Avon Racecourse
B4632
Cranhill
Sandfields Fm
Luddington
ALL SAINTS
Milcote Manor Fm
A422
Meer Hill
Orchard Hill Fm
A3400
ST PETER
Welford-on-Avon
Hillborough
River Avon
ALL SAINTS
Weston-on-Avon
Clifford Hill
ST HELEN
Clifford Chambers
Claydons
Atherstone on Stour
ST MARY
Ailstone
Leys Fm
Weston Hill
Sheep Leys Fm
Welford Hill
Rumer Hill
Atherstone Hill Fm
ST MARY
Whitehill Fm
Knobs Fm
ST PETER
Dorsington
Glebe Fm
Noleham Brook
Preston on Stour
Churchill Fm
Wincot
Disused Airfield
Wimpstone
Pebworth Downs
Pettiphers Fm
Long Marston
Radbrook
ST MARY & HOLY CROSS
Alderminster
The Bell
ST JAMES
Court Fm
Sweet Knowle
Nardeybush Hill
Crimscote
Long Marston Grounds
Lower Quinton
Crimscote Fields
Broad Marston
Upper Quinton
Admington
Crimscote Downs
Lower Meon
Lower Clopton
Fort
194
Meon Hill
Ardington Lane Fm
New York
Berry Field Fm
Kite's Hill
Church Honeybourne
ST EGWIN
Three Ways House Hotel (Pudding Club)
Norton Hall
Upper Clopton
Coleman's Hill
Mickleton
Kiftsgate Court Gardens
ST LAWRENCE
Hidcote Combe
Lark Stoke
Howard Arms
Scenic Village
Ilmington
ST MARY
Woodmead Fm
B4081
Norton Grounds Fm
Baker's Hill
Hidcote Bartram
Hidcote Manor
Nebsworth
Darlingscott
Dairy Hills
Aston Subedge
ST ANDREW
Hidcote Ho
Hidcote Boyce
Windmill Hill
Foxcote
Longdon Manor
Longlands Fm
Ebrington Hill
Weston Subedge
B4035
Hoarston
The Lynches
ST LAWRENCE
Dover's Hill (NT)
Mickleton Hills Fm
Ebrington
Compton Scorpion Manor
Noel Arms Hotel
ST EADBURGHA
Ebrington Arms
Gorse Hill
Market Hall
Grevel's House
Guild of Handicrafts
ST JAMES
Campden Gallery
Chipping Campden
Eight Bells Inn
Kiftsgate Stone
Almshouses
Vegetable Matters
A429
Cotswold House Hotel
Court Barn Museum
Marfurlong Fm
B4479
ST PETER
Weatington Hill
ST MICHAEL & ALL ANGELS
Bakers Arms
Churchill Arms
Blackdowns
Stretton-on-Fosse
Fosse Way
Paxford
Paddle Brook
Campden Ho
Broad Campden
Scenic Village
Tilbury Hollow
A44
Wellacre Fm
Upper Ditchford
Ditchford Hill
Stapenhill Fm
Knee Brook
Campden Hill Fm
Northwick Park
ST JOHN
Aston Magna
Northwick Hill
ST PETER & ST PAUL
Scenic Village
Blockley
Draycott
Dorn Hill
Oldborough Fm
Upton Wold Fm
Lower Lemington
Pasture Fm
Seven Wells
204
137

THE NORTHERN COTSWOLDS • Broadway, Chipping Campden

Row of Cottages

Broadway Tower Walk

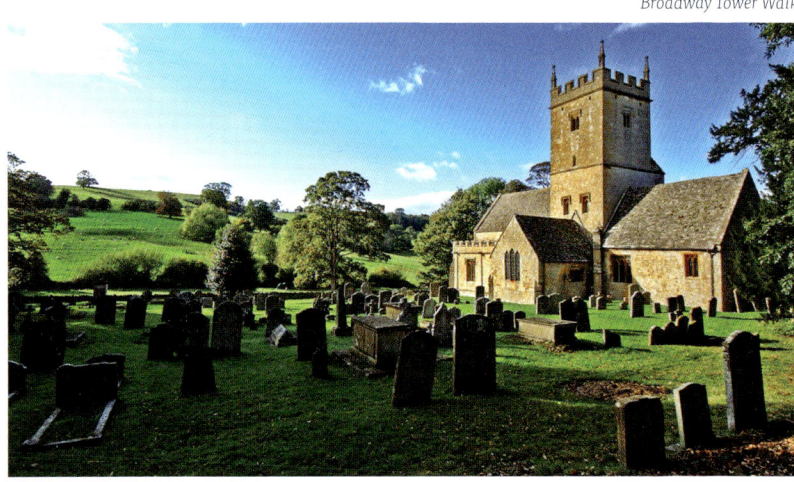

St Eadburgh's Churchyard

| 188 | 1902 | C R Ashbee sets up the Guild of Handicrafts in Chipping Campden by moving his 50 members from London | 1904 | Baker's the Jewellers shop front is built featuring Father Time and John Bull |

Broadway, Chipping Campden • THE NORTHERN COTSWOLDS

BROADWAY

'The Painted Lady of the Cotswolds' is a term often used to describe this beautiful village. The honey-coloured stone captivates the visitor today, as it did in the C19, when William Morris and his pre-Raphaelite friends settled here. A slow walk up the High Street will unfold some large, and impressive houses, former homes to Edward Elgar, JM Barrie (Peter Pan), Ralph Vaughan Williams, Sir Gerald Navarro MP and Laura Ashley's daughter. These great houses with bow windows, dormers and finely graduated stone roofs are usually hidden behind statuesque gates. There are a number of fine hotels, restaurants, tearooms, art galleries and a fine bookshop. (F9)

SPECIAL PLACES OF INTEREST…

Broadway Museum & Art Gallery, 65 High Street. Exhibits on display over 3-floors include decorative art from the C17-C21; paintings by Gainsborough and Millais, Armorial ceramics, and Sheldon tapestries. Much was donated to the University of Oxford in 1683, by Elias Ashmore. Open daily 10-4.30 (F9) 01386 859047
broadmuseum.org.uk

Broadway Tower Country Park. A unique Cotswold attraction: an C18 folly tower with historical and geographical exhibitions. Country retreat of the pre-Raphaelite, William Morris. Breeders of red deer with nature walks, Morris & Brown Café with quality giftshop. Superb views from the top of the Tower - a clear day gives a view of 12 counties. Nuclear Bunker open Apr-Oct W/Es & BHs 10-4.45. E-bike hire and new Visitor Centre in Tower Barn 10-4.30. The M & B Café opens from 9-5 & the Tower 10-5, all year. (F10) 01386 852390
broadwaytower.co.uk

Buckland Church, St Michaels. An exquisite church preserved with an almost undisturbed history from the C13 to the C17. Beautiful roof: painted and wood panelled. C14 tower with gargoyles. C15 stained glass in East window restored by William Morris. Not to be missed, the Wainscotting: medieval wooden benches along the far wall as you enter. The Hazel Bowl made in 1607 of Dutch maple with a silver rim. The Buckland Pall, C15 embroidered vestments from the V&A, London. Sadly, the medieval frescoes were removed by the restorer FS Waller in 1885. (E10)

Buckland Rectory. The oldest, and most complete rectory in the county. Notable Great Hall with timbered roof. Open occasionally for village events. (E10)

Fish Hill Woods. Attractive woodland providing superb views. (G9)

Gordon Russell Museum, 15 Russell Square. A collection spanning 60 years that is dedicated to one of the C20s finest furniture designers. With original design drawings and furniture embracing the 'Arts & Crafts' movement. Open Tu-Su & BH Ms 10-4 (F9) 01386 854695
gordonrussellmuseum.org

Haynes Fine Art, 42 High Street. One of the Cotswold's and England's finest galleries established in 1971 specialises in C19-20 Masters: paintings, sculpture and furniture. Open daily. (F9) 01386 852649
haynesfineart.com

St Eadburgh's Church. A rare architectural gem of almost perfect proportions with a mix of C12-C18 additions. Superb brass work, topiary in churchyard, interesting tombstones and a welcome retreat from the hustle and bustle of Broadway. (F10)

Trinity House Paintings, 35 High Street. Modern British Paintings are their speciality; Dame Laura Knight, Donald McIntyre, Edward Seago, amongst others. All from £2,000. Open daily. (F9) 01386 859329
trinityhousepaintings.com

High Street, Broadway

| 1907 | Major Laurence Johnstone begins the construction of Hidcote Manor Gardens | 1908 | W H Davies' Autobiography of a Super-Tramp is published | 189 |

THE NORTHERN COTSWOLDS • Broadway, Chipping Campden

Buckland Manor ss

EAT...DRINK...SLEEP...

Abbots Grange B&B, Church Street. If you seek one of the most romantic hideaways in the Cotswolds this may well fulfill your expectations. Step back in time to Medieval England to a Manor House built c. 1320 but with the comforts of the C21. 4-poster beds, log fires, Great Hall, croquet lawn, tennis court, parkland, rose gardens and heli-pad. A mere 2-3 minutes walk to the village. Breakfast, no Dinner. (F9) 020813 38698 abbotsgrange.com

Buckland Manor Hotel. The benchmark for the Country House Hotel: formal, quiet,

Bar & Grill 1, Lygon Arms ss

| 1909 | Henry F S Morgan founds the Morgan Motor Company | 1912 | Death of Edward Wilson on Scott's ill-fated Antarctic expedition |

Broadway, Chipping Campden • THE NORTHERN COTSWOLDS

LIGHT BITES...

On entering Broadway from the south along the Cotswold Way you will spy the **Crown & Trumpet Inn.** A necessary pit stop after a hard slog across the hills. You may be persuaded to stay (B&B) for the monthly jazz and blues nights. (F9) 01386 853202.

Then onwards to The Green, perhaps enter the **Broadway Hotel** for a relaxed and comfortable pint of ale, moving onto the RH pavement there is **Tisanes, 21 The Green.** A friendly tea room with garden set in a C17 Cotswold stone building full of charm. Homemade cakes. (F9) 01386 853296

Further up the High Street on your R, **Broadway Deli at No.16.** You can't miss it; the fruits and veg outside and once inside you will salivate at their mouth-watering cakes, pastries and pies. Open for breakfast at 8, brunch all day, lunch 12-4. (F9) 01386 853040 broadwaydeli.co.uk

Further up the Street, **Market Pie** for an alternate choice. If you seek a yearning for the grape, then turn down Kennel Lane for a glass, or two, of Champagne, Chardonnay, Pinot Noir at the **Broadway Wine Co.** Open M-Sa 10-5 where you can sit outside and smoke a cheroot. Further up the High Street, beyond Landmark is the **Hunters Restaurant and Tearoom** for a more conventional repast. If you hunger for a Stonebaked Pizza, a Sirloin Steak or Tapas, cross the road to **Number 32.** But, if you demand a grand location for afternoon tea, try the **Lygon Arms**, 2-5pm, where you can soak up some history, admire their recent refurbishments and wonder what happened to all their earlier, fine furniture?

understated luxury set within a 10-acre garden of sweeping lawns amidst stunning countryside. A lovely, modest-minded contrast to the ephemeral boutique hotel; oak-panelled walls, oil paintings, porcelain, antiques and traditional fireplaces with roaring log fires and discreet staff on hand. A formal dress code for dinner. Displays of flowers in abundance. Open all year. (E10) 01386 852626 bucklandmanor.co.uk

Dormy House Hotel & Spa, Willersey Hill. C17 farmhouse converted into a comfortable hotel with a multitude of leisure facilities. Adjacent, an 18-hole golf course. Popular dining room and barn owl bar. (G9) 01386 852711 dormyhouse.co.uk

Foxhill Manor. The old, (traditional architecture) meets the new, (bespoke baths, and beds) in a titanic clash that will seduce all those seeking a hedonistic break. Your very own private Cotswold retreat. Only 8-luxurious rooms. Butler service. 01386 854200 foxhillmanor.com And down a swirling drive you come to **The Fish** an exclusive up-market style of centre-parc. 01386 858000 thefishhotel.co.uk All part of the Farncombe Estate.

Lygon Arms. This former coaching inn of renown, has recently been re-branded into a luxurious Spa, and Country House Hotel. The centrepiece is the Great Hall with imposing barrel-vaulted ceiling, C17 Minstrel's Gallery, suits of armour and oak panels, and off the hall are cosy lounges with log fires and deep armchairs. Many additional, contemporary rooms, but when you book ask for a traditional bedroom. (F9) 01386 852255 lygonarmshotel.co.uk

Mill Hay House. An imposing Queen Anne house provides sophistication and luxurious B&B on the outskirts of Broadway. Beautiful garden. No children U-12. No dogs. Associated with Broadway Tower. (F9) 01386 852498 millhay.co.uk

Mount Pleasant Farm, Childswickham. 900 acre mixed family farm in a quiet rural area with stunning views from all of the en-suite bedrooms. Traditional farmhouse English breakfast. B&B and holiday cottages. 01386 853424 mountpleasantfarmbroadway.co.uk

Olive Branch Guest House, 78 High Street. A B&B of long standing, and one that has traded for 50 + years. It is convenient, comfortable and often doing great deals for 2/3 day breaks. 01386 853440 theolivebranch-broadway.com

Russell's, 20 High Street. This has gained quite a reputation, as a great place to eat in the North Cotswolds. So, feast on their food, then settle into one of their contemporary, comfy bedrooms with all the latest mod cons, and indulge yourselves. (F9) 01386 853555 russellsofbroadway.co.uk Fish and chips, behind.

THE NORTHERN COTSWOLDS • Broadway, Chipping Campden

CHIPPING CAMPDEN

If you choose to visit just one Cotswold village, make sure it's this one. There is no better introduction. The harmony of Cotswold stone mirrors the town's prosperity in the Middle Ages. The Gabled Market Hall was built in 1627 by the wealthy landowner Sir Baptist Hicks, whose mansion was burnt down in the Civil War, and the remains are the two lodges beside the Church. The Church of St James is a tall and statuesque 'Wool' church. William Grevel, one of the wealthiest wool merchants, is remembered in the church on a brass transcription which reads: 'the flower of the wool merchants of all England.' Opposite his house (Grevel's House) on the High Street, the Woolstaplers Hall, the meeting place for the fleece (staple) merchants. The Dovers Cotswold Olympick Games & Scuttlebrook Wake is held in June. (H8)

SPECIAL PLACES OF INTEREST...

Almshouses. You will pass these on your left as you make your way toward the parish church. Built about the same time as the Market Hall (in 1627) by the town's wealthy benefactor, Sir Baptist Hicks. (H8)

| 1924 | Edward Elgar made Master of the King's Music | 1926 | Shakespeare Memorial Theatre is destroyed by fire |

Broadway, Chipping Campden • **THE NORTHERN COTSWOLDS**

Almshouses, Chipping Campden

Campden Gallery, High Street. One of the most respected of Cotswold galleries has constant changing exhibitions of paintings, sculpture and prints. Open Tu-Sa 10-5. (H8) 01386 841555 campdengallery.co.uk

Court Barn Museum. A celebration of the town's association with the Arts & Crafts Movement. An exhibition of silver, jewellery ceramics, sculpture, industrial design and more, all beautifully set up by the Guild of Handicraft Trust. Open Apr-Sept Tu-Su 10-5, Oct-Mar Tu-Su 10-4. (H8) 01386 841951 courtbarn.org.uk

Cotswold Way. A long distance footpath covering 97 miles from Chipping Campden to Bath. It follows the edge of the escarpment, meanders through picturesque villages, past pre-historic sites and provides spectacular views. It is signposted. For short excursions set out from Cleeve Hill, Winchcombe, Broadway, Painswick, Coaley Peak or Brackenbury Ditches. (H8) cotswold-way.co.uk

Dover's Hill. A natural amphitheatre on a spur of the Cotswolds with magnificent views over the Vale of Evesham. The *Olympick Games & Scuttlebrook Wake* have been

| 1928 | Christians settle in Cranham Woods | 1928 | Benedictine monks acquire Prinknash Abbey |

THE NORTHERN COTSWOLDS • Broadway, Chipping Campden

Kiftgate Court Garden ss

Hidcote Manor Garden

Broadway, Chipping Campden • **THE NORTHERN COTSWOLDS**

held here since 1612, and take place on the Friday and Saturday, following the Spring Bank Holiday. (G8)

Grevel's House. Built by the wealthy wool merchant, William Grevel: 'The flower of the Wool Merchants of England.' The house has intricately decorated windows, gargoyles and a sundial. (H8)

Guild of Handicraft and The Gallery@The Guild - The Old Silk Mill. Founded in 1888 as part of the 'Arts & Crafts' movement. The Harts gold and silversmith workshops (open Tu-Su) remain in situ and the Gallery@The Guild is a co-operative of artists and craftspeople. Open daily, all year. Coffee shop 10-4. (H8) 01386 840345
thegalleryattheguild.co.uk

Hidcote Manor Garden (NT). One of the finest gardens of the C20 designed by Major Lawrence Johnston in the 'Arts & Crafts' style. It is made up of garden rooms with rare trees, shrubs, herbaceous borders and 'old' roses. The all-weather court has recently been restored. Barn café, plant sale and restaurant. Open daily 10-6, winter times vary. (J6) For other (more complex) times phone 01386 438333
nationaltrust.org.uk

Kiftsgate Court Garden. Rare shrubs, plants, and an exceptional collection of roses in a magnificent situation. Water Garden. Plants for sale. Tearoom. Open Apr & Sept Su, M & W. April 2-6, May-Aug also Th & Sa, Sept 12-6. (J6) 01386 438777 kiftsgate.co.uk

Market Hall. This iconic image of Chipping Campden was funded by Sir Baptist Hicks (merchant banker) in 1627, for the sale of cheese and butter. It is Jacobean, with pointed gables. (H8)

Autumn Sunshine, Seymour House, Chipping Campden

THE NORTHERN COTSWOLDS • Broadway, Chipping Campden

LIGHT BITES...

On entering the High Street you may be inclined for a glass of Prosecco, an Earl Grey tea, some Antipasti, a Bruschette, a salad, or breakfast, to start your day, then it has to be **Café Huxleys**, opposite where you can sit, alfresco, and watch the world come to you. 01386 849077 huxleys.org

In search of sandwiches, cheeses, charcuterie and fresh breads try **Fillet & Bone.** For value for money sarnies head toward the Church to **Maylams Deli.** Across the road is **Tokes** for ready meals, quiches, wines by the case, and cheeses galore. Their sausage rolls are delish. You won't go hungry in Campden!

See below for Tea Rooms and Inns.

Meon Hill. Iron-age hillfort. The locals keep well away from this spot for fear of the spookery of witchcraft. (J5)

Parish Church of St James. A fine old 'Wool' church, of Norman origin, restored in the C15, with a tall and elegant tower, and a large Perpendicular nave. The 'Brilliant' gold stone is startling in late summer afternoons. C15 Cope, and a unique pair of C15 Altar Hangings. Brasses of Woolstaplers. C15 Falcon Lectern. Open daily. (H8)

Vegetable Matters Farm Shop & Café, Ebrington. As the name suggests, vegetables (boxes) are the speciality. As well as flowers and seasonal fruit. Café for light lunches and coffees who welcome walkers, cyclists and passersby (horseriders, too). Open Tu-Sa 8.30-5. 01386 593226
vegetable-matters.co.uk

EAT...DRINK... SLEEP...

Badgers Hall (B&B). Charming C15 house with mullioned windows and exposed beams housing bedrooms and a tearoom. Light lunches or substantial afternoon cream teas available to visitors and guests. No pets or young children.(H8) 01386 840839

Bakers Arms, Broad Campden. Good old-fashioned, traditional Cotswold pub with no jarring modernities serving fine ales. (J9) 01386 840515
bakersarmscampden.com

Bantam Tea Rooms B&B. C17 building situated opposite the old Market Hall. Afternoon teas available inside or in the tea garden. Private guest lounge and off street parking. (H8) 01386 840386
bantamtea-rooms.co.uk

Cotswold House Hotel & Spa, The Square. Bespoke luxury, blissful comfort and informality, on hand for your every need. Two restaurants; **Fig Restaurant** (formal) and **Bistro On The Square**, innovative and deliciously sublime. Two bars. Spa with 6-treatment rooms, hydrotherapy pool and aromatic steam room. (H8) 01386 840330
cotswoldhouse.com

Eight Bells Inn B&B. Church Street. C14 inn, full of rustic charm, contrasts well with the modern cuisine and bright bedrooms. Fresh fare. (H8) 01386 840371
eightbellsinn.co.uk

Michaels Mediterranean Restaurant. Greek and modern Mediterranean cuisine, served in a relaxed setting. Open for coffee, lunches, takeaways and evening meals. (H8) 01386 840826
michaelsmediterranean.co.uk

Noel Arms Hotel, High Street. A C16 coaching inn that has been transformed into a luxurious contemporary hotel: it's all log fires, four-posters and fine ales. Event Nights; curry, mexican, beer...to keep you wanting more. (H8) 01386 840317
bespokehotels.com/
noelarmshotel

The Volunteer B&B. Named The Volunteer in the mid 1800's because local men used to visit to 'sign on' for the volunteer armies (mercenaries). A popular local pub not least because of the excellent curries available from the kitchen. B&B. (H8) 01386 840688
thevolunteerinn.net

EAT... DRINK...SLEEP... NEAR CHIPPING CAMPDEN...

Churchill Arms B&B, Paxford. Nick Deverell-Smith has transformed, brought new life and expertise, into this ancient C17 hostelry. British food, and a full panoply of pub characteristics; log fires, flagstone floors and local ales plus cosy, boutique bedrooms on hand. (K9) 01386 593159
churchillarms.co

Ebrington Arms B&B, Ebrington. An C17 traditional

1933 The Thames & Severn Canal closes   1937 Hailes Abbey given to the National Trust

Broadway, Chipping Campden • **THE NORTHERN COTSWOLDS**

inn full of charm, character and popular as a community pub with both locals, and visitors to the area. Luxurious, old-pine bedrooms. English breakfasts. Dogs welcome. Garden. (K8) 01386 593223
theebringtonarms.co.uk

Howard Arms B&B, Ilmington. Fine selection of local beers. Pubby atmosphere serving interesting food. Dining Room. (L6)
01608 682226
howardarms.com

Manor Farm, Weston Subedge. Beautifully restored, and renovated traditional oak-beamed farmhouse built in 1624, and set within an 800-acre working farm with pedigree Charolais cattle, and sheep. Bedrooms with power-showers. Also, self-catering cottage. (G7) 01386 840390
manorfarmcotswolds.co.uk

Three Ways House Hotel, Mickleton. If a desire for the pudding is your food to beget love then beat a course to their door, the Home of the Pudding Club since 1985. Walking tours arranged (to burn off the calories!). Special themed 'Pudding Club' bedrooms.
Randall's Bar Brasserie open daily for coffee, lunch and dinner. (J6) 01386 438429
threewayshousehotel.com

Cotswold House hotel ss

William Grevel's House, Chipping Campden

| 1941 | The Stroud Water Navigation Company closes | 1946 | Sir Peter Scott establishes the Wildfowl and Wetlands Trust at Slimbridge |

THE NORTHERN COTSWOLDS • Broadway, Chipping Campden

EVESHAM

An attractive market town with tree-planted walks and lawns beside the River Avon. Centre for the Vale of Evesham's fruit growing industries. Abbey remains. Simon de Montfort, who fell at the Battle of Evesham in 1265, is buried in the churchyard. (B6)

Almonry Heritage Centre. Displays of the Romano-British, Anglo-Saxon, medieval and monastic remains, in an exquisite C14 timber-framed building. TIC. Open Mar-Oct M-Sa, Nov-Feb M-Sa Except W, 10-5. (C6) 01386 446944
almonryevesham.org

The Valley, Evesham Country Park & Vale Wildlife Hospital. Wildlife rescue centre supporting animal welfare. Set in country park that has shopping outlet stores, fishing, light railway, walks and garden centre. Open daily. (C5) 01386 882288
valewildlife.org.uk

All Things Wild. A mini-zoo for young children with sheep, parrots, rabbits, foxes, lemurs, meerkats, reptiles and Dinosaurs, can you believe it? Open daily all year, 10-5. (F6) 01386 833083
allthingswild.co.uk

Middle Littleton Tithe Barn (NT). This C13 barn is considered one of the finest in the country with ten bays and 130 feet long. Open daily May to Oct 10-5. (F4) 01905 371006
nationaltrust.org.uk

EAT…DRINK…SLEEP…

Fleece Inn B&B, Bretforton. A half-timbered medieval farmhouse that became an inn in 1848. Fine collection of pewter. Morris dancing, and folk music are regular events. Pretty garden. Fine ales and menus using local produce. Moongazer Glamping. (E6) 01386 831173
thefleeceinn.co.uk

Salford Farm House, Salford Priors. A quintessentially English B&B. The owner has a fruit farm and farm shop nearby, and guests dine well on its produce, as well as that of other local farmers. (E2) 01386 870000
salfordfarmhouse.co.uk

Evesham Abbey

| 198 | 1948 | Hidcote Manor Gardens handed over to the National Trust | 1951 | Revival of Robert Dover's Cotswold Olympick Games |

STRATFORD UPON AVON

Holy Trinity Church

Narrow Boats

Holy Trinity Church

THE NORTHERN COTSWOLDS • Broadway, Chipping Campden

STRATFORD UPON AVON

The birthplace of William Shakespeare, home to the Royal Shakespeare Company and one of the great tourist destinations in England. The town was established as a Romano-British settlement beside the river crossing on the busy Exeter to Lincoln route. In 1086 during the Domesday survey Stratford was a manor house belonging to Wulstan, Bishop of Worcester. In 1196 Richard I granted permission for a weekly market thereby establishing Stratford's early days as a market town. This instigated the annual Mop Fair on October 12 where local labourers sought employment. The tradesman's society, the Guild of the Holy Cross, was later formed to promote the crafts and local industries. During Shakespeare's time Stratford was home to 1,500 persons and was a bustling centre for the marketing of corn, malt and livestock, as well as being a centre for local government, and proud to foster one of the country's finest grammar schools. The town's

LIGHT BITES…

Sheep Street has the best restaurants in town: **Lambs, The Vintner** (also teas and coffees) and **The Opposition**. Just around the corner, **The Shakespeare Hotel** where you can have morning coffee and afternoon teas in the hotel or next door at **Othello's Bar Brasserie**, or perhaps stay the night. Down by the Waterside is **Carluccio's**, an ideal spot for some pasta, Italian charm and people watching. Most or all eating places cater for pre-theatre suppers. (L1)

buildings were predominantly Elizabethan and Jacobean. Today, there are C15 half-timbered buildings on Church Street, and C16 to C17 timber-framed houses in Chapel Street, the High Street and Wood Street plus a number of C18 period buildings of re-frontings with brick and stucco. It is not strictly a Cotswold town, but is included as it lies on the edge of the map, and is worthy of a day's visit from Broadway, or Chipping Campden. (L1)

SPECIAL PLACES TO VISIT…

Butterfly Farm & Jungle Safari, Tramway Walk. The UK's largest butterfly farm where you can wander through a jungle of exotic plants, fish filled pools, and waterfalls amid hundreds of tropical butterflies. Open daily. (L1) 01789 299288
butterflyfarm.co.uk

Clopton Bridge. Built in late C15 by Sir Hugh Clopton who became the Lord Mayor of London, and who died circa 1496. (L1)

Gower Memorial (Shakespeare Statue). This was presented to the town in 1888 by Lord Gower. The statue is made up of figures depicting Hamlet, Lady Macbeth, Falstaff and Prince Hal, which in turn, symbolizes philosophy, tragedy, comedy and history. (L1)

Guild Buildings: Guild Chapel. This dates back to the C13, The nave and tower were rebuilt in the 1490s. Notable for the medieval wall paintings of the Last Judgement. These were covered up, whitewashed, in 1560 which preserved them and were uncovered and restored in 1804. **The Guildhall.** Built

from 1418-1420. A superb half-timbered building that reflects the prestige and wealth of the Guild in the C15. **Grammar School and Almshouses, Chapel Street.** Most probably built around 1500. The ground floor was sheltered housing for the poor, sick and infirm. Next door, the schoolhouse for the sons of the Guild members. A teacher called a Grammar Priest would teach the children. (L1)

Holy Trinity Church, Southern Lane. The burial place of William Shakespeare, and his family, and a magnificent building, too. Note the Clopton Chapel, C15 vestry screen, C15 misericords, C15 font, The Bible c. 1611, the stained glass windows and the Chapel of Thomas a Becket. Open daily. (L1) 01789 266316

Mason's Court, Rother Street. A beautifully preserved C15 domestic building of red brick and timber-framing. Views of exterior only. (L1)

Mason Croft, Church Street. C18 property of the Shakespeare Institute of Birmingham University. The home, until 1921, of Marie Corelli, the Victorian novelist. Open for academic studies. (L1) 01214 149500

Open Air Bus tours. Travel to 14 stops including all the Shakespeare landmarks. Tickets are valid for 24 hours and passengers can hop on and off. Main departure point outside the TIC. (L1) 01789 412680
visitstratforduponavon.co.uk

Royal Shakespeare Theatre, Waterside. The home of the Royal Shakespeare Company, was built in 1932 to Elizabeth

Broadway, Chipping Campden • **THE NORTHERN COTSWOLDS**

Smith's design, following the fire of 1926, and then fully renovated in 2010, known as the Transformation Project into a 1,040 +seat thrust stage, Rooftop Restaurant & Bar, Riverside Café and Observation Tower. Officially opened on 4th March, 2011 by HM Queen Elizabeth 11. Its dedicated to the works of the poet and playwright, William Shakespeare. (L1) 01789 301111 Box Office. rsc.org.uk

Town Hall, Sheep Street. Originally built in the reign of Charles I and throughout its chequered history has seen calamitous events including being extensively damaged from a gunpowder explosion in 1643. (L1)

Tudor World, 40 Sheep Street. A waxworks museum recreates Stratford's darkest hours. Ghost tours. Open daily 10.30-5.30.
01879 298070 (L1)
tudorworld.com

EAT...DRINK...SLEEP...

The Black Swan (or Dirty Duck), Waterside. An C18 pub and an institution that gets crowded and over run with tourists and Thespians from the RSC. Pub-grub, seafood a speciality. (L1)

The Phoenix, 38 Guild Street. A classy, contemporary bar and restaurant with a large al fresco area perfect for sundowners and cocktails. Open daily. (L1)
phoenixstraftford.co.uk

The Townhouse, 16 Church Street. Here we have a smart Bar and Restaurant with Rooms described as boutiquey (bright, colourful and fun). (L1)
01789 262222
stratfordtownhouse.co.uk

Mary Arden's House, Wilmcote

Shakespeare's Birthplace

The Garrick Inn

| 1960 | The Shakespeare Theatre is renamed the Royal Shakespeare Theatre | 1961 | Brook House Mills, Painswick is the last Cotswold cloth mill to close |

WILLIAM SHAKESPEARE

IVDICIO PYLIVM GENIO SOCRATEM ARTE MARONEM
TERRA TEGIT, POPVLVS MÆRET, OLYMPVS HABET

STAY PASSENGER, WHY GOEST THOV BY SO FAST,
READ IF THOV CANST, WHOM ENVIOVS DEATH HATH PLAST
WITH IN THIS MONVMENT SHAKSPEARE: WITH WHOME
QVICK NATVRE DIDE WHOSE NAME, DOTH DECK Y TOMBE,
FAR MORE, THEN COST: SIEH ALL, Y HE HATH WRITT,
LEAVES LIVING ART, BVT PAGE, TO SERVE HIS WITT.

OBIIT ANO DOI 1616
ÆTATIS 53 DIE 23 AP.

WILLIAM SHAKESPEARE

"The Swan of Avon" as Ben Jonson described his friend, was born in Henley Street on 23rd April, 1564. His father, John Shakespeare was the son of a yeoman farmer from nearby Snitterfield who traded as a glover and wool-dealer and who later was to become the town's mayor. His mother, Mary Arden married John Shakespeare in 1557 and was the daughter of a prosperous gentleman-farmer from an old Warwickshire family. Although we know little of William's early life we know that he attended the local Grammar School where he took a close interest in the touring actors who performed in the Guildhall below the Grammar School. In 1582 he married Ann Hathaway, a farmer's daughter from Shottery and six years older than he. Shottery is still today linked to Stratford by a footpath that the courting William must have trod.

One wonders at the success of their marriage for he soon fled to London in 1587 after being caught poaching Sir Thomas Lucy's deer in Charlecote Park. The more likely reason was to pursue his ambitions. In London he joined the Leicester Players and later the King's Company which was patronised by the Elizabethan court and men of the Inns of Court. Despite his success in London he retained a close association with Stratford. In 1597 he bought New Place, the finest house in Stratford and took up permanent residence in 1611. He died in 1616 on his 52nd birthday following a merry meeting with his fellow poets Ben Jonson and Michael Drayton. He is buried in Holy Trinity Church beside members of his family. The statue which overlooks his grave was placed there seven years after his death. But…? Some scholars wonder how a son of an illiterate glove dealer could write, at all.

WILLIAM SHAKESPEARE

PROPERTIES OF THE SHAKESPEARE BIRTHPLACE TRUST

This Trust was established in 1847 and is probably the oldest conservation society in Britain. Its purpose to promote the appreciation and study of William Shakespeare's plays and prose, to an international audience and to protect and care for the buildings associated with the poet for future generations. You can purchase a ticket that covers the three properties open to the public. 01789 204016 shakespeare.org.uk

Anne Hathaway's Cottage, Shottery. This is the picturesque home of Anne before her marriage to WS in 1582. A large 12-room farm house surrounded by a colourful and charming garden of perennial shrubs, box hedges and apple orchard. This cottage belonged to descendants of the Hathaway family until 1892. Open late March to end October. (K1)

Hall's Croft, Old Town. A fine Tudor house beautifully furnished with a walled garden. It was the home of WS's daughter Susanna and her husband Dr John Hall who in his day was considered an advanced medical practicioner. Closed for refurbishment. (L1)

Mary Arden's Farm, Wilmcote. Mary Arden was WS's mother and she lived in this beautiful C16 farmhouse with Jacobean furniture and bygones from a former time. There is a farm museum exhibiting carts, carriages and a 650-hole dovecote. Open only for Educational/School Learning groups. (North of map)

New Place & Nash's House, Chapel Street. Sir Hugh Clopton built New Place in 1483. In 1597 it was bought by WS and was one of the finest and most prestigious houses in Stratford. WS retired here in 1610, and it was where he died on 23rd April 1616 whilst celebrating his 52nd birthday. In 1702 it was almost completely rebuilt but was demolished by the Reverend Francis Gastrell in 1759 following a dispute with the corporation about his rates. The foundations of New Place remain in the garden adjoining Nash's House, formerly the home of Thomas Nash, husband of Elizabeth Hall, who was WS's granddaughter. It remains half-timbered with an ancient interior and is a museum of local history. The Great Garden of New Place has the original orchard and kitchen garden with a mulberry tree raised from a cutting of WS's tree. Adjoining, the Knot Garden, a replica of an enclosed Elizabethan garden with old English flowers and herbs. Open daily late March to end October. (L1)

Shakespeare's Birthplace, Henley Street. William Shakespeare was born here on 23rd April, 1564. The house was originally divided into two buildings and used as a home and a workshop for his father, a wool-dealer and glove maker. It is half-timbered with strong oak framing, leaded windows and wide sills. The building was restored in the C18 by the Actor- Manager David Garrick. There is a comprehensive collection of Shakespeariana and the garden displays flowers named in his plays and poems: daisies, violets, pansies, lady smocks and mary buds. Open daily. (L1)

Harvard House & Pewter Museum, High Street. Harvard House was built in 1596 by the wealthy townsman Alderman Thomas Rogers who had twice served as High Bailiff. His initials are carved on the front of the house (with a bull's head to denote his trade as a butcher) together with those of his wife Alice and his eldest son William and the date 1596. The elaborately carved facade by far the richest example in the town is testimony to Rogers's wealth and standing. From the mid C17 there was a succession of owners until the Shakespeare Birthplace Trust assumed responsibility for the building and in 1996 it became the Museum of British Pewter. No longer open. (L1)

QUOTES FROM HIS PLAYS:

"If music be the food of love, play on."
Twelfth Night

"The course of true love never did run smooth."
A Midsummer Night's Dream

"She is spherical, like a globe. I could find countries in her." **The Comedy of Errors**

"More of your conversation would infect my brain."
Coriolanus

"It is a tale told by an idiot, full of sound and fury, signifying nothing." **Macbeth**

"Death lies on her, like an untimely frost Upon the sweetest flower of all the field."
Romeo and Juliet

"Love is blind, and lovers cannot see, The pretty follies that themselves commit."
The Merchant of Venice

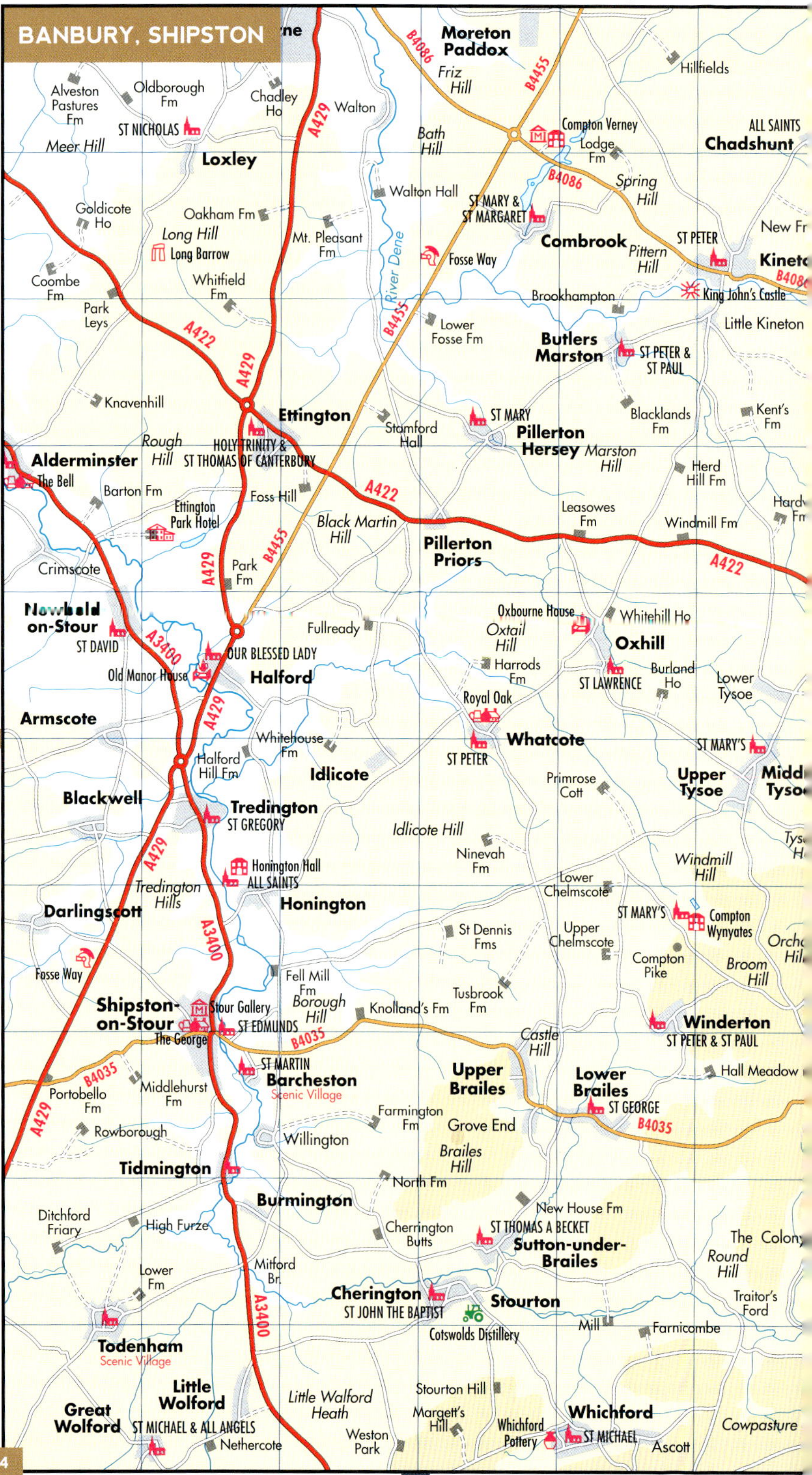
Moreton Paddox
Friz Hill
Hillfields
Alveston Pastures Fm
Oldborough Fm
Chadley Ho
Walton
ST NICHOLAS
Meer Hill
Loxley
Bath Hill
Compton Verney
Lodge Fm
ALL SAINTS
Chadshunt
Goldicote Ho
Oakham Fm
Walton Hall
ST MARY & ST MARGARET
Spring Hill
Long Hill
Long Barrow
Mt. Pleasant Fm
River Dene
Combrook
Pittern Hill
ST PETER
New Fr
Kineto
Coombe Fm
Whitfield Fm
Fosse Way
King John's Castle
Brookhampton
Park Leys
Lower Fosse Fm
Little Kineton
Butlers Marston
ST PETER & ST PAUL
Knavenhill
Ettington
Stamford Hall
ST MARY
Pillerton Hersey
Blacklands Fm
Kent's Fm
Rough Hill
HOLY TRINITY & ST THOMAS OF CANTERBURY
Marston Hill
Alderminster
The Bell
Herd Hill Fm
Barton Fm
Foss Hill
Ettington Park Hotel
Black Martin Hill
Leasowes Fm
Windmill Fm
Hardw Fm
Pillerton Priors
Crimscote
Park Fm
Newbold on-Stour
Oxbourne House
Whitehill Ho
ST DAVID
Fullready
Oxtail Hill
Oxhill
OUR BLESSED LADY
Harrods Fm
Burland Ho
Old Manor House
Halford
ST LAWRENCE
Lower Tysoe
Royal Oak
Armscote
Whitehouse Fm
Whatcote
ST MARY'S
Halford Hill Fm
ST PETER
Idlicote
Primrose Cott
Upper Tysoe
Middl Tysoe
Blackwell
Tredington
ST GREGORY
Idlicote Hill
Ninevah Fm
Tys H
Windmill Hill
Honington Hall
ALL SAINTS
Tredington Hills
Lower Chelmscote
Honington
Darlingscott
ST MARY'S
Compton Wynyates
St Dennis Fms
Upper Chelmscote
Orcha Hil
Compton Pike
Broom Hill
Fosse Way
Fell Mill Fm
Tusbrook Fm
Borough Hill
Shipston-on-Stour
Stour Gallery
Knolland's Fm
Winderton
ST PETER & ST PAUL
The George
ST EDMUNDS
Castle Hill
ST MARTIN
Barcheston
Scenic Village
Upper Brailes
Lower Brailes
Hall Meadow
Middlehurst Fm
Portobello Fm
ST GEORGE
Farmington Fm
Grove End
Rowborough
Willington
Brailes Hill
Tidmington
North Fm
Burmington
New House Fm
Ditchford Friary
High Furze
Cherrington Butts
ST THOMAS A BECKET
Sutton-under-Brailes
The Colony
Round Hill
Lower Fm
Mitford Br.
Cherington
ST JOHN THE BAPTIST
Stourton
Traitor's Ford
Cotswolds Distillery
Mill
Farnicombe
Todenham
Scenic Village
Little Wolford
Stourton Hill
Little Wolford Heath
Margett's Hill
Whichford
Great Wolford
ST MICHAEL & ALL ANGELS
Whichford Pottery
ST MICHAEL
Cowpasture
Nethercote
Weston Park
Ascott
A429
A422
A3400
B4086
B4455
B4035
187
124
A B C D E F
1 2 3 4 5 6 7 8 9 10

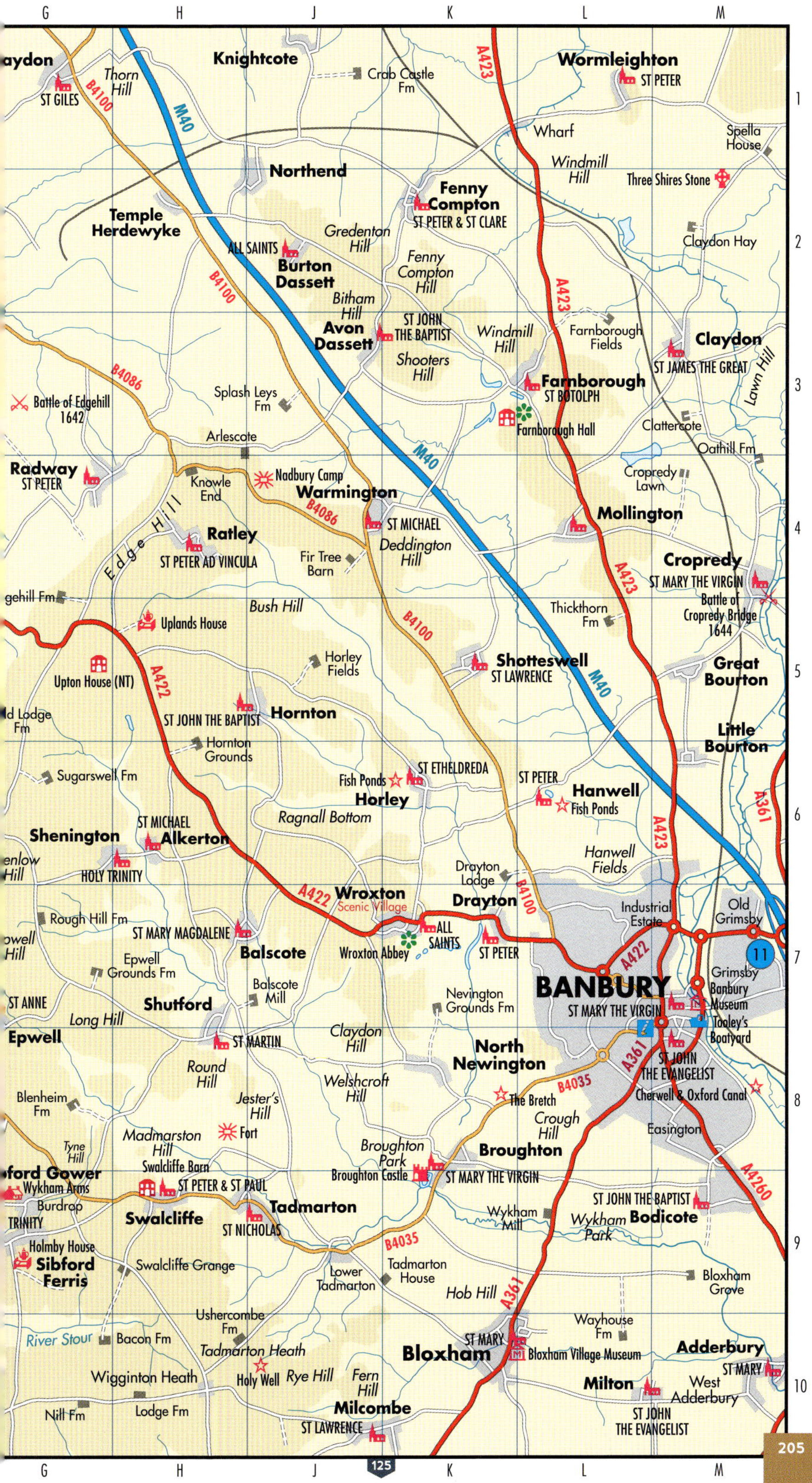
G H J K L M
1 2 3 4 5 6 7 8 9 10
aydon
ST GILES
Thorn Hill
B4100
M40
Knightcote
Crab Castle Fm
A423
Wormleighton
ST PETER
Wharf
Spella House
Windmill Hill
Three Shires Stone
Northend
Fenny Compton
ST PETER & ST CLARE
Temple Herdewyke
Gredenton Hill
Claydon Hay
ALL SAINTS
Burton Dassett
Fenny Compton Hill
Bitham Hill
Avon Dassett
ST JOHN THE BAPTIST
Windmill Hill
Farnborough Fields
Claydon
ST JAMES THE GREAT
Lawn Hill
Shooters Hill
B4086
Farnborough
ST BOTOLPH
Battle of Edgehill 1642
Splash Leys Fm
Farnborough Hall
Clattercote
Arlescote
Oathill Fm
Radway
ST PETER
Knowle End
Nadbury Camp
Warmington
Cropredy Lawn
ST MICHAEL
Mollington
Edge Hill
Ratley
ST PETER AD VINCULA
Deddington Hill
Fir Tree Barn
Cropredy
ST MARY THE VIRGIN
Battle of Cropredy Bridge 1644
gehill Fm
Bush Hill
Thickthorn Fm
Uplands House
B4100
Horley Fields
Shotteswell
ST LAWRENCE
Great Bourton
Upton House (NT)
A422
d Lodge Fm
ST JOHN THE BAPTIST
Hornton
Little Bourton
Hornton Grounds
Sugarswell Fm
Fish Ponds
ST ETHELDREDA
ST PETER
Hanwell
Fish Ponds
A361
Horley
ST MICHAEL
Ragnall Bottom
Shenington
Alkerton
enlow Hill
HOLY TRINITY
Hanwell Fields
Drayton Lodge
Wroxton
Scenic Village
Drayton
Industrial Estate
Old Grimsby
Rough Hill Fm
ST MARY MAGDALENE
ALL SAINTS
owell Hill
Balscote
Wroxton Abbey
ST PETER
11
Epwell Grounds Fm
BANBURY
Grimsby
Banbury Museum
Balscote Mill
Nevington Grounds Fm
ST ANNE
Shutford
ST MARY THE VIRGIN
Tooley's Boatyard
Long Hill
Epwell
ST MARTIN
Claydon Hill
North Newington
ST JOHN THE EVANGELIST
Round Hill
Welshcroft Hill
Cherwell & Oxford Canal
Blenheim Fm
Jester's Hill
B4035
The Brecht
Crough Hill
Easington
Madmarston Hill
Fort
Tyne Hill
Broughton Park
Broughton
Swalcliffe Barn
ford Gower
Wykham Arms
ST PETER & ST PAUL
Broughton Castle
ST MARY THE VIRGIN
A4260
Burdrop
Tadmarton
ST JOHN THE BAPTIST
TRINITY
Swalcliffe
ST NICHOLAS
Wykham Mill
Wykham Park
Bodicote
Holmby House
Sibford Ferris
B4035
Swalcliffe Grange
Lower Tadmarton
Tadmarton House
Bloxham Grove
Hob Hill
A361
Ushercombe Fm
Wayhouse Fm
River Stour
Bacon Fm
Tadmarton Heath
ST MARY
Bloxham Village Museum
Adderbury
Bloxham
ST MARY
Wigginton Heath
Holy Well
Rye Hill
Fern Hill
Milton
West Adderbury
Milcombe
Nill Fm
Lodge Fm
ST LAWRENCE
ST JOHN THE EVANGELIST
125

THE NORTHERN COTSWOLDS • Banbury, Shipston

BANBURY

A prosperous commercial and retail centre situated on the northern edge of the Cotswold escarpment. The extension of the M40 in 1991 has provided access to Birmingham, London and Oxford and thus given Banbury infinite opportunities. Since 2005 a massive influx of Polish immigrants has boosted the local economy and the congregation in the Catholic churches. Kraft Foods has the largest coffee processing plant in the world here. Famous for Banbury cakes (similar to Eccles cakes), and the celebrated 'Banbury Cross.' Man has lived here since an Iron Age settlement of 200 BC, a Roman villa at Wykeham Park around 250 AD and a Saxon stronghold in the C5. The Danes developed trade routes and the Salt Way came through Banbury. A focus of Civil War hostilities in the C17 - the first battle took place at Edgehill in 1642. Shortly after Banbury became a centre of Puritanism. From about 1700-1800 cloth making took a hold on the local economy producing shag, then plush. With the expansion of the Oxford Canal in 1790 Banbury again prospered. The Cattle Market was once the largest in Europe but sadly closed in 1998. You can follow a Town Trail around all the historic buildings. (M10)

Ride a cock horse to Banbury Cross,
To see a Fyne lady ride on a white horse.
With rings on her fingers and bells on her toes, She shall have music wherever she goes.

LIGHT BITES

S H Jones Wine Merchants, 27 High Street. Enjoy a coffee or snack in one of Banbury's oldest buildings, or sample a soupçon of fine wine. Open daily. (M7) 01295 251177
shjones.com

Ye Olde Reindeer Inn, Behind Parson Street. Visit this inn for its Civil War associations, and superb C17 panelling, and gate. (M7) 01295 270972
ye-olde-reindeer-inn.co.uk

Whately Hall Hotel, Horse Fair. A pragmatic destination for morning coffee, business meetings and lunch. The building is impressive from the exterior, and once inside look to the superb Jacobean staircase. It is an old fashioned hostelry with a long history of ghosts, Regal visits and town functions. Sadly, let down by the modern additions. (M7) 01295 253261
countrywidehotels.co.uk

SPECIAL PLACES TO VISIT...

Banbury Museum. The new canal side location features interactive art and historic exhibitions with some fabulous displays of clothes, bicycles, a timeline of events and changing exhibitions. Café open Tu-F 8-4, Su 10-3. Quay. Museum Open M-F 10-4, Sa 10-5, Su 11-3. (M7) 01295 236165
banburymuseum.org

Broughton Castle. Moated medieval manor house, substantially enlarged in the C16. Magnificent plaster ceilings, fine panelling and fireplaces. Interesting Civil War connections. In the family of the Lords Saye and Sele for over 600 years. Multi-coloured borders. The location for much of the film, Shakespeare in Love. Tearoom. Open Apr-Sept. See website for details. (K9) 01295 276070
broughtoncastle.com

Oxford Canal. Built by James Brindley in 1769 to connect the industrial Midlands with London via the River Thames. Financial problems delayed the construction but it was eventually to reach Oxford in 1789. Today, it runs for 77 miles from Hawkesbury Junction, south of Coventry to Oxford. You can enjoy a multitude of leisure activities, from solitary walks to boating, canoeing, cycling, fishing and, the wildlife. (M7) canalrivertrust.org.uk

Tooley's Boatyard & Tours, Spiceball Park Road. This is the oldest working dry dock boatyard on the inland waterways of Britain. Established in 1790 to build and repair the wooden horse-drawn narrow boats. 200-year old forge, chandlery and gift shop. Self-drive hire and private boat trips. (M7) 01295 272917
tooleysboatyard.co.uk

SHIPSTON-ON-STOUR

A working town with some attractive Georgian inns, as described below plus The Lazy Pug for a drink or two…. and handsome houses amidst some rich pastoral farmland. In the C16, it was a prosperous weaving centre holding one of the great sheep markets. There is even a Gentleman's Tailor and a Clocksmith to hand. (B7)

EAT...DRINK...SLEEP...

The George Townhouse, High Street. A handsome building that has been given a contemporary makeover. The downstairs has a pleasing

Banbury, Shipston • **THE NORTHERN COTSWOLDS**

ambience. Upstairs, the 15 boutiquey bedrooms have been designed to be classic, cosy, luxurious, superior, deluxe etc. Dog friendly. (B7) 01608 661453 thegeorgeshipston.co.uk

The Bower House, Market Place. Fast gaining a reputation as a little hotel or Restaurant With Rooms for its flair and flavours in the kitchen and comfortable, bright bedrooms. Ideally located close to Stratford and the North Cotswolds. 01608 663333 (B7) bower.house

SPECIAL PLACES OF INTEREST...

Adderbury Church. Early C13 cruciform. C14 West tower with massive carvings. Superb chancel and vestry. (M10)

Bloxham Church. C14 spire. Carvings. C15 wall paintings. East window by William Morris and Edward Burne-Jones. (K10)

Mrs Baldwin in Eastern Dress, Joshua Reynolds, Compton Verney ss

The Old Wine House

1964   Arkle wins the first of his three Cheltenham Gold Cups (1965 & 1966)   1968   Kelmscott Manor restored

THE NORTHERN COTSWOLDS • Banbury, Shipston

Broughton Castle

| 1969 | Death of the Rolling Stone, Brian Jones born in Cheltenham in 1942 | 1970 | The Cotswold Way designated a long distance footpath |

Banbury, Shipston • THE NORTHERN COTSWOLDS

Battle of Edgehill site. The Battle of Edgehill on Sunday 23rd October, 1642 was the first major battle of the English Civil War. It was fought in the open fields around the villages of Radway and Kineton in Warwickshire between the army of the Earl of Essex, the parliamentarian Lord General, and the King's army. The outcome was deemed indecisive. (G3)

Compton Verney. Art Gallery in C18 Robert Adam mansion set in parkland by 'Capability' Brown. Naples School, British portraits, folk art. Open mid-Feb to mid-Dec Tu-Su & BHs 10-5. (D1) 01926 645500
comptonverney.org.uk

Compton Wynyates. A Tudor dream house built 1460 with multi-coloured bricks; pale rose, crimson, blood red, shades of orange and bluish brown. Twisted chimneys. Panelled rooms. Plaster ceilings. Perhaps, the most romantic of all England's country houses. Sadly, no longer open. May be glimpsed through the trees from the nearby road. (F7)

Cotswolds Distillery, Stourton. The hopes of a dream came true…from the barley fields of the North Cotswolds; a Single Malt Whisky and later after 60 recipes, to this Dry Gin. Bottoms Up! Cafe. Open M-Sa 9-5, Su 10-5. (C9) 01608 238533
cotswoldsdistillery.com

Farnborough Hall (NT). A beautiful honey-coloured stone house sits in parkland crated in the 1740s. Noted for the exquisite C18 plasterwork. Parkland walks and lake views. Open Apr to Sept, W & Sa 2-5.30. (L3) 01295 670266
nationaltrust.org.uk

Swalcliffe Barn. Early C15 tithe barn with fascinating displays of Oxfordshire's agricultural and trade vehicles. Exhibition of 2,500 years of the area. Open East Su to Oct & BH Ms 2-5. (H9) 01993 814106

Upton House & Gardens (NT). This house exhibits the lifestyle of a 1930s millionaire. It also has an outstanding display of English and Continental Old Masters paintings plus a wealth of herbaceous borders, terraces and tranquil water gardens. See website for details. (G5) 01295 670266
nationaltrust.org.uk

Whichford Pottery. Hand-made English terracotta flowerpots of immense size. Thirty craftsmen and women. Shop. Open daily 10-4. (E10) 01608 684416
whichfordpottery.com

EAT… DRINK…SLEEP…

Ettington Park Hotel. Flamboyant Victorian Gothic hotel with rococo plasterwork, many leisure activities has recently undergone a massive renovation. Very much aimed at the corporate and wedding markets. Open all year. (B4) 01789 450123
handpickedhotels.co.uk

Holmby House B&B, Sibford Ferris. An elegant wisteria-clad Victorian house set in fragrant gardens complete with heated outdoor pool and tennis and croquet equipment for the restless. The en-suite bedrooms are spacious and light. Dinner available if pre-booked. (G9) 01295 780104

Old Manor House B&B, Halford. English country house style B&B at its finest. From lounging black Labradors to chintz and marmalade, and family antiques. Anyone for tennis? (B5) 01789 740264
oldmanor-halford.co.uk

Royal Oak, Whatcote. This is the ultimate dining pub or really a smart restaurant within a pub build. Richard Craven will pepper your taste buds to kingdom come and back and you will crave more until your hedonism explodes like the Savant in Le Grande Bouffe. Game in season, fish from Cornwall, cheeses from Neals Yard. Closed M-W. 01295 688100 (D5)
theroyaloakwhatcote.co.uk

The Bell B&B, Alderminster. Former C18 coaching inn now run by the Alscot Estate. It is spacious, comfortable and serves good, solid food. Perhaps, more restaurant than inn. B&B. (A4) 01789 335671
brunningandprice.co.uk

Uplands House B&B, Upton. The owners of this Country House B&B are former Olympic fencers with interesting stories, aplenty, as well as detailed, rapier-like knowledge to help you plan your break. A comfortable, and welcoming home-from-home. (H5) 01295 678663
cotswolds-uplands.co.uk

Wykham Arms, Sibford Gower. Thatched inn set in pretty North Oxford village. The proprietors, Damian and Debbie are chefs so expect pub-grub of the highest order. Open for coffee and pastries, lunch and dinner. Sundays are special. (G9) 01295 788808
wykhamarms.co.uk

DOORS

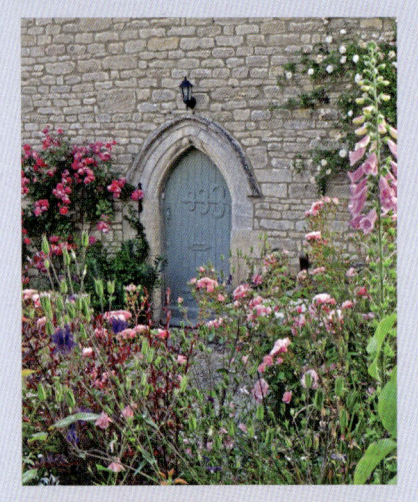

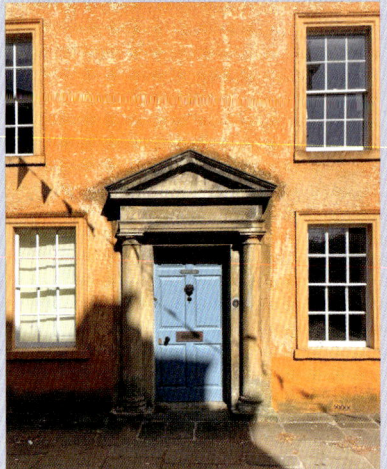

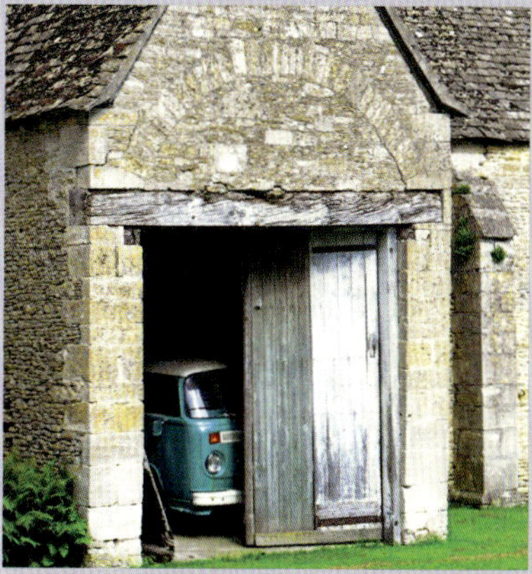
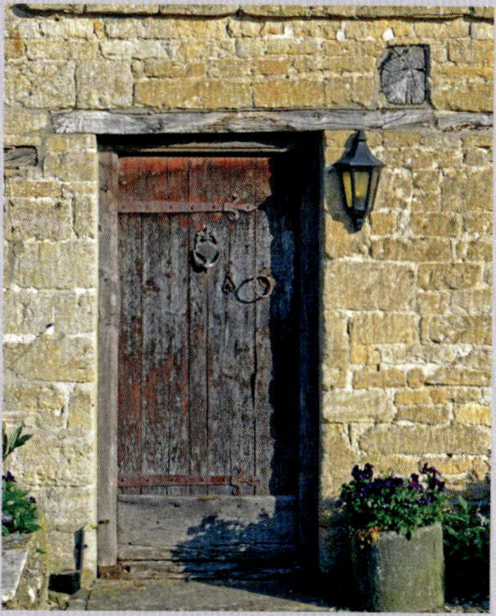
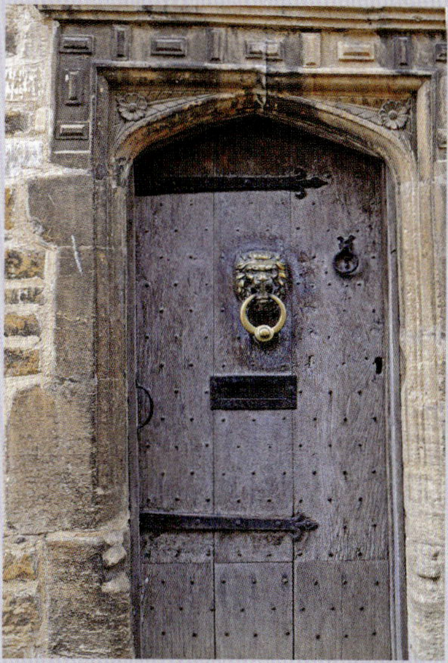
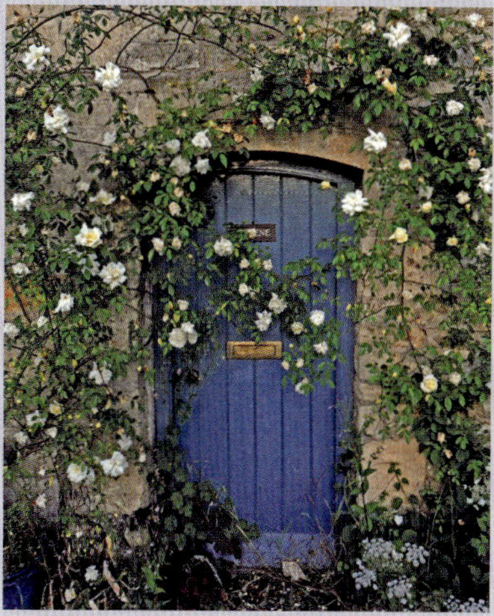
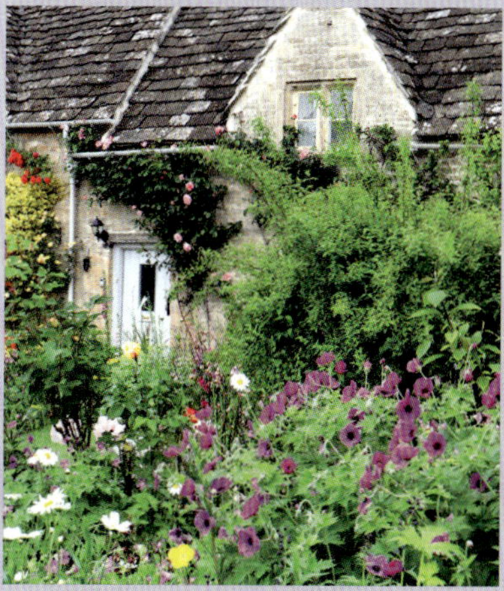
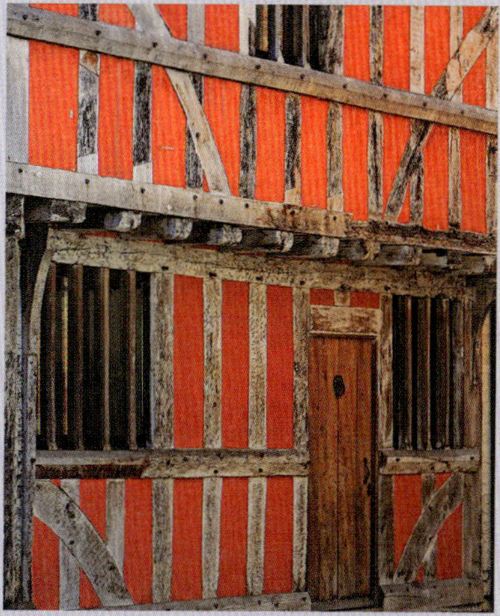

CONTEMPORARY ART

In the Studio by P J Crook MBE RWA FRSA Courtesy of Trinity House, Broadway

Saied Dai - Artist in Studio, Brian Sinfield Gallery, Burford

CALENDAR OF EVENTS

January
Gloucester Cajun & Zydeco Festival
Royal Shakespeare season ends

February
Snowdrops at Colesbourne Park
Snowdrops at Rococo Gardens, Painswick

March
Cheltenham National Hunt Festival
Chipping Norton Music Festival cnmf.org.uk
Evesham Spring Regatta
Lambing, Cotswold Farm Park cotswoldfarmpark.co.uk
Royal Shakespeare Theatre season begins
West Country Game Fair, Royal Bath & West Showground

April
Adderbury Day of (Morris) Dance adderbury.org
Broadway Spring point-to-point
Cheltenham Int. Jazz Festival cheltenhamfestivals.co.uk
Evesham Vintage Easter Gathering shakespearesrally.com
Great Blenheim Palace Easter Egg Challenge
GWR Toddington Spring Diesel Gala
Shakespeare Birthday celebrations, Stratford

May
Badminton Horse Trials badminton-horse.co.uk
Banbury Beer & Cider Festival northoxfordshirecamra.org.uk
Bath International Music Festival bathfestivals.org.uk/music
Burford Levellers Day levellersday.wordpress.com
Chipping Campden Music Festival campdenmayfestivals.co.uk
Coopers Hill Cheese Rolling
Kemble Great Vintage Flying Weekend
Longborough Festival Opera (May-Aug) lfo.org.uk
Malvern Arts Festival
Malvern Spring Gardening Show threecounties.co.uk
Nailsworth Festival nailsworthfestival.org.uk
Pershore Carnival
Prescott Hill Classic Car Event cleevevale.org.uk
Randwick Cheese Rolling
South Cerney Street Fair BHM
Stow Horse Fair
Stratford-Upon-Avon Lit. Festival stratfordliteraryfestival.co.uk
Tetbury Woolsack Races BHM
Upton Folk Festival uptonfolk.org

June
Banbury Show banbury.gov.uk
Bledington Music Festival bledingtonmusicfestival.co.uk
Bloxham Steam Rally bloxhamrally.com
Cheltenham Science Festival cheltenhamfestivals.com/science
Deddington Festival deddingtonfestival.org.uk

June (continued)
Dover's Olimpick Games olimpickgames.co.uk
Gloucester Tall Ships Festival gloucestertallships.co.uk
Kemble Air Day
Longborough Festival Opera (May-Aug) lfo.org.uk
Pershore Festival of Arts
Severn Project severnproject.com
Sudeley Castle Rose Week
Tewkesbury Food & Drink Festival
Three Counties Agricultural Show, Malvern
Wychwood Music Festival wychwoodfestival.com

July
Banbury Hobby Horse Festival
Cornbury Riverside Festival Charlbury cornburyfestival.com
Cotswold Show, Cirencester Park
Fairford Air Tattoo airtattoo.com
Fairport Convention, Cropredy fairportconvention.com
Gloucester Festival
Gloucester Rhythm & Blues Festival
Hook Norton Festival of Fine Ales hookybeerfest.co.uk
Longborough Festival Opera (May-Aug) lfo.org.uk
Music Deo Sacra, Tewkesbury Abbey
Music At The Crossroads, Hook Norton hookymusic.co.uk
Tewkesbury Medieval Festival tewkesburymedievalfestival.org
Three Choirs Festival 3choirs.org

August
Bourton Water Games BHM
Evesham Flower Show
Longborough Festival Opera (May-Aug) lfo.org.uk
Prescott Vintage Hill Climb
Winchcombe Country Show winchcombeshow.org.uk

September
Banbury Cavalcade of Sport
Battle of Britain Weekend, Kemble Airfield
Cheltenham Carnival
Chipping Norton Mop Fair
Moreton-in-Marsh Show
Painswick Church Clypping and Puppy Dog Pie

October
Banbury Canal Day
Cheltenham Literary Festival cheltenhamfestivals.com/literature
Shipston Medieval Fun Fair
Stratford Mop Fair
Tewkesbury Mop Fair

November
Bonfire Show, Cheltenham Racecourse

TOURIST INFORMATION CENTRES

Banbury
c/o Banbury Museum Spiceball Park Rd, OX16 2PQ
01295 236165

Bath
visitbath.co.uk

Bourton-on-the-Water
Victoria Street, GL54 2BU
01451 820211
bourtoninfo.com

Bradford-on-Avon
The Greenhouse, 50 St. Margaret's Street, BA15 1DE
01225 865797
bradfordonavon.co.uk

Broadway
Unit 14 Russell Square, High Street, WR12 7AP
01386 852937
broadway-cotswolds.co.uk

Cheltenham
The Wilson, Clarence Street, GL50 3JT
01242 237431
visitcheltenham.com

Chippenham
Yelde Hall, Market Place, SN15 3HL
01249 665970

Chipping Campden
The Old Police Station, High Street, GL55 6HB
01386 841206
chippingcampdenonline.org

Cirencester
Corinium Museum, Park Street, GL7 2BX
01285 654180
cirencester.co.uk

Corsham
Arnold House, 31 High Street, SN13 0EZ
01249 714660
corsham.gov.uk

Evesham
The Almonry, Abbey Gate, WR11 4BG
01386 446944
almonryevesham.org

Gloucester
Brunswick Rd, Gloucester GL1 1HP
01452 396572
gloucester.gov.uk

Malvern
The Lyttelton Well Courtyard, 6 Church St, WR14 2AY
01684 892289
visitthemalverns.org

Moreton-in-Marsh
Moreton Area Centre, High Street, GL56 0AZ
01608 650881

Nailsworth
Old Market, GL6 0DU
01453 839222

Pershore
Town Hall, 34 High Street, WR10 1DS
01386 556591
visitpershore.co.uk

Stow-On-The-Wold
St Edwards Hall, The Square, GL54 1AG
01451 870998
stowinfo.co.uk

Tetbury
33 Church Street, GL8 8JG
01666 50355
visittetbury.co.uk

Tewkesbury
Tewkesbury Heritage & Visitor Centre
100 Church Street, GL20 5AB
01684 855040
visittewkesbury.info

Upton upon Severn
4 High Street, WR8 0HB
01684 594200
visituptonuponsevern.co.uk

Winchcombe
High Street, GL54 5LT
01242 602925
winchcombe.co.uk

Woodstock
Oxfordshire Museum, Park Street, OX20 1SN
01993 813276
woodstock.vic@westoxon.gov.uk

Wotton-Under-Edge
The Heritage Centre, The Chipping, GL12 7AD
01453 521541
wottonheritage.com

ACKNOWLEDGMENTS

I would like to thank my wife, Caroline, for her constant support and encouragement. To Phil Butcher for his design skills and enthusiasm for this project, to my daughter, Izy for her proof reading skills and to Richard Martin for allowing me to print extracts from his essay on the Golden Fleece. Thank you to Richard Vaughn-Davies (novelist) for encouraging me to include an extract from my Long Walk's Journal. Not to be forgotten, all the kind persons at the many attractions, places to stay and eat, for showing me around their establishments, and for putting up with my endless questions.

And, thank you, to Sebastian Faulks for permitting me to quote his praiseworthy comments on the cover of this book.

LOAN OF IMAGES:

Goldeneye would like to thank the following for allowing us to photograph their property, or for providing us with an image to illustrate their property. It is now not uncommon for a tourist attraction (e.g. Blenheim Palace) or a charitable organisation (The National Trust) to charge a fee for photographing their property. Goldeneye makes it a policy not to pay a fee given that: a) We are promoting these properties (free of charge), and b) The cumulative expense would make this book an unfeasible production. We would hope that this policy may change, and that a more mutually beneficial outcome may arise. A good number of illustrations used in this book were shot with permission before these organisations had a policy change at head office. Goldeneye would therefore prefer to illustrate a lesser-known property, rather than the expected. Therefore, if you wonder why we have not illustrated the obvious key attraction in a town (a rare occurrence) that is the reason:

Barnsley House, Bath Priory Hotel, Beaufort Polo Club, Bennetts Fine Wines, Bibury Trout Farm, Blenheim Palace, Bliss Tweed Mill, Buckland Manor Hotel, Burford Parish Church, Calcot Manor & Spa, Cerney House Gardens, Chipping Campden, Parish Church, Colin Carruthers Red Rag Gallery, Compton Verney Trust, Corsham Court, Cotswold Inns, Cotswold Motoring Museum, Cotswold Woollen Weavers, Daylesford Organic Farm, Dyson, Earl of Wemyss & March Stanway, Fairford Parish Church, Frocester Estate Barn, Gallery Pangolin, Gloucester Cathedral, Great Tew Estate, Guiting Power Parish Church, Henson, Cotswold Farm Park, Holy Trinity Church, Jack Russell Gallery, Jeremy George of The Glebe, Kelmscott Manor Trust, Kiftgate Court Gardens, Lords of the Manor Hotel, Lords Saye & Sele Broughton Castle, Lower Slaughter Manor, Mike Finch Winchcombe Pottery, Morgan Motor Company, Bourton House Garden, National Trust Ltd, Nature In Art Museum, New Inn Coln St Aldwyn, No 1 Royal Crescent, Owlpen Manor, Oxford Canal Trust, Oxfordshire Museums Trust, Painswick Rococo Garden, Pershore Abbey, Royal Crescent Hotel, Edward Peake of Sezincote, Shakespeare Birthplace Trust, Sudeley Castle, Tewkesbury Abbey, The Wheatsheaf, Westonbirt Arboretum, Wild Garlic, Wildfowl & Wetlands Trust, William Grevel's House, Winchcombe Parish Church. Johnny Chambers at Kiftgate Court, Kardien Gerbrands of Stroud Farmer's Market, Abigail of Museum in the Park, Elena of Frampton Court, Rousham Park Gardens, Amelia Bird of The Wild Rabbit, Nina Lloyd-Jones of Badminton HT, Caroline Lowsley-Williams of Chavenage, Tof Milway Conderton Pottery, Beckford Silk, Foxhill Manor, Mill Hay, Holy Trinity Church, Brian Sinfield Gallery.

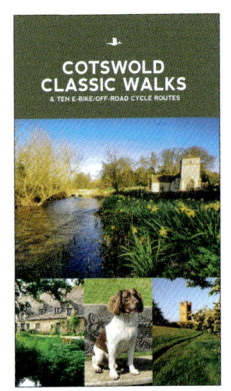

CALLING ALL WALKERS!

Herewith, the new edition of our Cotswold Classic Walks…

This book contains 25 circular routes (& 10 E-Bike/Off-Road cycle routes) including recommendations for the best walks for families, dogs, pub lovers, views, weekends away…and so much more.

"Now you can take a hike the easy way… Each map has easy-to-follow directions, clear navigational reference points and details of places to eat, drink, stay and visit along the way."
Gloucestershire Echo

INDEX

A

Abbey House Gardens 58
Abbey Mill 43
Abbey Road Cafe 183
Abbotswood 147
Acorns Vegetarian Restaurant 38
Adderbury Church 209
Adventure Café 39
Akeman Street 96
Almonry Heritage Museum 178
Almshouses, Chipping Norton 126
Amberley Inn 85
Ampney Crucis Church 107
Ampney St Mary Church 107
Anderson's Coffee House 161
Angel Inn Hotel, Pershore 184
Anne Hathaway's Cottage 203
Apple Tree Park 85
Arlingham Peninsula 69
Arlington Mill 87
Arlington Row 87
Ashleworth Court 168
Ashleworth Manor 168
Ashleworth Tithe Barn 168
Ashmolean Museum 189
Ashmolean Museum 189
Assembly Rooms, Bath 35
Aston Pottery 121
Athelstan Museum 58

B

Back Lane Tavern 129
Badminton 57
Badminton House 57
Bagendon Church 107
Bagendon Earthworks 96
Bakers Arms, Broad Campden 195
Bakery On The Water 142
Banbury 206
Banbury Museum 206
Barnsley House 96
Barrow Wake 85
Barton Farm Country Park 43
Barton House 122
Bath 35
Bath Abbey, Church of St Peter & St Paul 35
Bath Aqua Theatre of Glass 36
Bath Boating Station 36
Bath Contemporary 36
Bath Priory Hotel 34
Bath Rugby Club 36
Bathurst Arms, North Cerney 101
Bathwick Gardens 40
Batsford Arboretum 142
Battle of Edgehill site 209
Baunton Church 107
Bay Tree Hotel 118
Bear at Bisley 85
Beckford Silk 189
Beckford's Tower 36
Beehive 162
Belas Knap Long Barrow 149
Bell at Sapperton 85
Bell, Alderminster 212
Bell Inn, Langford 122
Benvenuti 184
Berdoulat 39
Berkeley 69
Berkeley Castle 69
Berkeley Parish Church of St Mary's 69
Beverston Castle 54
Beverston Church 54
Bibury 92
Bibury Parish Church of St Mary 92
Bibury Trout Farm 92
Bird in Hand Inn 120
Birdland 139
Bishops Palace, Witney 121
Bisley 82
Black Cat Café 104
Black Horse, Naunton 153
Blanket Hall 120
Blenheim Palace 128
Bliss Tweed Mill 126
Bloxham Church 209
Bourton House Garden 142
Bourton-On-The-Water 139
Bowers Hill Farm 196
Brackenbury Ditches 48
Bradford Canal Wharf & Lock 37
Bradford-on-Avon 43
Brawn Farm 168
Bredon Barn 185
Bredon Hill 184
Bredon Hill Fort 185
Brian Sinfield Gallery 113
Bridge Tea Rooms 44
Broadway 189
Broadway deli 193
Broadway Hotel 191
Broadway Tower 189
Broadway Wine Co 191
Brook Cottage 209
Brothertons 129
Broughton Castle 206
Browns 32
Buckland Church 189
Buckland Manor Hotel 191
Buckland Rectory 189
Bugatti Trust 159
Building of Bath Collection 36
Bull Inn, Charlbury 127
Bullocks Horn Cottage 59
Burford 117
Burford House 119
Burford Parish Church of St John the Baptist 117
Burford Priory 117
Buscot Old Parsonage 121
Buscot Park 121
Butcher's Arms, Sheepscombe 85
Butterfly Farm 200
Butts Farm 96

C

Café 6 152
Café Deli & Art 161
Café Huxleys 196
Café Lucca 39
Calcot Manor 57
Cam Long Down 84
Campden Coffee Co 196
Campden Gallery 192
Canal Wharf & Lock 43
Canary Gin Bar 40
Castle Combe 45
Castle Combe Church of St Andrew's 45
Castle Combe Motor Racing Circuit 45
Castle Inn Hotel 45
Caswell House 121
Cattle Country Park 69
Cerney House Garden 96
Chalford Valley Nature Trail 84
Champignon Sauvage 162
Charlbury 126
Charlbury Museum 131
Charlton Park 58
Chastleton House 131
Chavenage 54
Chedworth Church 101
Chedworth Roman Villa 107
Chedworth Woods 107
Chef Imperial 129
Chef's Table 53
Cheltenham 159
Cheltenham College 160
Cheltenham Gallery 160
Cheltenham Ladies College 160
Cheltenham Racecourse Hall of Fame 160
Chequers Inn 126
Chipping Campden 192
Chipping Campden Almshouses 192
Chipping Campden Parish Church of St James 195
Chipping Norton 126
Chipping Norton Museum 126
Chipping Sodbury 48
Churchill Arms, Paxford 201

217

INDEX

Churn Valley 107
Cirencester 93
Cirencester Abbey 93
Cirencester Parish Church of St John the Baptist 93
Cirencester Park 93
City Museum & Art Gallery, Gloucester 164
Clapton Manor 142
Classic Motor Hub 92
Claverton Church 41
Claverton Manor 41
Claverton Pumping Station 41
Cleeve Common 161
Cleeve Hill 160
Clopton Bridge 200
Close Hotel 57
Coaley Peak 84
Coates Church 84
Coconut Tree 162
Coffee Hub 142
Cogges Manor Farm Museum 121
Coleshourne Inn 98
Colham Farm Trail 45
Coln St Dennis Church 107
Coln Valley 107
Colonna & Hunter 39
Colonna & Smalls 39
Combe Grove Estate 41
Combe Mill 129
Compton Verney 209
Compton Wynyates 209
Conderton Pottery 185
Coombe Hill Canal Nature Reserve 161
Cooper's Hill 84
Corinium Museum 93
Cornbury Music Festival 128
Corsham 46
Corsham Court 46
Cote Brasserie, Cirencester 96
Cotswold Baguettes 149
Cotswold Canals 83
Cotswold Distillery 209
Cotswold Falconry Centre 142
Cotswold Farm Park 139
Cotswold House Hotel & Spa 195
Cotswold Lion Café 104
Cotswold Motoring Museum 139
Cotswold Perfumery 139
Cotswold Pottery 139
Cotswold View Campsite 126
Cotswold Water Park 107
Cotswold Way 193
Cotswold Wildlife Park 117
Cotswold Woollen Weavers 118
Cottage In The Wood 183
Court Barn Museum 192
Cowley House B&B 191

Cowley Manor 85
Cranham Wood 84
Crickley Hill Country Park 161
Croft Farm Leisure 185
Croome Park 182
Crown & Trumpet Inn, Broadway 193
Curry Corner 162

D

Daffodil 162
Daglingworth Church 84
D'Ambrosi Fine Foods 149
Daylesford Organic Farmshop 131
Decou 107
Deerhurst B&B 168
Deerhurst St Mary 168
Demuths Vegetarian Restaurant 32
Devil's Chimney 161
Diddly Squat Farm Shop 126
Dix's Barn 85
Donnington Brewery 147
Dorian House 40
Dormy House Hotel 191
Double Red Duke 122
Dover's Hill 193
Dower House 45
Dragonfly Maze 139
Dukes Hotel 40
Dunkirk Mill Centre 78
Duntisbourne Rouse Church 84
Dursley 70
Dyrham Park 42
Dyson Factory 58

E

Eastgate 164
Eastleach 95
Eastleach Churches 98
Eastleach Martin Church 107
Ebrington Arms 196
Ebworth Estate 84
Eckington Bridge 185
Eckington Manor Cookery School 183
Edgeworth Church 84
Edgeworth Polo Club 87
Edward Jenner Museum 69
Eight Bells Inn 195
Elkstone Church 84
Elmore Court 83
Elver Fishing 70
Enstone Tithe Barn 1131
Ermin Way 85
Estate & Tithe Barns 131
Ettington Chase Hotel 209
Evesham 198

F

Fairford 101
Fairford Parish Church of St Mary 101
Falkland Arms 128
Falstaff's Experience 200
Far Peak Camping 104
Farnborough Hall 209
Fat Fowl Restaurant 44
Feathers Hotel 130
Fillet & Bone 196
Fish Hill Woods 189
FishWorks 33
Five Alls 122
Five Mile House 85
Fleece Inn 198
Flynns Bar 161
Folk & Police Museum 149
Folk Museum 164
Folly Farm Cottage 196
Food Fanatics 152
Fosse Farm B&B 45
Fosse Manor Hotel 154
Fox Inn, Broadwell 153
Fox Inn, Oddington 153
Foxhill Manor 191
Frampton Court 70
Frampton Manor 70
Frampton-on-Severn 70
Francis Gallery 36
Frocester Court's Medieval Estate Barn 83
Frocester Hill 84

G

Gallery Nine 36
Gallery Pangolin 77
George Inn, Lacock 46
George Townhouse, Shipston-on-Stour 209
Georgian Garden 29
Georgian House B&B 39
Gigg Mill 78
Ginger & Garlic 162
Glevum 164
Gloucester & Sharpness Canal 165
Gloucester 164
Gloucester Cathedral 165
Gloucester Services 74
Gloucestershire Wildlife Trust 84
Golden Heart, Birdlip 85
Golden Valley 84
Gordon Russell Museum 189
Gower Memorial 200
Great Malvern 182
Great Tew 126
Greenway 166
Grenville Monument 42

INDEX

Grevel's House 193
Grey Cottage 85
Grey Lodge 34
Greyhound B&B 119
Grim's Ditch 129
Grouch Coffee 144
Guild Buildings, Stratford 200
Guild of Handicraft 193
Guiting Power 153
Gustav Holst Birthplace Museum 160
Gusto Deli & Café 161

H

Hailes Abbey 149
Halfway at KIneton 151
Hall's Croft 203
Hampers Food & Wine 129
Hanover House B&B 162
Haresfield Beacon 84
Harvard House 203
Hayles Fruit Farm 149
Haynes Fine Art 189
Henna 144
Henry's Seafood Bar & Grill 96
Herschel Museum 36
Hetty Pegler's Tump 85
Hidcote Manor Garden 195
Highgrove Royal Gardens 57
Highnam Woods Nature Reserve 161
Highway Inn, Burford 118
Hobbs House 78
Holburne Museum of Art 37
Hollow Bottom, Guiting Power 153
Holmby House 209
Holy Trinity Church, Bradford 43
Holy Trinity Church, Stratford-Upon-Avon 200
Hook Norton Brewery 128
Hook Norton Pottery 128
Hop Pole 33
Horse & Groom, Bourton–On–The-Hill 144
Horse & Groom, Upper Oddington 149
Horse and Groom Inn, Charlton 59
Hotel du Vin 162
Hotel On The Park 166
Howards Arms 196
Hudson Steakhouse Bar & Grill 33
Huffkins 113
Hunters Restaurant 191

I

Imperial Garden Bar 161
Inn For All Seasons, Great

Barrington 98
Iona House Gallery 129
Isbourne Manor B&B 158
Ivydene House 183

J

Jack Russell Gallery 48
Jacks's Coffee Shop 96
Jaffe & Neale 126
Jake Sutton Clockmaker 101
Jane Austen Centre 37
Jesses Bistro 96
Jet Age Museum 165
John Davies Gallery 142
John Gordons 161
John Moore Countryside Museum 168
JRool 76

K

Kebles' Bridge 95
Kelmscott Church 122
Kelmscott Manor 121
Kempsford Manor 101
Kibou 161
Kiftsgate Court Gardens 195
King William, Bath 33
Kings Arms Hotel, Woodstock 130
Kings Arms, Chipping Campden 195
Kings Arms, Stow 149
Kings Head Hotel & Spa 96
Kings Head Inn, Bledington 130
Kings Head Inn, Wootton 131
Kingston Bagpuize House 121
Kingswood Abbey Gatehouse 48
King's Arms, Didmarton 57
Kneed 96

L

La Galleria Ristorante 129
Lacock 46
Lacock Abbey 46
Lacock Pottery 46
Lamb Inn, Burford 119
Lansdown Pottery 77
Lazy Grace 161
Le Maitre du Pain 196
Le Patissier Anglais 149
Lechlade & Bushleaze Trout Fisheries 107
Lechlade 107
Leckhampton Hill 161
Lion Inn 152
Little Malvern Court 182
Little Stocks Coffee Shop 149
Little Theatre Cinema 36
Littledean Hall 72
Lloyd Baker Countryside

Collection 104
Lodge Park 107
Lola & Co 56
Lords of the Manor 145
Lower Slaughter 144
Lower Slaughter Manor 145
Lucknam Park 42
Luggers Hall 191
Lygon Arms, Broadway 191

M

Macaroni Downs 98
Magallaria 37
Malmesbury 58
Malmesbury Abbey 58
Malvern Hills 182
Malvern Priory of St Mary & St Michael 183
Manfred Schotten Antiques B&B 119
Manor Farm 196
Manor Farm House, Ab Lench 198
Manor House Hotel 144
Market Cross, Malmesbury 59
Market Cross, Stow 147
Market Hall, Chipping Campden 195
Market House Tetbury 54
Market House, Minchinhampton 77
Market Pie 191
Marlborough Arms 130
Mary Arden's House 203
Mason Croft 200
Mason's Court 20
Matara Centre 54
Mayfield Park 96
Mayflower Chinese Restaurant 96
Maylans Deli 196
Meon Hill 195
Merchant's House 168
Meticulous Ink 37
Middle Littleton Tithe Barn 198
Mill Hay House 191
Mill House Hotel 124
Mills Café 76
Milsom Hotel 40
Minchinhampton 77
Minchinhampton Common 77
Minster Lovell 120
Minster Lovell Hall 120
Misarden Park Gardens 83
Miserden Church 84
Miss Muffets Deli 168
MMB Brasserie 96
Moda House 48
Model Village, Bourton 139
Montpelier Café 161

219

INDEX

Montpelier Wine Bar 161
Morans Eating House 162
Moreton-In-Marsh 142
Morgan Motor Company 182
Mount Pleasant Farm 191
Mrs Bumble of Burford 118
Mrs Potts Tea House 144
Mulberry Tree Restaurant 183
Museum In The Park 77
Museum of Bath at Work 37
Museum of East Asian Art 37

N

Nailsworth 78
Nan Tow's Tump 54
National Waterways Museum 165
Nature In Art Museum 165
Naunton 145
Naunton Church 145
New Brewery Arts 93
New England Coffee Shop 149
New Inn, Coln St Aldwyn 93
New Place & Nash's House 203
New Wave Brasserie 107
Newark Park 60
No 1 Royal Crescent 37
No. 131 Promenade 162
No. 38 Evesham Road 162
No.28 Café 78
Noel Arms Hotel 195
North Cerney Church 107
North Farmcote 152
North Leigh Roman Villa 121
North Street Bakery 152
Northleach 104
Northleach Parish Church of St Peter & St Paul 104
Number 8, Pershore 188

O

Odda's Chapel 168
Old Baptist Chapel 175
Old Bell Hotel, Malmesbury 59
Old Manor House, Halford 209
Old Mill 144
Old Post House 128
Old Prison Café 104
Old Rectory, Lacock 47
Old Rectory, Meysey Hampton 101
Old Stocks Inn 149
Olive Branch Guest House 191
Olive Tree, Bath 33
Olive Tree, Nailsworth 78
Oak Vegetarian Restaurant 38
Open Top Bus Tours, Stratford 200
Organic Farm Shop 96
Owlpen Manor 83

Oxford Bus Museum 121
Oxford Canal 206
Oxfordshire Museum 129
Oxfordshire Way 139
Ozleworth Park 60

P

Pack Horse Bridge 43
Painswick 79
Painswick Beacon 79
Painswick Parish Church of St Mary 79
Painswick Woodcrafts 79
Pershore 183
Pershore Abbey 183
Peter Martin Gallery 147
Pinetum Lodge 165
Pittville Pump Room 160
Plough Inn, Ford 153
Plough, Kelmscott 122
Postal Museum 37
Postlip Hall 152
Potting Shed Pub, 59
Prego 191
Prema 83
Prinknash Abbey Park 79
Prior Park Landscape Garden 37
Priory Garden 189
Prithvi 162
Pulteney Bridge 38

Q

Quayles 56
Queen Elizabeth Inn 185
Quince & Clover 129

R

RAF Rudloe Manor 40
Railway Museum 157
Rectory Kitchen 92
Red Lion, Long Compton 129
Red Rag Gallery 147
Redesdale Arms, Moreton 144
Rendcomb Church 107
Rococo Garden 79
Rodborough Common 85
Rodmarton Manor 83
Rollright Stones 126
Roman Baths 37
Rousham Park 131§
Royal Crescent Hotel 41
Royal Oak, Ramsden 122
Royal Shakespeare Theatre 200
Ruskin Mill 78
Russell's 191

S

S H Jones Wine Merchants 206
Salford Farmhouse 198
Sally Lunn's House & Museum 38

Salmonsbury Camp 139
Salt Way 152
Santhill Fisheries 139
Sapperton 82
Sapperton Church 84
Saxon Church of St Laurence 43
Selsey Church 84
Seven Springs 160
Seven Tuns, Chedworth 101
Sezincote House 144
Shakespeare's Birthplace 203
Sheepscombe 82
Sherborne Park Estate 107
Shipston-on-Stour 207
Sign of the Angel, Lacock 47
Slad 82
Snowshill 145
Snowshill Hill Estate B&B 144
Snowshill Manor 145
Society Café 39
Soho Farmhouse 128
Soldiers of Gloucestershire Museum 165
Southrop Church 107
Spetchley Park 183
St Andrew Church 45
St Anne's B&B 82
St Augustine's Farm 61
St Eadburgh's Church 189
St John's Hospital 96
St Mary's Mill 83
Stanton 145
Stanton Church 145
Stanton Harcourt Manor 122
Stanway 145
Stanway House 145
Stinchcombe Common 62
Stour Gallery 207
Stow Horse Fair 147
Stow Parish Church of St Edward 147
Stow-On-The-Wold 147
Stowell Church 107
Stratford-Upon-Avon 200
Stroud 76
Stroud Brewery 77
Stroud Farmer's Market 77
Stroud House Gallery 77
Stroud Valley Cycle Trail 77
Stroud Wine Co 76
Studio Pottery 117
Studio Works Gallery 78
Sudeley Castle 152
Sudeley Hill Farm 153
Suffolk Kitchen 161
Suffolk Parade 160
Swalcliffe Barn 209
Swallow Bakery 161
Swan Hotel, Bibury 93

INDEX

Swan Inn, Swinbrook 122
Swinbrook Church 122
Swinford Museum 122

T

Tasburgh House 41
Tetbury 54
Tetbury Parish Church of St Mary 54
Tewkesbury 168
Tewkesbury Abbey 168
Tewkesbury Museum 168
The Angel, Burford 119
The Beckford Bottle Shop 39
The Bell B&B 209
The Boot (Inn) 101
The Bottoms 61
The Bower House 207
The Bull, Fairford 101
The Chantry 43
The Chequers 130
The Chequers, Chipping Norton 122
The Circus 38
The Circus Restaurant 39
The Cotswold Cheese Co 118
The Cotswold Guy 152
The Cotswold Horse 78
The Crown 96
The Dark Horse 40
The Duntisbournes 82
The Fish 191
The Fleece, Witney 120
The Foodie Bugle Shop 39
The George 207
The Grove 34
The Halfway at Kineton 151
The Hide 168
The Lady Jane 152
The Lakes, Bourton 139
The Lakes By Yoo 107
The Marlborough Tavern 39
The Maytime, Asthall 122
The Old Brewery 83
The Old Passage Inn 69
The Old Spot Inn 70
The Ormond 57
The Ox House 104
The Painswick 82
The Paragon Gallery 160
The Phoenix 201
The Plough at Kingham 130
The Porch House 149
The Priory Tea Room 118
The Promenade 160
The Rectory 59
The Retreat Cheltenham 161
The Retreat Stroud 76
The Royal Crescent 38
The Shambles 43
The Slaughters Country Inn 145
The Swan, Southrop 101
The Theatre, Chipping Norton 126
The Townhouse 201
The Three Horseshoes 120
The Trout, Tadpole Bridge 122
The True Heart 70
The Valley 198
The Volunteer 196
The Wheatsheaf, Northleach 107
The Wild Rabbit 130
The Wildings Campsite 142
The Wilson - Cheltenham Art Gallery & Museum 159
Theatre Royal 38
Thermae Bath Spa 39
Thirty Two Imperial Square 166
Three Ways House Hotel 196
Tilleys Tea Room 144
Timbrell's Yard 44
Tinto 69
Tisanes 194
Tite Inn, Chadlington 129
Tithe Barn 43
Tolsey Museum 117
Tooley's Boatyard 206
Tortworth Chestnut 48
Town Bridge 43
Town Hall, Stratford 200
Trinity House Gallery 189
Trouble House, Tetbury 53
Tyndale Monument 48

U

Uley 82
Uley Bury 85
Uley Church 84
Uplands House 209
Upper Court 185
Upper Slaughter 144
Upton Heritage Centre 184
Upton House 209
Upton-Upon-Severn 184

V

Victoria Art Gallery 39
Volunteer Inn 196

W

Waterfowl Sanctuary & Rescue Centre 131
Weigh Bridge Inn, Minchinhampton 78
Well Farm 85
Wellington Aviation Museum 144
Wesley House 152
Westbury Court Garden 72
Westley Farm 85
Weston Farm 107
Westonbirt Arboretum 55
Westonbirt School 55
Westward B&B 158
Whatley Hall Hotel 206
Whatley Manor 36
Wheelright Arms Hotel, Monkton Combe 42
Whichford Pottery 209
White Hart, Castle Combe 45
White Hart, Winchcombe 152
White House B&B 45
Whiteway Coloby 83
Whittington Court 153
Whittington Lodge Farm 153
Wild Garlic 78
Wild Thyme Restaurant 131
Wildfowl & Wetlands Trust 72
William Shakespeare 202
Williams Food Hall & Oyster Bar 78
Willow Pottery 42
Wiltshire Music Centre 44
Winchcombe 149
Winchcombe Pottery 152
Winchcombe's Gargoyles 150
Winchcombe's Parish Church of St Peter 152
Windrush Valley 107
Windrush Valley 139
Winstone Glebe B&B 81
Witney 120
Witney Museum 121
Woodchester Roman Villa 77
Woodruffs 76
Woods 33
Woodstock 129
Woodstock Arms 128
Woodstock Wallhangings 129
Woolley Grange 44
Woolpack Inn, Slad 85
Wooodchester Mansion 83
Wortley Roman Villa 61
Wotton Heritage Centre 61
Wotton Parish Church of St Mary 60
Wotton-under-Edge 60
Wren House 144
Wyatts Countryside Centre 131
Wykham Arms, Sibford Gower 209

Y

Ye Olde Reindeer Inn 206
Yew Tree Inn, Conderton 185

Z

Zuleika Gallery 129

221

Autumnal Pathway to Tyndale Monument

MAP SYMBOLS EXPLAINED

- Abbey/Cathedral
- Battle Site
- Bed & Breakfast Accomodation
- Café
- Castle
- Church/Chapel of Interest
- Cinema
- Craft Interest
- Cross
- Cycleway
- Fun Park/Leisure Park
- Hill Fort/Ancient Settlement
- Historic Building
- Hotel
- Industrial Interest
- Karting
- Lighthouse
- Mining Interest/Engine Houses
- Miscellaneous/Natural Attraction
- Museum/Art Gallery
- Pottery

- Pub/Inn
- Railway Interest
- Restaurant
- Self Catering Accommodation
- Standing Stone/Barrow
- Theatre/Concert Hall
- Tourist Information
- Tumulus/Tumuli
- Viewpoint
- Windmill/Wind Farm
- Airfield
- Aquarium
- Boat Trips
- Camping Site (Tents)
- Caravan Site
- Ferry (Pedestrians)
- Ferry (Vehicles)
- Fishing Trips
- 9/18 Hole Golf Course
- Harbour
- Inshore Rescue Boat

- Leisure/Sports Centre
- Lifeboat
- Parking
- Picnic Site
- Tents & Caravans
- Sailing
- Surfing
- Tourist Information
- Windsurfing
- Youth Hostel
- Agricultural Interest
- Arboretum
- Bird Reserve
- Garden of Interest
- Vineyard
- Walks/Nature Trails
- Wildlife Park
- Zoo
- National Trust Car Park

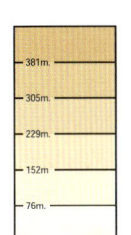

381m.	
305m.	
229m.	
152m.	
76m.	

- A Road
- B Road
- Minor Road
- Other Road or Track (not necessarily with public or vehicular access)
- Railway
- Cycleway

- Open Space owned by the National Trust
- Built-up Area

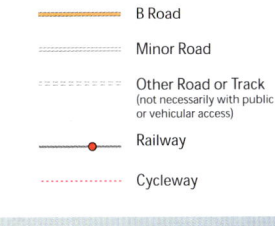

Scale 1:100,000

0   1   2 (miles)
0   1   2 (km)

Stanway in Winter

223

ABOUT THE AUTHOR & PHOTOGRAPHER

William Fricker, photographed by his son Harry, checking out an off-road route.

William Fricker was born in Somerset and educated at Stonyhurst College, Lancashire and in various places of learning in Austria and Germany. He has worked in publishing for many years.

William first worked for William Collins (now Harper Collins) in London where he became a Creative Director in their paperback division before taking a sabbatical to make a 4,000 mile trek across Europe (France-The Alps-Italy, to Greece) along the old mule tracks, footpaths and pilgrim's routes. Inspired by Patrick Leigh Fermor's A Time of Gifts, and Laurie Lee's As I Walked Out One Midsummer Morning. On reaching Greece, his original plan was to then head south and walk up the Nile but he believes his better judgement prevailed and returned on a bicycle via North Africa, Spain and France. He would like to record that he found walking a lot easier than cycling. An extract from his Journal is featured on page 22. For the past thirty-five years he has built up Goldeneye compiling the research, editorial and photography for more than two hundred UK travel guides and books; on cycling, touring and walking. More recently, he has been re-developing his Guidebook series to The Cotswolds, Cornwall, Devon and The Lake District.